and the perfectability of man. The purpose of Deborah Thomas in "Dickens' Mrs. Lirriper and the Evolution of a Feminine Stereotype" is to discover if Dickens did present feminine stereotypes.

Robert Lougy, David Marcus, and Frank Smith also take modern approaches to three of Dickens' novels. Lougy's essay is a contribution to phenomenological meditation on *David Copperfield*. Marcus shows that in *Dombey and Son* Dickens was aware of pre-twentieth-century phenomenological assumptions. And in his interpretation of *Hard Times* Smith finds that order is the central formal structure of the novel.

Taken together, the contributions widen the dimensions of Dickens scholarship and thus broaden our understanding of the man and his work. The essays, of permanent value, will b
as well as students and

Robert B. Partlow, Jr.,
is Chairman and Profes
nois University, Carbonc

DICKENS STUDIES ANNUAL

Robert B. Partlow, Jr., *Editor*

DICKENS
STUDIES
ANNUAL

VOLUME
6

Edited by

ROBERT B. PARTLOW, JR.

SOUTHERN ILLINOIS UNIVERSITY PRESS

Carbondale and Edwardsville

FEFFER & SIMONS, INC.

London and Amsterdam

COPYRIGHT © 1977 *by* Southern Illinois University Press
All rights reserved
Printed in the United States of America
Designed by Andor Braun
International Standard Book Number 0-8093-0806-1
Library of Congress Catalog Card Number 78-123048

Contents

Preface

MOST UNIVERSITY instructors with even a few years of experience have had to cope with the bright undergraduate who offers a reading of a piece of literature which is quite impossible, say an insistence that *Wuthering Heights* is really a religious allegory based on *Pilgrim's Progress* or that Heathcliff must be viewed as a proletarian hero whose heroism consists in his recognition and defeat of his bourgeois oppressors. The wise instructor politely puts such a reading on the list of possibilities to be discussed, but, in one way or another, he gets around to pointing out the difference between "reading out" meanings and "reading in" meanings, that is, between arriving at an interpretation which takes account of the factual details of the text and the inferences which may legitimately be drawn from those facts, and interpretations which impose meanings, values, and systems of thought more or less alien to that text. At this level, the instructor can pontificate with reasonable certitude.

But when that same professor changes his role and reads the books and articles of his confreres, he faces a different set of circumstances. "Reading out" and "reading in" become less easy to discriminate: the author-critics are usually more sophisticated, more aware of critical pitfalls, more widely read. Even now, however, the professor more or less consciously rejects some readings flatly, accepts others with enthusiasm, notes that this essay reinforces his own views, and that that essay observes only a part of what is really important. I suspect that, for the most part, these reactions are subcritical, i.e., that the professor-reader does not deliberately keep his own critical values and assumptions in the forefront of his consciousness, as he does when he writes a review article. I further suspect that many writers of articles do not have a completely developed, coherent critical theory always present when they initiate a new article; they do what they "feel" is the right thing to do in the presence of a given literary object at a given moment. The stimulus of a book, a character, a symbol, a situation, a relationship, or whatever, triggers certain reactions, perhaps the urge to tell others what he sees there, what he thinks it signifies, where it fits into some pattern of the author or the critic or some third person, how it relates to other meaningful matters in literary history or cultural history or biography, or how it came into being. As he organizes his thinking, his reactions to the object, there is seldom doubt in his mind that he is "reading out" what is actually there in the context he has chosen. So he submits the manuscript to the editor of a learned journal to be considered for publication.

Editors—whose motives for becoming editors we generously assume are noble—face the ultimate situation: how to act as a referee and judge, how to determine who and what is published (in effect, a censor's job), how to be a critic of critics. No matter how tough-minded he is, the redactor's lot is not an 'appy one. If he accepts only established, well-known critics, he may be accused of snobbishness or exclusiveness; but if he regularly accepts the work of unknowns, he may be accused of lowered standards. If he prints too many articles which use similar methodologies or base themselves on the same philosophy, he may be accused of partisanship, propagandizing, and narrowness; but if he accepts articles with widely varying methodologies or value-judgments, he may be found guilty of eclecticism or lack of principle. Therefore most editors refer papers to a staff of readers or referees for opinions about the merits and defects of a submission in order to protect themselves against claims of unfairness or prejudice, to take advantage of the expertise of others, sometimes even out of an awareness of their own frailty.

Theory would have it that although there may be differences of opinion about the merit of a manuscript, there should be general agreement about its plausibility, that is, about its grasp of the essential facts buttressing the argument, the adequacy of its organization and style, and the acceptibility of its conclusions. In practice there is seldom unanimity of opinion. On the contrary, there is more often than not a wild diversity. One reader says, "Accept by all means; this is a brilliant phenomenological interpretation, gracefully written, in command of the latest criticism, and completely persuasive." The second reader says, "I simply cannot read papers like this: the initial premises are unsound, vitally significant elements of the text are ignored or explained away, other important passages are completely distorted, there is no logical organization that I can see—in short, this paper tells me far more about the author than it does about Dickens." The third reader, whom the editor wistfully hopes will mediate between these extreme reactions, does not want to commit himself, for reasons that are not made clear: "This kind of paper is not my cup of tea; I seldom get much out of them, though I do read them with great interest; he really ought to have a tighter thesis statement, and his conclusions ought to be spelled out more clearly; there are several awkward sentences [which he rewrites]; I rather object to his handling of commas [all of which are corrected]; the choice of words is sometimes unfortunate [alternates are suggested]; and, really, the fellow ought to have taken my 1961 article into account."

If this situation, which has been overstated of course, but not made parodic, were unusual, no one would be surprised—but it occurs more often than not. And this leads one to consider not only the function of a journal devoted to scholarship and criticism but the very nature of the critical process. Obviously this Preface is not the place for such an analysis, but I would like to remark on one aspect of the critical process that has forced itself on my attention as an editor of the *Dickens Studies Annual* more and more strongly: the personality of the critic. I recommend to your attention the fine *Yearbook of Comparative Criticism* edited by Joseph P. Strelka (The Pennsylvania State University Press), especially volume 6 of the series, entitled *The Personality of the Critic* (1973), and particularly the fine article of Murray Krieger, "The Critic as Person and Persona." Most of the authors in this volume tend to agree with Professors Strelka and Krieger that three entities meet in the critical process: the novelist (with his personality), the created work, and the reader-critic (with *his* personality). Put in slightly different form, the novel may be considered the meditation by a specific, unique human being of a set of human situations and problems embodied in created characters in created situations which reflect real-life situations; criticism is the stated result of a consideration of that meditation by another unique human being. These two humans overlap to a greater or lesser extent: they share certain conventions about language; they share certain agreements about the nature and form of the novel; and they share certain cultural, historical, social, political, economic, psychological, ethical, and so forth, convictions—but, though somewhat similar, they are never congruent. The same observation also applies to the critic, the criticism he produces, and the reader of that criticism. It follows, then, as theoreticians from Kant on have made clear, the comprehension, analysis, and evaluation of a piece of literature are inevitably personal and idiosyncratic to some degree.

Theories of, or rather personal opinions about, the nature and function of literary criticism have ranged all the way from complete subjectivity (e.g., Housman's determination of poetic greatness by physical and emotional reactions) to at least the possibility of an objective assessment (as with Wellek's insistence that the critic can "discover a structure of determination in the object itself"). Certainly a good deal of scholarship achieves a high level of objectivity in such matters as literary history, the establishment of true texts, rhetorical and linguistic analysis—in so far as these are descriptive and nonevaluative; and efforts during the last hundred years, as in the New Criticism, to make the critical assay emulate the objectivity of the scholarly. But as Krieger points out, a "nagging skepticism" accompanies the honest and aware critic even when he is trying to be most objective, when trying to curb or obliterate the vagaries of his own personality.

> Are the literary works we read our teachers, shapers of our visions and our persons, or are they reflections of our needs? Do they seize upon us and mold us, creating for us and in us the forms which become the forms of all our imaginations, or do we seize upon them, forcing them to be what our persons require them to be, putting them into a rude service for us? And, if the latter, do we then, worst of all, read these caterings to our needs back into the works and claim that they have been there all the time for us to discover them where they lay? Are we doomed only to project our own imaginative forms outward, peopling all works with the single cast of monsters created by our own imagination, and so turning all works into essentially the same work? . . . In his hermeneutic circularity, does the critic's every claim to objectivity reduce to this charade played out by his own personality in order to deceive—most of all—himself? (P. 71)

Candor must force the critic to admit that he does not have direct access to the object, but only to that version of the work which is filtered through his own personality, automatically a refractor rather than a reflector. Even if it is possible for a given critic to be so much in tune with a given text, say Mill's *On Liberty,* that he can produce accurate, objective analyses and evaluations, can we legitimately expect equally accurate, objective treatment of Carlyle's *Latter-Day Pamphlets* or must we admit that the critic's personal social, political, and psychological commitments and believed-as-true values are warping factors? We are all familiar with the critic who writes with magnificent clarity and persuasiveness about one author or work, and then provokes feelings of uncertainty, fumbling, or sheer wrongheadedness when he writes about another author or work.

Why is one person drawn to specialize in the late medieval period while another is aggressively twentieth-century American? Why is Poe more attractive to some as a subject for years of study than Joyce? Why do some sneer at science fiction while others take it seriously? Why do some find it virtually impossible to read Ruskin or Hooker or Spenser or Ferlinghetti or James Baldwin or Albee while others cheerfully devote years of valuable time exploring the aesthetic and moral universes of these same writers? Surely no one would be brash enough to claim that only *his* preferences merit the title of real literature and few are courageous enough to declare that some people are wasting time and intelligence on dead authors or, even worse, subversive authors. But, in the critical process, the critic, whether naïvely or deliberately, implicitly demands that the reader assume *his* code of values as the only, true code, at least for the moment. Thus, to take one glaring example, recall all the work done to show that Dickens was a radical, work ranging all the way from the massive effort of Jackson in his *The Progress of a Radical,* which makes of Dickens a sort of proto-Communist, to various smaller studies showing that, in effect, Dickens found the Victorian period deficient in almost exactly the same ways that a critic of the 1970s finds our civilization deficient. In considering such pieces, one is led to wonder if these critics are objectively coming to terms with a particular Victorian's social, political, religious, and moral stances, or whether these critics are writing a sermon for these hard times in back of a façade of seemingly objective analysis. *Hard Times* makes a neat test case. What, for example, is one supposed to make of Dickens' dedication of the novel to Carlyle and his remark in a letter to Carlyle requesting permission to make that dedication: "I know it contains nothing in which you do not think with me, for no man knows your books better than I" (Nonesuch *Letters,* II, 567)? Given the fact of the dedication and the actuality of at least some likeness in their system of values, on what part (since he probably cannot transport the whole) of Carlyle's far-ranging system of ideas, values, judgments, observations, and prejudices should the critic concentrate?—the hatred of laissez faire? the detestation of playacting and circuses? the failure of democracy to find leaders and heroes? the failure of the present to measure up to the past? the need for a return to a transcendental religious belief? the condition-of-England question? the fear of a bloody revolution? the necessity of hierarchy? what? and why *that*?

Suppose our poor editor receives a nicely written article which has as its basic assumption that the major Carlylean element in *Hard Times* is the master's concept of leadership, especially leadership in the new industrial society, dramatized in the failure of Bounderby to lead his troops properly, his inability to be a real Captain of Industry, a hero-leader, and that therefore *Hard Times* can best be understood as an antidemocratic plea for political and social guidance. The other characters and events of the novel can be fitted into this pattern: Slackbridge is the false demagogue-leader; Mrs. Sparsit and Harthouse are the remnants of an outworn aristocracy, parasites and dilettantes; Gradgrind is the archenemy, the Utilitarian, the rationalist, the logician, the antitranscendentalist, the distorter of human nature, the sifter of ashes in the Parliamentary dust pile; most of the other characters are victims of a floundering system which cries out, with Stephen Blackpool, for the leadership of a new Abbot Sampson, or a Cromwell, or the Ironmaster out of *Bleak House*. It is almost a certainty that many readers would be outraged by this essay and would reject it out of hand as totally alien to the spirit of Dickens, not at all what he was saying in the novel. If there is right criticism and wrong criticism, who is right and who is wrong? who is "reading out" and who is "reading in"? Or is literary criticism forever doomed to be solipsistic, forever involved in an attempt to consider subjectively imposed structures as basically objective?

Put another way, the general tendency of the trained human mind is to move rapidly beyond perception of individual objects or facts, to the marking out of constellations of percepts, to an estimate of the universe of meaning of those constellations within a given context. Ideally, the receptive mind should perform these operations objectively and rationally, without the interposition of percepts and meanings outside the context. This is of course possible in the pure sciences, because, for all practical purposes, no universe of meaning is in or emerges from the percepts. In varying degrees in the soft sciences and in the humanistic disciplines, universes of meaning exist not only within the object itself being observed but within the mind acting as observer. The observer-critic does not come to the reading or criticism of a novel with an empty or open mind; on the contrary, the receiving mind is a more or less closed universe, or series of universes, of meanings and values. The operative metaphor is not that of a passive receptor, like a sound-recording camera, being snapped into activity by a complex set of stimuli, but rather that of one nebula impinging upon another, one system interacting with another—Karl Marx debating with Thomas Jefferson, Freud talking with Dear Abby, Sylvia Plath convincing St. Augustine that he is a trifle passé, Effie Ruskin listening to her husband define the glories of Venetian Gothic architecture. Criticism is not the same thing as recording sunspot activity or measuring the exact composition of a rock; it is the personal, idiosyncratic response of a unique mind in the presence of certain facts and details, certain patterns, structures, references. Instead of exact knowledge, literary criticism is a reflection of the real world of facts existing in a human imagination and embodied in a fiction, or construct, which is itself a reflection of a fiction created by another human imagination; the critic writes glosses on a work which is itself a gloss on reality.

The mind of the critic is made up not only of individual desires, needs, experiences, emotions, and so on, but also of larger or smaller bits and pieces absorbed from the minds of others, congenial "frozen" systems of thinking which the critic applies more or less consciously as instruments for the investigation and weighing of a piece of literature:

Marxism, socialism, democracy in any one of its several forms, Christianity in *its* many forms, liberalism, Freudianism, Jungianism, mythology, feminism, phenomenologicalism, contextualism, semanticism, etc., etc., perhaps as part of an organized, coherent philosophy of life, more often as fragments shoring up an incomplete mental structure, but most often with the implicit assumption that the system of values selected at the moment for the analysis of the piece of literature has some universal truth capable of being universally applied. Thus we have made possible studies of the Christian elements in *The American Senator*, existential treatments of *Daniel Deronda*, Marxist denunciations of *John Halifax, Gentleman*, analyses of *Vilette* as evocations of the sun myth, a Women's Lib reading of *Little Dorrit*, sermons of the necessity of brotherhood as exhibited in *Vanity Fair*, and apologies for the racism in "The Perils of Certain English Prisoners." The interrelationships are very complex. There exists the personal universe of the writer: his personality, intelligence, sensitivity, educational training, value system; his existence in a social, historical, literary, and cultural matrix; the psychological pressures acting on him. The reader-critic has his own universe shaped by similar qualities and pressures, but the further apart he is in time and space from the author, the less likelihood there is of the two universes doing more than overlapping. And, if the critic adopts, say Marxism, as a true (or at least usable) set of explanations of the human situation, there is added a third universe, again one impinging on the needs and experiences of the critic and not fully absorbing his beliefs and values. A first-rate critic is fully aware that he does, and must, operate within these interlocking sets of universes, and is consequently careful to speak with humility, to avoid absolute statements, to suggest that what he observes and evaluates is *a* possible way of seeing, a vision of reality that has only *some* claim to validity.

Nothing that has been said to this point, however, is meant to suggest that literary criticism must automatically fail, that it is a form of self-justification on the one hand and more or less effective propaganda on the other. We can agree that some readings of a given work are closer to the truth of that work than are other readings. We can agree that some readings are so completely subjective, so far removed from the object, that they are merely daydreams stimulated by some aspect of the novel or large constructs based on a few details rather than on the masses of details that make up the universe of that novel. We also agree, though seldom unanimously, that some readings manage to draw the universe of the critic and that of the author into close proximity, that some readings penetrate more deeply and fully into the central significances of the novel than do most other readings. Finally, except for a few extremists caught in a "frozen" system like Marxism or Freudianism, most of us can agree that there should be an

open forum for the discussion of ideas: whether or not we can fully accept the reading or evaluation of another critic, we believe with Mill
that out of the clash and roar of conflicting opinions and prejudices will
emerge clearer understandings of the truth. To paraphrase Krieger (p.
75), we strive to grasp and to share a work of art even as we acknowledge the epistemological and phenomenological shambles that is criticism; we try to save enough of the work to convince ourselves that it is
not a rationalization of one's private needs, a recital of self-conscious-
ness, or a preachment.

These considerations, plus a Millean diffidence about censorship
and a humanistic respect for the opinions of others, make possible the
professional life of an editor. The life of an editor who is a zealot of
any persuasion is relatively easy—all he must watch for is heresy. An
editor of Dickens studies, because of the very nature of the subject and
the people involved in the venture, cannot think in terms of orthodoxy
or heresy. He must act with a decent humility, a willingness to allow all
points of views and all conclusions to be expressed, in the hope that the
false, the shoddy, the shaky, the partial, the prejudiced, and the useless
will not prevail finally. Perhaps the modest, semifacetious remark of
another editor, a colleague of mine, hits the mark: "I am willing to accept any article that is reasonably well written, even if I disagree, if I
can see any possibility that *someone* will be able to use it in his classroom
or will be stimulated to think out the same problem himself." This has
been the general policy of the *Dickens Studies Annual* since its inception
in 1970 and remains in force in this volume: like earlier issues, there is
no preestablished theme or topic or critical set. Instead there is presented a sampling of different reactions to Dickens and his work, ranging from cool, scholarly studies which keep a severe eye sharply on the
subject, to meditations, or subjective reactions, sparked by selected elements of a fiction considered vital by the critic.

As the title suggests, William Burgan's "The Refinement of Contrast: Manuscript Revision in *Edwin Drood*" is a careful, scholarly analysis of Dickens' prose in his last novel. Burgan has gone to specific passages in the original manuscript, analyzed the changes Dickens made in
his initial statements and ideas, and then drawn several carefully re-
stricted conclusions about the peculiar excellence of this last composition. The reasoning is so exact and detailed that it cannot be sum-
marized, but the scope can be indicated by noting that Burgan
discovers five major aspects of stylistic refinement: symbolic enhancement, tension through paradox and unconventional tropes, tonal control, imagistic elaboration, and isolation of contrasting elements. Obviously Burgan cannot present his analysis of every revision in the
whole manuscript nor can he discuss the significance of every revision
in those passages he does select, but, by choosing characteristic passages

skillfully and by sharing his subtle, sophisticated insights into what Dickens did while converting his original through revision into final form, Burgan indeed persuades us that the prose style of *Edwin Drood* has its own "peculiar excellence," that Dickens remained a careful craftsman to the end, and that this last work is not the production of a tired old man but a new departure with "a sense of fine-grained distinctness different in the quality of its appeal from the startling solidity and aggressively physical presence of the material world in the other novels."

Albert Hutter's "Reconstructive Autobiography: The Experience at Warren's Blacking" goes beyond a strictly scholarly approach to offer a psychoanalytic explanation of the episode which has been widely accepted as of crucial importance in the life of Dickens. After outlining the views of such significant biographers as Forster, Edmund Wilson, Lindsay, and Marcus, Hutter proceeds to suggest the limitations, distortions, and omissions of each, and then goes on to meld the insights of Leonard Manheim, Ian Watt, and Warrington Winters into his own Eriksonian-Freudian interpretation of *all* the events and factors pressing on the adolescent psyche of Dickens. Perhaps more than any previous analyst, Hutter offers a full, credible, and objective explanation of this traumatic experience.

Freudianism, this time in combination with some of the insights of G. B. Shaw, is again used as an investigative tool by Randolph Splitter in his "Guilt and the Trappings of Melodrama in *Little Dorrit*." The key to the central meaning of this study is probably the close association seen by the critic between money and guilt, the identity of guilt and indebtedness. Splitter sees Dickens viewing the possession of money as somehow charged with guilt, whether felt or unfelt, for the society of all England as for the individual or small social groups. The characters, their interrelationships, and the events which they precipitate are all interpreted in terms of this equation and explained as "a child's vision of parental authority or, worse, of no authority at all, of children abandoned to a world run on mysterious, magical principles and sustained by guilt." The melodramatic elements in the novel are seen on the one hand as signs of "a compulsive, guilt-ridden attempt at liberation," a kind of childish exorcism of a nightmare, the nightmare of contemporary civilization, and on the other hand, following Northrop Frye, as post-Romantic and post-Revolution, and as looking forward to Freud, Marx, and the existentialists. The combination of psychoanalytic and socioeconomic analysis is not entirely new, but it does show that one investigative or explanatory technique can powerfully reinforce another in trying to reach the inner core of meaning of a novel as complex as *Little Dorrit*.

Peter Christmas, like Splitter, concerns himself with the social, economic, and political aspects of *Little Dorrit,* with such matters as class distinctions, the cash nexus, the structure of governance, social conventions and evasions, religion, prisons, and the condition of England. The angle of his approach is not Marxist or Freudian, however, but moral and epistemological. He sees the real struggle in this novel as a transformation of the earlier, simpler conflict of good and evil into a conflict between reality and gentility (neither carefully defined except as metaphysical principles). The conflict is therefore "quasi-theological": it starts from a moral dichotomy but moves rapidly to subsume the moral into the political. Mr. Christmas thus brings together two approaches hitherto used separately, with somewhat surprising rereadings of characters and events.

Another essay in this volume that bridges two approaches is Robert McCarron's "Folly and Wisdom: Three Dickensian Wise Fools." Its starting point is obviously the work of Leonard Manheim, Hillis Miller, and Jerome Meckier, all of whom have written brilliantly on the function of Dick Swiveller, Barnaby Rudge, and Tom Pinch. McCarron's purpose is, however, not to rephrase their insights but rather to place these wise fools in the long literary tradition stemming from the folk-fool and Shakespearian drama and to demonstrate the significance such characters have in Dickens' artistic and moral vision. The recurrent fool-figure in Dickens, from Sam Weller onward, in all his diverse functions (as living character, as humorist, as exposer of social faults, as antisentimentalist) is, as McCarron carefully explains, among the most complex and "innovative" representations of this cliché of literary history, almost equal to those of Shakespeare.

William Palmer's "Dickens and the Eighteenth Century," while not as broad as the title suggests, is a more ambitious essay than any yet considered. Starting from Camus' definition of the novel as "a philosophy expressed in images," then putting aside serious consideration of Dickens as a radical, a Marxist, a radical Christian, or existentialist, Palmer proceeds to offer a long, detailed argument designed to prove that Dickens' *Weltanschauung* was fundamentally and lastingly the eighteenth-century philosophy of natural benevolence and the perfectibility of man. In so doing he attacks the popular division of Dickens' novels into "light" and "dark," preferring instead the view that all the novels, even the later ones, are centrally concerned with positive and imaginative ways to find order and happiness even in an absurd world—in short, that all Dickens' novels from *Pickwick* to *Edwin Drood* present an optimistic, benevolent vision of life and its possibilities. Many readers will find the most useful part of this long analysis is Palmer's investigation of Dickens' theory of benevolence and its probable roots in the eighteenth-century novelists we know he read, especially Fielding, Sterne, and Goldsmith, with the later Godwin as a parallel or possible source. Probably not as convincing is his insistence that *Little Dorrit* is a good deal less than pessimistic, claustrophobic, "dark." One can agree with Palmer that many of our contemporaries are "reading in" the darkness and exhaustion of our own age and the critic himself; one can also agree that it is time to consider other aspects of the novel, and to remember constantly that Dickens was not writing for us but for and within the Victorian period; it is even plausible to insist that Dickens' philosophy was derived in some measurable part from his eighteenth-century reading (or, at a minimum, that he found that reading more or less agreeable)—certainly these are, as Palmer assumes, necessary elements in any objective consideration of the *Weltanschauung* embodied in all Dickens' fictions. But a belief that his later novels, such as *Little Dorrit,* are essentially optimistic, seeing, in spite of all aberrations, man as fundamentally benevolent and perfectible, will undoubtedly persuade relatively few.

So too will, in a lesser degree, Deborah Thomas' article on "Dickens' Mrs. Lirriper and the Evolution of a Feminine Stereotype," even though there is a faint tinge of the Women's Lib movement buried in the discussion. Mrs. Thomas' intention is not, however, to rescue women from the Victorian clutches of Dickens or, in her admiration for his work generally, to explain away his "femininities." Her purpose is rather to discover by analysis of one of the stereotypes he used (i.e., a recurrent character, in this instance a middle-aged, comically talkative person like Mrs. Nickleby and Flora Finching) whether Dickens actually did present stereotyped characters or whether he remained steadily creative and developing during his career. Mrs. Lirriper is chosen because she is relatively untouched by critics, because she comes late in the canon (in the 1863 and 1864 Christmas Numbers), and because she serves neatly to demonstrate that such recurrent characters are successive, evolving transmutations of typical human beings.

The last three essays to be considered are definitely *au courant.* Robert Lougy's "Remembrances of Death Past and Future: A Reading of *David Copperfield*" is a phenomenological meditation on the novel deriving primarily from Heidegger, Barthes, and Laing, with support from Lukács, Manheim, and Wordsworth, that is, a combination of Romanticism, philosophy, psychology, and Marxist theory, none of which overwhelms his personal reaction to the object. No summary of this study is possible; its merit lies less in any sustained argument, or in the development of a single basic insight, or in any single set of conclusions, than in being permitted to brood with the critic about the inner meanings of this novel, meanings perhaps only partially understood by the narrator himself.

David Marcus' "Symbolism and Mental Process in *Dombey and Son*" does not refer specifically to Heidegger or Laing and does not seem fundamentally phenomenological; in fact, it looks at first glance like a typical study of image-patterns in the novel, the images of the sea and the railroad, done so often earlier on with techniques adapted from New Criticism analysis of poetry. Marcus' intent, however, seems to be to demonstrate that Dickens himself was well aware of phenomenological assumptions before they were articulated in the familiar forms of the twentieth century. He suggests that Dickens employed symbols "as a method of representing dramatically the act of perception, of showing the interaction of the mind and the world around it," as a means of showing the subjectivity of perceptions, and eventually of making an epistemological insight into a moral insight; to focus attention on the fact that a person's moral nature exhibits itself in the unconscious ways he observes people and things. Since neither other characters in the novel nor the reader sees these people and things exactly as does the character being presented, Dickens forces a kind of moral irony: "what the character sees as reality, the audience sees as solipsism." Such a literary approach fuses literary theory, epistemology, and moral standards.

Finally, there is a clearly reasoned example of formal criticism in Frank Edmund Smith's "Perverted Balance: Expressive Form in *Hard Times*." His avowed intention is to interpret that novel as a unified work of art, to find the means of considering it as holistic, organic, "not merely [to see] a lesson that Dickens preaches but the formalization of the materials with which he presents it." The central formal structure he finds is order, but an order whose balance is too often precarious, endangered, perverted. Within this framework Smith sees what is almost painting: structures and relationships which are repetitive, duplicative, balancing, sometimes grotesquely mirroring, sometimes distorted analogues, polar opposites, strange growths and transformations of people, places, events, and relationships.

One final announcement is called for at this point in the life of the *Dickens Studies Annual*. The senior editor plans to retire in 1979; unless another professor-editor is chosen, the subvention offered by Southern Illinois University for eight years stops with volume 7. All of those involved in the production of the volumes—the editors, the Advisory Board, the readers, the scholar-critics who have submitted their work, and the critics and students who have been able to draw upon the analyses and insights published—all owe a debt of gratitude to the administrators of the university who had the wisdom to see the merit of such a series, the professional desire to encourage professional activity, and the courage to offer personal and financial support in a time of increasingly limited funds and heavier demands on those funds. Especially to be thanked are the chairmen of the Department of English (Drs. Howard Webb, William Simeone, and Ted Boyle), the deans of the College of Liberal Arts (Drs. Roger Beyler and Lon Shelby), Vice-Presidents Charles Tenney, Willis Malone, John Leasure, and Frank Horton, and the director of the University Press Vernon Sternberg. Support of scholarly and professional activity is of course a major part of the task of any university that presumes to be a university, but support of a publication that demands substantial commitments of finances over a number of years is evidence of more than lip service: it is evidence of stubborn devotion to the fundamental purpose of higher education. It is unfortunate that this print shop may close down—indications are that the *Annual* series has served a need reasonably well—but we can hope that the precedent of supporting a journal or a series of volumes devoted to Charles Dickens will be followed by others.

Carbondale, Illinois   *Robert B. Partlow, Jr.*
January 1977

Notes on Contributors

WILLIAM M. BURGAN, Associate Professor of English at Indiana University, received an American Philosophical Society grant for study of Dickens' manuscripts which enabled him to prepare this article; he has also written three other major articles on Dickens and is presently at work on a book entitled "The Identity of Things: Dickens and the Fictional Setting."

PETER CHRISTMAS was a graduate student at Stanford University when he wrote this article.

ALBERT D. HUTTER, Assistant Professor of English and Comparative Literature at the University of California at Los Angeles and a Clinical Research Associate with the Southern California Psychoanalytic Institute, has also published on detective fiction and on *Hamlet*.

ROBERT E. LOUGY, Associate Professor of English at The Pennsylvania State University, wrote this article while a recipient of a NEH Younger Humanist Fellowship working on twentieth-century philosophy; in addition to articles on Swinburne, Morris, and Thackeray, he published a book on Maturin. He is now completing a book on the artist, art, memory, and fantasy in nineteenth-century literature.

ROBERT M. MC CARRON here publishes for the first time a portion of his master's thesis, "A Study of Dickens and the Fool Tradition," submitted at Simon Fraser University.

DAVID D. MARCUS, Assistant Professor of English at the University of Illinois at Chicago Circle, has previously published two articles on Dickens; he is now at work on a book on Dickens, an essay on Henry Fielding, and a research project on Victorian popular fiction and its conventions.

WILLIAM J. PALMER, Associate Professor of English at Purdue University, has published extensively: articles on Dickens, Richardson, Faulkner, Camus, Hardy, and Fowles, as well as a book entitled *The Fiction of John Fowles*.

FRANK EDMUND SMITH, Assistant Professor of English at William Rainey Harper College, is now at work on a book on the short fiction of A. E. Coppard.

RANDOLPH SPLITTER, Assistant Professor of English at the California Institute of Technology, has published on James Joyce and is now preparing a study of Proust and the psychology of art and the artist.

DEBORAH A. THOMAS, Coadjunct Assistant Professor of English at University College, Rutgers University, has published other articles on Dickens, edited his short fiction for the Penguin English Library, and is currently investigating the novels and short stories of Shirley Jackson as well as completing a book on Dickens and the short story. A version of the essay in this volume was delivered during the 1973 MLA seminar on "Women in Dickens."

Dickens Studies Annual

Albert D. Hutter

RECONSTRUCTIVE AUTOBIOGRAPHY:
THE EXPERIENCE AT WARREN'S BLACKING

ANY AUTOBIOGRAPHICAL statement is a fabrication. Facts are distorted, relationships colored, not necessarily to deceive or persuade an audience, but rather because of the individual's desire to make sense out of the past as he understands it—and always incompletely understands it—in the present. I hope to clarify and redefine the central issues in the autobiographical account to Forster of Dickens' childhood experience at Warren's Blacking Factory. I have, in fact, three aims: to outline the significant approaches taken by critics and biographers toward the period at Warren's; to describe the limitations of these earlier approaches; and to suggest further considerations which must become part of our reading if we are to do justice to Dickens' full experience.

One group of biographers, beginning with Forster, reproduces and fully accepts Dickens' account, or distorts it much as Dickens himself distorted it; a second group accepts Edmund Wilson's now famous description of a "trauma, from which [Dickens] . . . suffered all his life"; and a final group of critics and biographers, which includes Jack Lindsay and Steven Marcus, regards these events as primarily a disguise for something earlier and deeper.[1]

Each of these approaches has contributed to our understanding of Dickens, but each also limits and distorts Dickens' rendering of his own experience. Forster, of course, is essential—and his loyalty to Dickens is so apparent that he often unintentionally clarifies his friend's emotional attitudes. When Dickens recalls crying over Fanny's prizewinning, in such sharp contrast to his own "humiliation and neglect," he finds it necessary to deny what seems a natural and obvious feeling: "There was no envy in this," he writes. Forster instantly seconds him: "There was little need that he should say so." Forster then provides good evidence of his friend's overreaction, citing Charles' "extreme enjoyment" and "utmost pride" in Fanny's success, "manifested always to a degree otherwise quite unusual with him." The quality of excess ("extreme," "utmost," "otherwise quite unusual with him"), like Dickens' "most affecting proof of his tender and grateful memory of her in the childish days" at Fanny's funeral (Forster, I, 31), may suggest a reaction formation. But we do not require a pathological label for behavior which would seem perfectly natural in any child who feels neglected and sees his sister praised. Even without the dramatic difference between his sister's life and his own at the time of Warren's, we would now expect a high degree of rivalry and aggression between siblings. The real pathology here is cultural: it denies the normalcy of envy and aggression and reinforces Dickens' own overwhelming need to make himself helpless and pitiable as he remembers this episode.

Forster's special pleading falsely objectifies Dickens' internal conflicts and reactions. And even his finest modern biographer, Edgar Johnson, reflects this tendency when he repeats Dickens and Forster about the prizewinning, without quoting them directly or commenting on their statements. Johnson simply writes, as if it were now accepted fact, that Charles "loved Fanny, he was proud of her, and he felt no envy" (I, 41). Chesterton was also sympathetic to Dickens, although not necessarily convinced by the direct denial of envy: "I do not think that there was [any envy], though the poor little wretch could hardly have been blamed if there had been." [2] Less skilled biographers translate other emotional statements from the autobiographical fragment into fact in more strikingly distorted ways. W. Robertson Nicoll, for example, describes "the miserable three years which [Dickens] spent in tying up pots of blacking." Margaret Lane lets him out in nine months, while Thomas Wright keeps Charles at work for a full year. [3] In evaluating the length of Dickens' stay and his age at the time, Forster notes that David Copperfield was ten when he worked for the firm of Murdstone and Grinby, while Dickens "could hardly have been more than twelve years old when he left" Warren's (I, 33). Forster defends the blurring of ten and twelve by adding that Charles "was still unusually small for his age" (I, 33). Charles seems in fact to have started in at Warren's just after his twelfth birthday (Johnson, I, 45), although he claimed: "I have no idea how long it lasted; whether for a year, or much more, or less" (Forster, I, 32). Less careful biographers have continued to confuse Dickens' quoted statements from the autobiographical fragment with his fiction and with their own sympathetic response to the child's predicament.

Most biographers before 1940—such as A. W. Ward (1882) or Robert Langton (1883)—uncritically reflect Forster and Dickens himself. The exception, as usual, is Chesterton, who anticipates Wilson in a variety of ways: "About any early disaster there is a dreadful finality; a lost child can suffer like a lost soul"; "I think we can imagine a pretty genuine case of internal depression. And when we add to the case of the internal depression the case of the external oppression, the case of the material circumstances by which he was surrounded, we have reached a sort of midnight" (pp. 34–37). George Gissing suggests that "the true reason for . . . [Dickens'] shrinking from this recollection lay in the fact that it involved a grave censure upon his parents." [4] My own argument will develop the conflict and aggression implicit in this censure. Gissing, however, assumes that the censure was perfectly merited by the circumstances as Dickens describes them and, similarly, that Dickens' silence in later years showed "the most natural reserve" (p. 15). In other words, Gissing's full acceptance of the Forster/Dickens view of Warren's prevents him from making an independent judgment. His conclusions are weak and anticlimactic: "An unpleasant topic; enough to recognize in passing, that this incident certainly was not without its permanent effect on the son's mind" (p. 15). Critics after 1941 are clearly influenced by Wilson and blend all three approaches outlined here—although they do not necessarily clarify their theoretical assumptions.[5]

Edmund Wilson's account has become the most widely accepted psychological analysis of Dickens' ordeal. Wilson writes:

> These experiences produced in Charles Dickens a trauma from which he suffered all his life. It has been charged by some of Dickens's critics that he indulged himself excessively in self-pity in connection with these hardships of his childhood; it has been pointed out that, after all, he had only worked in the blacking warehouse six months. But one must realize that during those months he was in a state of complete despair. For the adult in desperate straits, it is almost always possible to imagine, if not to contrive, some way out; for the child, from whom love and freedom have inexplicably been taken away, no relief or release can be projected. Dickens's seizures in his blacking-bottle days were obviously neurotic symptoms; and the psychologists have lately been telling us that lasting depressions and terrors may be caused by such cuttings-short of the natural development of childhood. For an imaginative and active boy of twelve, six months of despair are quite enough. (Pp. 5–6)

But what the psychologists had been telling us, even by 1941, made it impossible to give this incident the status of a *formative* trauma. Wilson overvalues the external events and underplays the extent to which they seem to have touched much earlier feelings. Because he speaks of "traumas" and "neurotic symptoms," most critics tend to assume that he articulates a psychoanalytic position, but such statements as these are alien to analytic thought because they tend to treat "the child" as a single, static entity, whether that child is three or twelve: "For the child, from whom love and freedom have inexplicably been taken away, no relief or release can be projected." Such an assertion, for a twelve-year-old, depends very much on the preceding eleven years, and especially on the first five years. In this respect Lindsay is much more sensitive than Wilson to the premises of psychoanalysis.

Yet Lindsay is also something of an embarrassment, and his use of psychoanalysis reveals the limitations we all face when we disregard the immediate circumstances and context of an event and choose instead only those elements which may be translated back into earlier meanings.[6] Psychoanalytic criticism is now being retried on the old charge of reductionism, and Lindsay's work reminds us of both the possibilities and limitations of the most powerful diagnostic tool of psychoanalysis: its ability to derive unconscious and infantile meanings from a conscious, adult text. This reductive principle may also lead to significant distortion, whereby all events begin to look the same when seen through the analyst's peculiar prism. For critics familiar with psychoanalytic constructs, Dickens' autobiographical fragment seems to provide the perfect conditions for psychoanalytic inference: a detailed description of Charles' first real separation from his family and his own intense emotions during that period. But so far these events have been used to substantiate some other thesis (Lindsay's "lost Eden" or Marcus' primal scene memory), while most critics, including Johnson, offer only a vague and sentimentalized evaluation: "But it is more than a mere unavailing ache in the heart, however poignant, and however prolonged into manhood, that gives the Marshalsea and Warren's Blacking their significance in Dickens's life. They were formative. Somewhere deep down inside, perhaps unconsciously, he made the decision that never again was he going to be so victimized. He would fall prey to none of the easy slipshodness of financial imprudence that had been his father's undoing. He would work and subject himself to a steel discipline."[7]

What, then, constitutes a fuller psychoanalytic reading? We may begin by adding, or properly emphasizing, developmental aspects of Dickens' personality which are brought out in this account with great intensity, particularly its focus on orality. Charles' continual preoccupation with food—saveloys and penny-loaves and beef and cheese and beer and milk and puddings, and the various people who serve them—reflect, as Ian Watt has recently noted, a falling back "on the oral patterns of the distant past."[8] A closer reading of the characteristic flavor and gustatory detail of the autobiographical fragment links it with Dickens' fiction and reinforces the truth of Lindsay's conjectures: the landlord's wife, "all womanly and good," who serves Charles ale on "a festive occasion" and follows it with "a kiss that was half-admiring and may also have reflected the boy's aggression against John Dickens which was repressed and directed back against himself. Both meanings are consistent with Charles' tendency, at this time, to suppress any evidence of his own aggression and to avoid blaming his father for the family's distress. Charles' physical symptoms were real enough, but they may have also been used to express deeper and more complicated feelings about himself and his relations to his father. The mind, at such times, naturally exploits appropriate bodily weaknesses, initiating a process of "somatic compliance" which characterizes psychosomatic disorders in general.[19] I believe that Dickens' childhood spasms may best be treated as *both* a physical reality and a symptoms of helplessness and oppression, like Oliver's weakness from starvation or Little Nell's more fatal illness. Even at the time of Warren's they stood symbolically for the child's neglected state.

Charles' illness, however, was only one of a number of devices he used to make himself a passive sufferer, whether from parental cruelty, external circumstances, or internal weakness and need. Yet the period young Charles was about to enter is characterized by active conflict and turmoil. Indeed, a healthy adolescence requires conflict for its successful development and resolution:

> Too little attention has been paid to the fact that adolescence, not only in spite of, but rather because of, its emotional turmoil, often affords spontaneous recovery from debilitating childhood influences, and offers the individual an opportunity to modify or rectify childhood exigencies which threatened to impede his progressive development. The regressive processes of adolescence permit the remodeling of defective or incomplete earlier developments; new identifications and counter-identifications play an important part in this. The profound upheaval associated with the emotional reorganization of adolescence thus harbors a beneficial potential.[20]

This is what Erikson refers to as the "normative crisis" of adolescence. Viewed from this perspective, Dickens might have used the sudden shift in his life situation, and his subsequent memory of that shift, to reorder his earlier experiences, and perhaps, as well, to justify later competitiveness and aggression. Put another way, we need to see Warren's both as something that happened to Dickens and as something he did to himself, something that he used positively in his own self-development. He had no control over the actual events, but his reactions to his new environment, and to the old family environment, reflect specific modes of coping with separation and independent development; Dickens' subsequent memory of this period, particularly in ways we know to be distorted, further indicates the uses he made of his experience, rather than simply the way in which he was used.

When Dickens wrote the autobiographical fragment, his eldest child, Charles Culliford, was somewhere between ten and twelve, that is, between the ages when David went to work at Murdstone and Grinby and when Charles actually went to work at Warren's.[21] It is tempting then to believe that the growth of his son stimulated the father's desire to work through an unresolved crisis of his own early adolescence.[22] Fanny's fatal illness must have similarly stimulated Charles' memories of his relationship to her during the time of Warren's—and before. Her tuberculosis was discovered in 1846 and, as Johnson writes, she "had long been in delicate health" (II, 650); she died in 1848.

But Dickens' powerfully melodramatic tone urges us to forget, as far as possible, his adult perspective: we see him only as child and victim, someone who suffered agonies. He omits from his account virtually any reference to self-assertive activity. And the act of growth in adolescence is very definitely a form of self-assertion: "In the unconscious fantasy," writes D. W. Winnicott, "growing up is inherently an aggressive act. . . . If the child is to become adult, then this move is achieved over the dead body of an adult." [23] Winnicott's language is intentionally strong because it is an attempt to translate the meaning of adolescent unconscious fantasy. The adult is so shocked by the power and potential threat of that fantasy that he tends strongly to repress this element in the memory of his own adolescence and to suppress or rebuke it in the adolescence of others. But its presence is critical for the growth of the child to adulthood: "In the total unconscious fantasy belonging to growth at puberty and in adolescence, there is *the death of someone*. A great deal can be managed in play and by displacements, and on the basis of cross-identifications; but, in the psychotherapy of the individual adolescent . . . there is to be found death and personal triumph as something inherent in the process of maturation and in the acquisition of adult status" (p. 145).

Acceptance of this symbolic murder is difficult for the parent, but more difficult for the child himself. And when this universal difficulty is exaggerated by external circumstance, the normative crisis may become a neurotic one. Dickens did not simply suffer a sudden act of deprivation (although it was that, too); he was placed quite abruptly in the role of his father. John Dickens had failed as a provider, and now suddenly this boy of twelve was the one person in the family who was both earning money and living outside of debtor's prison. We can speculate that in addition to the long hours and the separation from his family, the boy would have been frightened by the realization of a normal fantasy of his age—the replacement of his own father. Charles recoiled from this fantasy and re-created himself as a much younger and weaker boy; he defended his father and softened the implications of his father's improvidence. As described above, Charles' spasms not only symbolize his helplessness and neglect: they also suggest an identification with his father, and perhaps a redirection of any aggression he felt toward John Dickens back upon himself. Certainly, this illness helped to intensify the feeling he later re-created through the pathos of his adult memory: "I was so young and childish, and so little qualified— how could I be otherwise?—to undertake the whole charge of my own existence" (Forster, I, 24). And when he later remembered this time, that memory rendered him helpless and childlike; to use the appropriate Victorian expression, it "unmanned him": "My whole nature was so penetrated with the grief and humiliation . . . that even now, famous and caressed and happy, I often forget in my dreams that I have a dear wife and children; *even that I am a man;* and wander desolately back to that time of my life" (Forster, I, 23—my italics). We can see a similar tendency in his fiction, to relive not simply the child's oppression but its innocence. Indeed, his purest heroes are heroines—Nell and Amy Dorrit and Esther Summerson—all of whom intensify the quality of passive and innocent suffering which Dickens tries to elicit in the fragment.

Elements of his own aggressiveness, however, are also present. He ironically compares himself, for example, to a "small Cain"; he reveals his envy for his sister; and even the description of Bob Fagin betrays an indirect aggression toward his real-life protector, transformed later into his most famous villain. The boy's resolve never to forgive his mother for her part in these events—a resolve he maintained throughout his life—also betrays both the strength of his aggression and an anger founded on a sense of separation and loss rather than a realistic judgment of Elizabeth's actions.

We now begin to see how complex Charles' experience at Warren's must have been: in itself a painful period of separation and readjustment, it would naturally encourage a defensive reaction and a regression to earlier developmental conflicts. In addition, it came at a critical period of Dickens' own growth, and his reaction may have been particularly intense because Warren's brought out elements of aggressiveness and fantasies of replacing the father which are part of every boy's adolescence but, in this case, were frighteningly realized through external events. However, by the time we learn anything directly about Warren's Dickens has grown up and, in the process, learned to use the experience as a part of that growth. This is apparent in the autobiographical fragment and in the reiteration of its theme throughout Dickens' fiction. Dickens portrays himself as he wishes to be seen, and as he needs to see himself, so that the values of innocence and an unaggressive childhood emerge as a significant part of his adult and creative vision.

Perhaps Dickens' critics and biographers have tended to overemphasize the traumatic elements of Warren's and to ignore the normal and even healthy aspects of this event because they fail to place Dickens in a developmental framework. Certainly, they do not compare Dickens to other similarly "traumatized" figures. For example, when Coleridge's father died, young Coleridge was sent away to a charity school, where he felt himself cut off from his mother and family: an "orphan," as he repeatedly described himself in adult life. For Coleridge, too, isolation and neglect are transformed into a detailed menu, but Coleridge's list is entirely unleavened by humor: "Our diet was very scanty—Every morning a bit of dry bread & some bad small beer—every evening a larger piece of bread, & cheese or butter, whichever we liked—For dinner—on Sunday, boiled beef & broth—Monday, Bread & butter, & milk & water—on Tuesday, roast mutton, Wednesday, bread & butter & rice milk, Thursday, boiled beef & broth—Friday, boiled mutton & broth—Saturday, bread & butter, & pease porritch—Our food was portioned—& excepting on Wednesdays I never had a belly full. Our appetites were *damped* never satisfied—and we had no vegetables." [24] Both Dickens and Coleridge experienced a painful period in their childhoods when they were abruptly separated from their families and felt isolated and neglected; and both tended to express their neglect through images of feeding. But Coleridge was three years younger than Dickens, his father had died, and the abrupt separation from the rest of his family was far more extensive than Dickens' period at Warren's. Dickens was in a better position to cope with a much more limited crisis and integrate it into a normal process of growth.

It is of course impossible to sustain a comparison of this kind. I am intentionally focusing on a single, apparently traumatic moment common to both biographies, in order to emphasize that the impact of Warren's was relatively limited and that it points to the range of Dickens' unneurotic response, as well as to its pathological side. Coleridge, on the other hand, would suffer throughout his life from screaming nightmares, some of them actually set in Christ's Hospital, and many of his fantasies reflect a combination of anal and oral imagery far more pathological than anything we know of in Dickens: "Instantly there appeared a spectrum, of a Pheasant's Tail, that altered thro' various degradations into round wrinkly shapes, as of [Horse] Excrement, or baked Apples—indeed exactly like the latter—round baked Apples, with exactly the same colour, the same circular intra-circular Wrinkles—I started out of bed, lit my Candles, & noted it down, in order to state these circular irregularly concentric Wrinkles, something like Horse dung, still more like flat baked or [dried] Apples, such as they are brought in after Dinner." [25] This passage shows the transformation of oral images into something directly anal. Dickens employs anal character traits to guard against the dangers of separation and loss of love;

Coleridge's anal imagery more directly renders a complete and irrecoverable loss.[26] Similarly, we must assume an oral predisposition to Coleridge's ultimate neurotic dependency, his opium addiction; any possible psychosomatic illness of Dickens, such as the recurrent spasms, is almost trivial by contrast.

In fairness to Coleridge, and in recognition of his lifelong achievements, we need to use the label "pathological" with great care. But the potentially misleading effects of labeling Warren's as pathological become clearer when we look at someone whose conflicts in childhood were even more extreme. Perhaps a final comparison should be made not to another great writer but to a great neurotic: Freud's "Rat Man." Dickens disguised and transformed his aggression against the father, whereas Freud's patient feared and hated his father intensely. He felt "an ineradicable grudge against his father," whom he construed as the block to his own growth and sexual enjoyment, and whose death merely intensified a pathology designed to suppress the aggressive wishes of the son. Once, when his father gave him a beating, the child responded with such uncontrollable rage and "elemental fury" that his father stopped and directly anticipated Edmund Wilson's pronouncement about Dickens: " 'The child will either be a great man or a great criminal.' " Freud adds, dryly: "These alternatives did not exhaust the possibilities. His father had overlooked the commonest outcome of such premature passions—a neurosis." [27]

To summarize: the earlier descriptions of Dickens' experience at Warren's, beginning with Forster and Dickens himself, have been incomplete and distorted. The events, and Dickens' reaction to them, reflect a significant external reordering of the child's life, a pressure which reactivated the needs and the characteristic defenses built up in the child throughout his earlier life; this pressure intensified an experience common to adolescent development. I have analyzed the seemingly neurotic components in this affair but have finished by stressing the normality of some of Dickens' reactions. I have suggested that he used this experience to manage and resolve earlier crises and that he continued to use his adult memory of Warren's to preserve a sense of his own boyishness, his own identity as a child—elements that say as much about the idiosyncratic nature of his personality and charm as about neurosis. Throughout his life Dickens absorbed experiences—bizarre, painful, unexpected—recreating and controlling them through his fiction. We know he did this when Maria Beadnell returned as Maria Winter, or with the disintegration of his marriage and his affair with Ellen Ternan. We are prepared to see, in his response to the apparent traumas of adult life, a dynamic quality: he changes loyalties and viewpoints and reflects those changes as he writes, always attempting to understand his behavior and, implicitly, to justify it. But in considering his experiences at Warren's, we have been inclined to read those events, and Dickens' much later account of them, as static. We tend to forget that Warren's was not, as most biographers would have us believe, the beginning; it is subject to that autobiographical reconstruction which characterizes so much of Dickens' fiction, and Dickens' account is a crucial attempt to redefine real-life events through the "fiction" of biography.

William J. Palmer

DICKENS AND THE EIGHTEENTH CENTURY

"A NOVEL is never anything but a philosophy expressed in images," Albert Camus began his review of Sartre's *La Nausée* in the *Alger républicain* (20 October 1938).[1] No one would question the philosophicality of Sartre's novels (after all, "Society" knows that Sartre was a professional philosopher who occasionally dabbled in literature) but Dickens' novels are something quite different. Dickens criticism has persistently portrayed Dickens' mind as a rich cornucopia overflowing with abundant comic senses and ripening satiric powers, with ever-fresh images and blooming characterizations and growing social consciousnesses, but rarely do the critics write of his basic philosophical beliefs. In those rare instances when Dickens had been considered philosophically, he has been characterized as a radical Marxist,[2] as a radical Christian,[3] and recently (a charge to which I personally plead guilty) as an existential writer.[4] However, while Dickens' philosophical sympathies may warm toward a Marxist polemic or an existential concern in a novel here or a novel there, he never consistently affirms any one of those philosophical positions throughout all of his novels. The first focus of this essay is upon the definition of the basic Dickens philosophy: its origins, its beliefs and ideas, and its consistent expression in images.

Another group of modern Dickens critics, while not labeling Dickens either a radical or an existentialist, has used general descriptors to characterize his world view. These critics (principally Edmund Wilson and Lionel Stevenson in the early 1940s)[5] defined the Dickens canon as made up of "light" and "dark" novels with the sun sinking at *Bleak House* and never rising again. This division in terms of tonal metamorphosis has been rather docilely accepted throughout the last three decades of Dickens criticism. In the fifties Edgar Johnson's fine biography fully endorsed the "dark" novel descriptor.[6] In volume II of the biography, Johnson's critical essays on *Bleak House, Hard Times,*

Little Dorrit, and *Our Mutual Friend* repeatedly emphasize the negative, pessimistic imagery as opposed to the positive images of light and imagination and love.[7] One of the otherwise most intriguing and innovative Dickens books of the sixties, Taylor Stoehr's *The Dreamer's Stance,* reiterates the "dark" novel theory by underlining again the importance of the blacking factory experience which Edmund Wilson had first emphasized two decades earlier.[8] No Dickens critic should minimize the shattering effect of the blacking factory upon the young Dickens, but is it not entirely possible that Dickens sufficiently exorcised that particular devil in *David Copperfield* before the so-called "dark" novels even began with *Bleak House?*

The most obvious facts that the simplistic "light/dark" descriptors overlook are that Dickens' early novels, especially *The Pickwick Papers,* are not unregenerately optimistic, and the later novels are hardly as pessimistic as they have been painted. In the later novels, Dickens' interest in the urban crisis in Victorian England certainly has matured. Tom-All-Aone's, the festering slum of *Bleak House,* is much more vivid and infecting than the slums in *Oliver Twist,* and the manufacturing city in *The Old Curiosity Shop* is but a shadow of the symbolic and physical reality of Coketown in *Hard Times.* But though his novelistic world changes, his world view doesn't. Though his social consciousness matures, Dickens still finds his eighteenth-century philosophy of natural benevolence and the perfectibility of man applicable to the changing Victorian world. J. Hillis Miller analyzes at length the heightened sense of the existential "absurd" in Dickens' later novels. However, Miller recognizes that Dickens' novels are not about the implacable pall which absurdity casts over the world but about the positive and imaginative ways that Dickens' characters cope and find order and happiness in spite of the absurdity of existence.[9] Perhaps Dickens realized what Camus later realized about Sisyphus: man can exist, be happy, alive, human, even in a darkly absurd world. Thus, the second major intention of this essay is to attempt to overturn that "dark novels" descriptor by examining the consistent operation in both early and late novels of Dickens' optimistic philosophical vision. This essay will deny that any drastic change from picaresque carefreedom and benevolence to dark "bitterness and frustration"[10] really occurred in Dickens' vision.

The third major concern of this essay is that of applied criticism. After describing the optimistic eighteenth-century cast of Dickens' mind—its origins, its moral values and beliefs, its ways of solving human problems—the focus will turn to the analysis of the consistently optimistic vision present in both early and late novels (specifically, *The Pickwick Papers, The Old Curiosity Shop,* and *Little Dorrit*). The discussion of each of these novels will include comparative study of specific eighteenth-century influences (particularly *Joseph Andrews, The Vicar of*

Wakefield, Tristram Shandy and *Caleb Williams*) upon the novel in question. By means of his reading of these major works of the previous century, Dickens developed the eighteenth-century attitudes and beliefs that later formed the philosophical base for his own characters' actions.

Thus, this essay hopes to do three things. First, it wants to describe what J. Hillis Miller would call the "consciousness of [the] consciousness" [11] of the artist. Secondly, it will attempt to define the origins of the novelist's "vision," the eighteenth-century philosophical and novelistic influences upon his art. And thirdly, it will analyze those influences at work in individual Dickens' novels, both early and late novels, both supposedly bright, comic novels and seemingly "dark," pessimistic novels, therefore showing that the vision is consistent throughout. The goal of this essay is to place Dickens at the fulcrum of a history of ideas, to show how the Dickens "vision" is a connecting link between eighteenth-century and twentieth-century views of human existence. The definition of this "vision" and the analysis of individual novels will reveal the way Dickens felt and his tendency to act (and to write) on emotion rather than practicality, on belief rather than rational analysis, on often unrewarded faith rather than the empirical evidence of ugly fact. Hobbes and Shaftesbury fought this same war in the eighteenth century, the Romantics sustained a rearguard action, and Dickens, an isolated guerilla, is merely carrying on the fight a century later. Dickens' "vision" derives from an eighteenth-century philosophical view which all his life he tried to apply to an unaccommodating Victorian world. He would have felt quite comfortable in the company of Camus' Sisyphus.

The Philosophy

The Dickens vision begins with Mr. Pickwick, Dickens' first major character, who is introduced to the world almost as if he were an ambulatory philosophical abstraction. "The praise of mankind was his Swing; philanthropy was his insurance office," the esteemed Secretary of the Pickwick Club first introduces the venerable Tittlebatian to the accompaniment of "(Vehement cheering)." [12] And later, the narrator describes how Pickwick's "countenance glowed with an expression of universal philanthropy" and how "general benevolence was one of the leading features of the Pickwickian theory" (16). This opening of Dickens' first novel shows Pickwick to be a firm believer in benevolence as a viable mode of social action. And Dickens, at the very outset of his writing career, is bodying forth his own central beliefs in his first major character. Unlike a Sartre, however, who creates and synthesizes a philosophy for his own times, Dickens is not defining a unique, self-engendered world view, a philosophical vision strictly his own. Rather, he is entering a stream of ideas that had been flowing from a source one hundred and fifty years in the past, meandering tortuously from Hobbes to Shaftesbury through most of the novelists of the eighteenth century to Godwin and the Romantics and then, its current dwindling, on into the nineteenth century to Dickens. Therein, bending back into the past, are the origins of the Dickens vision, a Dickensian headwater which has never adequately been explored.

Two eminent Dickensians, Humphry House and Louis Cazamian, have looked at the surface of the theme of benevolence in Dickens' novels. House defines the "main symptoms of Dickens' benevolence" as

> 1) Generosity, in money and kindness that costs nothing. Both kinds of generosity are chiefly shown by the poor towards each other or by the benevolent well-to-do towards the poor.
> 2) An acute feeling for suffering in all forms, whether caused by poverty, sickness, cruelty (mental or physical) or injustice. The feeling becomes most acute when all these causes of suffering are combined in the sufferer, and there is somebody who has the power to relieve them all.
> 3) Righteous, if ineffectual, indignation against all anomalies, abuses, and inefficiency in social organizations or government which cause suffering of any kind. This is the Benthamite strain, found more in Dickens's own words than in the words of his characters.
> 4) An equable and benign temper in the benevolent person, which is on the whole immune from the changing moods which make human beings interesting in themselves.[13]

This definition briefly mentions the benevolence of the poor but concentrates upon what House sees as the major Dickensian emphasis: the charitable motives of the rich. And, throughout his book, House, when discussing the Dickensian concept of benevolence, considers only that of the rich arbitrarily giving to the randomly selected poor.

Cazamian, writing long before House, first placed this emphasis upon Dickens' benevolence as being the sole property of the open-handed rich with his "Philosophie de Noël."

> C'est une forme vague and sentimental du socialism Chrétien. Timide dans se partie positive, plus hardie dans ses critiques, elle prêche l'interventionisme au nom d'un idéalisme religieux.[14]
> Avec les chef de la philanthropie nouvelle, Dickens reconnaît le droit à l'assistance. Les classes dirigeants sont responsables du mal social; elles ont sur les ignorants et les faibles l'autorité naturelle du père sur ses enfants. Il faut que l'individu et l'État

interviennent dans la vie des classes inférieures; la charité pri-
vée ou publique, l'action dévouée, sincère, patiente, doivent
sans relâche soulager et guérir.[15]

Certainly, flowing from the benevolent Pickwick and coursing through
the Cheeryble brothers and Scrooge to John Jarndyce and Noddy Bof-
fin, the Father Christmas figures who need only reach into their
pockets to bring relief are prominent. But if benevolence were the sole
property of the rich in the Dickens world, then that world would be
truly dark. There would be no opportunity for moral decision-making
among the wide range of characters and no genuine human involvement on the most basic personal level, that of survival. The Dickens
world would be a randomly patriarchal welfare state. The only welfare
recipients would be those lucky enough to be blundered upon by a rich
benefactor like Brownlow or Jarndyce.

But in the Dickens world the poor as benevolists far outnumber
the rich. Dickens repeatedly affirms the moral value of the act of benevolence in which the giver is an active participant, in which the gift is
not just an effortless dole, and in which an equal flow of love is generated between giver and receiver as each participates in the other's
misery or meager abundance. Cazamian does not recognize the benevolence of the poor in the novels of Dickens at all, and, while House
briefly recognizes this phenomenon in his definition, he subsequently
ignores it while proceeding to discuss the Dickensian rich man as a stereotyped caricature. Both of these studies of benevolence in Dickens'
novels neglect more than half of the subject. Dickens' philosophy of benevolence which begins with that embodied abstraction, Pickwick, ef-
fectively and consistently represents one of the major trends of thought
of the eighteenth-century view of man.

In the first decade of the eighteenth century Lord Shaftesbury
began this trend. His was a reaction against the rationalism of Hobbes
who had posited in *Leviathan* that all human action was "self-regard-
ing." For Lord Shaftesbury, Hobbes' empirical, unsentimental view of
the world was antithetical to the real nature of man. Hobbes, writes
Shaftesbury, dwells only on fear and "forgot to mention Kindness,
Friendship, Sociableness, love of Company, and Converse, Natural Affection." [16] Thus, Shaftesbury started the eighteenth-century rebellion
against the Puritan ethic which defines man as naturally sinful and life
in the world as a constantly self-centered struggle for salvation. He did
not deny the idea of personal salvation; he simply changed the emphasis from the struggle of the isolated, self-centered man as the only
means of salvation to the concept of universal benevolence as the more
natural means of salvation. In 1711 Shaftesbury wrote of that marvel-
ous clockwork orange, eighteenth-century man—

A thousand other Springs, which are counter to *Self-Interest,* have as considerable a part in the Movements of this Machine. . . . The Students of this Mechanism must have a very partial Eye, to overlook all other Motions besides those of the lowest and narrowest compass. 'Tis hard, that in the Plan or Description of this Clockwork, no Wheel or Ballance shou'd be allow'd on the side of the better and more enlarg'd Affections: that nothing shou'd be understood to be done in *Kindness* or *Generosity;* nothing in pure *Good-Nature* or *Friendship,* or thro any *social* or *natural Affection* of any kind: when, perhaps, the main Springs of this Machine will be found to be either these very *natural Affections* themselves, or a compound kind deriv'd from them.[17]

Thus, Shaftesbury saw men as naturally benevolent and he began a philosophical movement against Hobbesian empiricism which would be sustained throughout the rest of the eighteenth century.

Lord Shaftesbury and those moral philosophers of the eighteenth century who followed his lead, principally Francis Hutcheson and Bishop Joseph Butler, articulated the concepts of the innate moral sense and natural benevolence for their age. But only near the very end of the century, with the writings of William Godwin in the 1790s, did this optimistic philosophy of man begin to take on political implications. What Rousseau had preached in France, Godwin was arguing in England: if man is naturally good, then the evils of the world must be attributable to a flawed society.

Not only does Godwin specifically align his thought with the tradition of Shaftesbury and Butler, he goes one step further than his predecessors by discussing the natural goodness of man in relation to society: "Neither philosophy, nor morality, nor politics, will ever show like itself, till man shall be acknowledged for what he really is, a being capable of rectitude, virtue and benevolence, and who needs not always to be led to actions of general utility, by foreign and frivolous considerations."[18] For Godwin, society's recognition of man's innate moral sense, and the movement thereafter of the habit of benevolence toward universality, would make possible the establishment of an egalitarian society in which repressive institutions would be unnecessary.

In *The Pickwick Papers* the natural benevolence of man is stressed, in the character of Pickwick, throughout the first half of the novel. However, the confrontation with society appears in the form of Dodson and Fogg and the Fleet. By the end of *The Pickwick Papers* universal benevolence has not permeated the Dickens world, though Pickwick's benevolence has drawn a number of converts—principally Sam Weller, Mr. Jingle, and Job Trotter—to the realization of the essential nature of man and of the impact which benevolence can have upon a repressive world. Pickwick descends into the underground of the Fleet, no longer just an openhanded gentleman slumming among the poor, but an actual prisoner putting on the shoes of the oppressed. Though Pickwick eventually retreats from the realities of personally involved benevolence, a casualty of the heart-to-heart combat of personal involvement in the battle for survival, he emerges a wiser man and no longer a simplistic Father Christmas. Dickens, therefore, reveals in his first novel an ambivalence toward the reality and efficacy of the Father Christmas figure. The thematic movement of *The Pickwick Papers,* from a group of episodes which emphasizes the natural benevolence of man embodied in Pickwick alone to a group of episodes emphasizing Pickwick's benevolence in confrontation with society, underlines Pickwick's deepening understanding of the nature of benevolence. His progress from an embodied philosophical abstraction to a sobered prisoner practicing and receiving personal benevolence among the poor represents Dickens' already maturing conception of the nature of true benevolence. And that realization, that true benevolence results only from close personal involvement, mirrors the central conception that developed out of the eighteenth-century philosophy of perfectibility.

However, there is one problem. Unlike his contemporary George Eliot, Dickens was virtually unacquainted with and uninterested in philosophy.[19] George Eliot's companion, George Henry Lewes, after having been shocked at the emptiness of Dickens' bookshelves, wrote, "Compared with that of Fielding or Thackeray, his was merely an animal intelligence. . . . He never was and never would have been a student." [20] Almost certainly, Dickens never read Shaftesbury's *Characteristics* or Butler's *Sermons* or even Godwin's *Enquiry Concerning Political Justice.* But Dickens did read the novels of Fielding, Sterne, and Goldsmith, and the novels of William Godwin, and these works all stand as firmly built bridges between the dominant philosophical tradition of the eighteenth century and the Dickens vision.[21]

In the preface to *Joseph Andrews* and the dedication and introductory chapters to the books of *Tom Jones,* Fielding intentionally speaks as a philosopher of natural benevolence and invokes the name of Lord Shaftesbury as a supportive authority. Sterne was a preacher as well as a novelist. His sermons, like those of Bishop Butler, emphasize that "a charitable and benevolent disposition is so principal and ruling a part of a man's character, as to be a considerable test by itself of the whole frame and temper of his mind, with which all other virtues and vices respectively rise and fall, and will almost necessarily be connected." [22]

But Godwin is perhaps the strongest bridge, especially to the later, supposedly "dark" Dickens. Godwin intentionally uses the novel form as a vehicle for the presentation of *his own* philosophy. For example, in *Caleb Williams* Falkland fluctuates between two poles of moral value.

The natural qualities which Falkland esteems most highly, his humanity and benevolence, are always at war with the artificial, society-imposed value of which he is so constantly aware, his honor. Falkland's characterization displays the conflict which Shaftesbury, Bishop Butler, and then Godwin himself (in *Enquiry Concerning Political Justice*) saw as the basic tension within the nature of man, self-love as opposed to benevolence.

Fielding, Sterne, and Godwin, as well as other important novelists—Smollett, Goldsmith, Henry Mackenzie—all represent in the characters and themes of their fiction the eighteenth-century philosophical view of man. Dickens may not have been directly acquainted with the original philosophical treatises, yet that eighteenth-century vision is repeatedly affirmed in all his novels. He was closely acquainted with the novels of the middle and late eighteenth century, and their created worlds directly influenced the birth and development of the Dickens world. Because of this chain of influence, Mr. Pickwick appears as a philosophical abstraction at the beginning of *The Pickwick Papers* and at the very beginning of Dickens' novelistic career. Also, because of this chain of influence the theme of the natural goodness of man as objectified in benevolence appears in all of Dickens' works, from *The Pickwick Papers* to the alleged "dark" novels, and remains essentially the same.

The Pickwick Papers

The characters and scenes of *The Pickwick Papers* are a striking example of the strong eighteenth-century influence on the Dickens vision. Pickwick's characterization and the plot movement of *The Pickwick Papers* are dependent upon the composite influence of three characters from eighteenth-century novels: Abraham Adams of Fielding's *Joseph Andrews,* Uncle Toby of Sterne's *Tristram Shandy,* and Dr. Primrose of Goldsmith's *The Vicar of Wakefield.* All of these eighteenth-century characters and Pickwick possess the same Shaftesburian natural goodness and feel the need to practice perpetual benevolence toward their fellowman. Like each of his three predecessors, Pickwick's inclination to benevolence often draws him into situations in which he is a comic dupe before the ultimate triumph of his good heart is accomplished. Luckily for Pickwick, these many episodes usually leave him only with the glow of embarrassment on his cheek rather than with the contents of a chamber pot dripping from his beard, the typical fate of Parson Adams.

Early in *The Pickwick Papers* Dickens refers to Fielding as an authority (103) and many of the episodes which involve Pickwick in the early parts of the novel are directly reminiscent of the misadventures of Parson Adams. At his first introduction Adams is described as "a man of good sense, good parts, and good nature; but at the same time as entirely ignorant of the ways of this world as an infant just entered into it could possibly be." [23] Like Pickwick, Adams has "benevolence visible in his countenance" (129) and as the members of the Pickwick Club feel toward Pickwick, so also do Adams' parishioners know "that he had their good entirely at heart, so they consulted him on every occasion" (34).

Pickwick and Adams are alike in innocence and in benevolent countenance, and they are also very alike in action. The comic finale of *Joseph Andrews* is the game of mistaken bedrooms which Adams finds himself playing during the night in the confusing rooms and passageways of Booby Hall. Pickwick undergoes a variation of this same experience in his nighttime encounter with the lady in the yellow curlpapers at the Great White Horse Inn at Ipswich. Dickens, however, because he is writing for an audience much different from Fielding's, is greatly restrained in the handling of the sexual overtones of his comic situation. He cannot reproduce the tactile methods of recognition which first Adams experiences with Madam Slipslop and then Fanny experiences with Adams, but both scenes are based on the same general premise. Each of the innocents becomes confused as to the whereabouts of his own room in the middle of the night in a strange building; each enters a room which is very similar to his own, undresses, and lies down to sleep in a woman's bed; and each is discovered by the lady (or ladies). Subsequently, each must face the wrath of the lady's suitor. Adams is discovered in bed with Fanny by Joseph, who is momentarily enraged, and Pickwick must face the jealousy of the formidable Peter Magnus in the morning. Finally, both episodes end when the two confused innocents are led back to their rooms by their two comparatively worldly-wise companions, Joseph and Sam Weller. Sam's comment to Pickwick upon the whole situation would serve equally well for Parson Adams: "You rayther want somebody to look arter you, sir, wen your judgment goes out a wisitin' " (312).

Thus Dickens used one of the outstanding comic events of *Joseph Andrews* as a prototype for the misadventures of Pickwick and he does the same thing with Sterne's *Tristram Shandy,* but the influence of Sterne's novel upon *The Pickwick Papers* is much greater. Instead of just imitating a comic episode of the earlier work, Dickens chooses an episode from *Tristram Shandy* which serves as the basis for the whole plot movement of *The Pickwick Papers.*

The character of Pickwick is modeled more closely upon Uncle Toby Shandy than upon any other literary character except Don Quixote. The central focus of Toby's characterization is upon the operation of his mind; and Toby's is a mind, emotionally and intellectually, very close to Pickwick's. Tristram pays tribute to Toby's nature in these

terms: "Thou envied'st no man's comforts—insulted'st no man's opinions,—Thou blackened'st no man's character,—devoured'st no man's
bread: gently with faithful Trim behind thee, didst thou amble round
the little circle of thy pleasures, jostling no creature in thy way;—for
each one's sorrows, thou hadst a tear,—for each man's need thou hadst
a shilling." [24] Both Pickwick and Toby Shandy are emotionally dedicated to helping others who are less fortunate than themselves while at
the same time they are intellectually dedicated to the spreading of
"hobbyhorsical" confusion. Riding one's hobbyhorse is the act of describing something which is absurdly simple in the most complex and
circumspect terms. Mr. Pickwick's speculations on the inscription—

+

B I L S T
U M
P S H I
S. M.
A R K

—which he finds on a rock in an innyard (217), are certainly of a
hobbyhorsical nature. The inscription is only the name and mark of a
rural stonecutter who, due to the shape of the rock, was forced to
break up the normal configuration of letters and to omit the spaces between words. Pickwick, however, feels that he has found an ancient
rune, a table which holds the key to knowledge of early British civilization.

Both *Tristram Shandy* and *The Pickwick Papers* focus upon the theme
of "meaning," which is both symbolic and ironic in each novel. Symbolically, the comedy of meaning becomes an analogue for human inadequacy, man's inability ever to find real certainty, true meaning, in his
world, in his life. In both novels, characters, especially Toby and Pickwick, attempt to invest the world with meaning, but invariably, because
of their own hobbyhorsical minds and the elusiveness of the world itself, they fail. Their perceptions never correspond with those of others
who similarly look for meaning in objects; their meanings, though well
meant, are always erroneous. Ironically, both Toby and Pickwick vio-
late meaning in their attempts to communicate it. When they talk or
speculate, no one ever understands what they mean. Their words are ill
chosen; their lives are plagued by ambiguity. Their words become
weapons which others, twisting those words' meanings, use against
them.

The closest similarity between *Tristram Shandy* and *The Pickwick
Papers* lies in Toby Shandy's and Pickwick's amorous adventures. And
these scenes are also the best illustrations of the identical themes of

meaning which operate in both novels. Uncle Toby Shandy's affair with the Widow Wadman is the prototype for Mr. Pickwick's unlucky misunderstanding with Mrs. Bardell. Mrs. Wadman first fell in love with Uncle Toby when that gentleman "was constrained to accept a bed at Mrs. Wadman's, for a night or two" (546) while Corporal Trim was building a bed for Toby. Pickwick also is a gentleman lodger at Mrs. Bardell's when their unfortunate misunderstanding takes place. Like Mr. Pickwick, Uncle Toby stands in complete "ignorance of the plies and foldings of the heart of woman" (455). Both Widow Wadman and Mrs. Bardell are in love with their gentleman boarders and are thus open to the power of the slightest suggestion; Mrs. Bardell "had long worshipped Mr. Pickwick from a distance, but here she was, all at once, raised to a pinnacle to which her wildest and most extravagant hopes had never dared to aspire" (152). Thus, the circumstances and characters in both scenes are essentially the same and the premise for the comic misunderstandings—the male talking about a harmless subject and the female interpreting his words, relative to her own amorous inclinations, as meaning something completely different from what is intended—is developed in exactly the same manner. The Widow Wadman mistakes Toby's maps for his groin, and the Widow Bardell mistakes Pickwick's benevolent proposal toward her son for an amorous proposal toward herself. Dickens, as in his handling of the episode modeled on *Joseph Andrews*, could not present this scene with all of the sexual implications present in Sterne's version. Dickens had to make the basic misunderstanding more general and less physical in order to make the joke acceptable to his audience.

This misunderstanding with Mrs. Bardell in *The Pickwick Papers* serves as the cornerstone for the plot structure of the whole work and, significantly, the novel's whole plot from this scene on is based upon a simple act of benevolence which Pickwick wished to undertake. But benevolence in the Dickens world is not always easy, as it was for Uncle Toby who could provide for Le Fever's son without any complications. The influence of the Widow Wadman episode from *Tristram Shandy* upon the conception of the Pickwick-Bardell misunderstanding also points to Dickens' use of *The Vicar of Wakefield* as the inspiration for the plot movement and theme of the second half of *The Pickwick Papers*.

The influence of the prison episodes of Goldsmith's *The Vicar of Wakefield* has been described by Steven Marcus as the main reason for the tonal change which takes place in the second half of *The Pickwick Papers*. But Dickens had a better reason for turning to Goldsmith than Marcus' theory that any novelist would naturally turn from Smollett and Fielding to Goldsmith when he feels like "becoming self-consciously serious." [25] Dickens turned to Goldsmith because he had gone as far as he could go with Sterne's Widow Wadman episode. Imitation

of the prison scenes from *The Vicar of Wakefield* offered a fitting resolution to the theme of benevolence, which had been the cause of all of
Pickwick's trouble with Mrs. Bardell, and would show the power of the
good heart in the hardest possible circumstances.

Since *Tristram Shandy* ends abruptly in the midst of the Widow
Wadman episode, Dickens was forced to look for a means of resolving
what he had begun. The central character of *The Vicar of Wakefield*
stands directly in the tradition of natural benevolence which had inspired the whole conception of Pickwick and thus was an appropriate
choice. One other important reason might well have figured in Dickens'
turning to *The Vicar of Wakefield*. Mr. Jingle and Job Trotter, the
highly entertaining swindlers of the first half of the novel, had been absent from the scene since Pickwick's encounter with them at Squire
Nupkins'. The prison scenes in *The Vicar of Wakefield* give Dickens a
means of reintroducing these established characters and of giving Pickwick the opportunity for accomplishing his greatest act of benevolence.

Throughout the novel, whenever outsmarted by Jingle, Pickwick
publicly levels dire threats of revenge against his archenemy: "Whenever I meet that Jingle again, wherever it is, . . . I'll inflict personal
chastisement on him, in addition to the exposure he so richly merits. I
will, or my name is not Pickwick" (226). These threats of Pickwick, however, seem artificial even as they are being shouted. To take physical
revenge on anyone or even to nurture the seeds of hatred within himself for longer than the briefest moment of anger would be an abrupt
movement out of character for Pickwick. The utter inconsistency of his
threats is evident as soon as Pickwick is given the opportunity to carry
them out. Pickwick's definitive "wherever it is" evidently does not include the degradation of the Fleet and instead of publicly vilifying
Jingle and Job, he "was affected . . . and said: 'I would like to speak to
you in private' " (597). Thus, as Dr. Primrose had done to Ephraim
Jenkinson, Pickwick forgives, forgets, and redeems through selfless benevolence.[26]

But the actions of Jenkinson in *The Vicar of Wakefield* also can serve
as the inspiration for another and greater act of benevolence in *The
Pickwick Papers*. Goldsmith's character, Jenkinson, is split in two by
Dickens' creative imagination. Half of him informs the repentant character of Jingle, but the other half motivates the benevolent action of
Sam Weller. A perceptive inmate in the Fleet recognizes Pickwick's naïveté immediately: "If I knew as little of life as that, I'd eat my hat and
swallow the buckle whole" (592). And Tony Weller confidently and
graphically images what Pickwick's relation to the new environment will
be: "Why, they'll eat him up alive, Sammy" (607). These assessments of
Pickwick are important because these are the voices of reality speaking.
If anything, Pickwick is a transparent character, and these men can see

immediately that he has never really felt the heat of the world, passed through the fiery furnace of reality. Pickwick is clearly too naïve to survive in a world in which men are scratching and clawing for existence. Sam and Tony Weller and the inmates know the territory and they also know Pickwick even better than he knows himself. Primrose, just as naïve as Pickwick, had a ready-made protector in the repentant Jenkinson, but Dickens, who has created a much more realistic prison world than Goldsmith could ever conceive, realized the absurdity of suddenly changing a disheartened Jingle into a strong protector who could stand between Pickwick and the hostile world. So Dickens turned to his already established strength, the one immovable force in the novel, Sam. Hope dies for the Pickwickian world if Sam is unwilling to give up all the prospects of his life for love of Pickwick. The Dickensian philosophy of benevolence and perfectibility is never more evident than when Sam does make this sacrifice joyfully and comically with no false emotion.

The Pickwick Papers is Sam Weller's novel. He was the savior when lack of interest threatened to end the adventures of the club and he was the prime mover behind Dickens' rise to fame. Fittingly, then, the theme of benevolence finds its most telling expression in the benevolence of Sam Weller. He doesn't fling coins randomly about like Father Christmas; his action involves no sort of monetary giving at all. He simply commits his life to another human being and, in the process, to a way of life, which, despite his solidly pragmatic nature, he has come to believe in.

Benevolence on the Road: *The Old Curiosity Shop*

In *The Pickwick Papers* Dickens' imitation of specific characters and situations from eighteenth-century novels highlights the affirmation of the eighteenth-century philosophy of benevolence which is his major theme. In another early novel, *The Old Curiosity Shop,* Dickens carries even further this philosophical theme. At the end of *The Pickwick Papers,* Dickensian benevolence is not the giving of money to the poor but rather the benevolence of the poor themselves, a Sam Weller sacrificing his own freedom to help Pickwick. The benevolence of the poor, especially in Fielding and Smollett, was a consistent occurrence in the plots of eighteenth-century picaresque or "road" novels, and is still a factor in the twentieth-century British picaresque. Listen to Gulley Jimson just out of jail and looking for a loan: "I was in trouble and people in trouble, they say, are more likely to give help to each other than those who aren't. After all, it's not surprising, for people who help other people in trouble are likely soon to be in trouble themselves." [27] No matter whether the unfortunate traveler is in a Smollett or Fielding or Dickens or Joyce Cary novel, the benevolent world he traverses always takes the same form: the rich are, more often than not, hypocritical and penurious; the poor are naturally benevolent and openhanded.

In the British picaresque or "road" fiction, the survival of the hero is always reliant upon someone's benevolent nature. When a young traveler such as Roderick Random or Joseph Andrews sets out on his journey toward fortune and love, he is invariably penniless. At appropriate times in the story, just when the hero is in a situation of the highest peril or the lowest degradation, a benevolent character appears and saves him. The operation of this convention is not always so trite, however. More often than not the benevolent character who rescues the hero is almost as destitute as the hero himself. Usually, the benevolent character cannot afford to rescue anyone, and after the act is accomplished, the rescuee is left better provided for than his rescuer. Frequently, the benevolent transaction has either nothing to do with money or involves an amount so small that before another day passes the hero is again in need of benevolent assistance. Fielding's *Joseph Andrews* and Smollett's *Roderick Random* both demonstrate the operation of this theme of the benevolence of the poor.

In *Joseph Andrews,* Parson Adams is a poor man, yet upon finding Joseph ill at Mrs. Tow-wouse's inn he immediately places at Joseph's disposal all his money, "nine shillings and three pence" (15). As the novel progresses Adams displays his natural goodness many times, but his are not the only acts of benevolence. With Joseph's departure from Lady Booby's London home, Fielding also departs from his original plan to parody Richardson's *Pamela* and begins to write his own novel of the road. And repeatedly, he depends upon the concept of the benevolence of the poor (as opposed to the unnatural class-consciousness and penury of the rich) for many of his finest satiric effects. Just outside of London, Joseph is beaten, stripped, and left in a ditch to die. A coach stops but a shocked lady, a well-dressed gentleman, and a lawyer refuse poor, naked Joseph admittance. The whole episode becomes a satiric travesty of the parable of the Good Samaritan. Ironically, the Good Samaritan who materializes is the poorest of all the occupants of the coach: "The postilion (a lad who has since been transported for robbing a hen roost) voluntarily stripped off a great coat, his only garment, at the same time swearing a great oath (for which he was rebuked by the passengers) 'that he would rather ride in his shirt all his life than suffer a fellow creature to lie in so miserable a condition' " (39). This is the first example of the benevolence of the poor which sustains Joseph, Fanny, and Adams on their journey. Later, after Trulliber refuses them, a "poor pedlar" (161) pays their bill, and after a seemingly benevolent gentleman refuses Adams a loan, an honest innkeeper trusts them for his bill. In each case the ability of the poor to feel and act is opposed to the hypocrisy and selfish irresponsibility of the rich. Fielding certainly is indulging in class antagonism and creating stereotypes of hypocrisy in *Joseph Andrews*, indulgences which Dickens, who creates both good and bad rich people and good and bad poor people, will avoid. Fielding also will balance his view by creating Squire Allworthy in *Tom Jones*.

Similar characters and events influence the plot movement of *Roderick Random*. Roderick is much more a real *picaro* than Joseph Andrews. Roderick is disreputable, lecherous, and, worst of all, he makes a habit of exploiting the good natures of the benevolent characters in the novel. The one character most exploited by Roderick Random is the ever-faithful Strap, who at one juncture gives Roderick all of his savings and says: "I'll beg for you, steal for you, go through the wide world with you, and starve with you: for though I be a poor cobbler's son, I am no scout." [28] Also, as in *Joseph Andrews*, the rich are portrayed as unfeeling and unnatural (the most unnatural of all is Lord Strutwell, who treats Roderick benevolently in order to attempt a homosexual seduction).

The parable of the Good Samaritan also appears in *Roderick Random* as Roderick, after a shipwreck, is set upon, robbed, and left to die by the crew members and the sadistic Captain Crampley. After being found alive by some country people who refuse to help him, he is taken to the parson who not only refuses to help him but threatens to excommunicate him as well. Finally, the only person who will give him refuge is a poor old woman "who was suspected of witchcraft by the neighborhood" (240). In the world of the eighteenth-century novel, natural benevolence seems to be much more accessible to the unenlightened and financially deprived lower classes. However, one does not have to be poor to be good. The well-established character type of the benevolent squire—Squire Allworthy, Matthew Bramble in *Humphrey Clinker*, and Toby Shandy—demonstrates that the rich also can be benevolent. The benevolent squire, however, does not appear so frequently as the figure of the good-hearted poor person.

In this eighteenth-century mode and with this view of what constitutes real benevolence, Dickens wrote *The Old Curiosity Shop*. Nell starts her journey to the supposedly green and pastoral north almost penniless and utterly defenseless. As she and her hapless grandfather travel, however, they are protected and sustained by a succession of good-hearted people along the way. Outside of London a poor woman notices that one of Nell's feet is "blistered and sore, and being a woman and a mother too she would not suffer her to go until she had washed the place and applied some simple remedy" (120). The travelers are next befriended by the poor schoolmaster and the lady proprietor of Jarley's waxworks, neither of whom can properly afford to be charitable.

After leaving Mrs. Jarley's, penniless because grandfather has lost the money at cards, the travelers find themselves isolated and destitute among the heartless crowds of a large manufacturing city. An underground man, the tender of one of the huge fires which generate power in the city, rescues them and leads them to shelter in his miniature inferno. The scene and the character are ironically symbolic and underline the parodoxical quality of Dickens' theme of benevolence. The fireman is a devil and yet his heart is benevolent. He comes out of an underground hell into the daylight world of the living to find Nell and save her; ironically, that daylight world contains only a drifting, faceless crowd of people whose hearts are dead and eyes blind to the plight of Nell, while in the dark inferno men can still feel and give. As Nell and her grandfather leave, the fireman says, "I wish I could do more" and presses "two old, battered, smoke-encrusted penny pieces" into her hand. The narrator cannot help saying, "Who knows but they shone as brightly in the eyes of angels, as the golden gifts that have been chronicled on tombs?" (333). The pennies symbolically represent an important quality of the novel's theme of benevolence, a quality that was repeatedly stressed in the novels of Dickens' eighteenth-century predecessors. Appearances often belie that reality which lies beneath the surface, and in this episode love comes more quickly out of hell to redeem than it ever can come from the rich who, like Quilp (or Ralph Nickleby or Jonas Chuzzlewit or Bounderby or Casby or Fledgeby), corrupted by a money lust which corrodes all natural instincts, often seek only to destroy.

Finally, as in the eighteenth-century novels of the road, the old schoolmaster appears just at that moment when Nell has reached the very limit of her endurance and has fainted from exhaustion. Like the Good Samaritan, he takes her up from the side of the road where she has fallen, carries her to an inn where she is restored, and makes it clear "that I am the paymaster for the three" (343).

All of these episodes reiterate that confidence in the essential goodness of man absorbed by Dickens in his reading of the eighteenth-century road novels. The very existence of the benevolence of the poor in the industrialized nineteenth-century world of *The Old Curiosity Shop* is, in itself, a forceful statement of the enduring power of man's intrinsically good nature. The industrial world, to which Dickens will later return in *Hard Times*, attempts to grind men into parts of the machines they operate, yet some of them have not allowed their ability to feel to be burned away by the blazing fires of the industrial metropolis.

This same emphasis upon the greater ability of the poor to feel and act also occurs in *Dombey and Son,* where the poverty-stricken crew of the Wooden Midshipman does not hesitate a moment at taking in Florence Dombey who has been rejected by her rich, unfeeling father, and in *Bleak House,* where Mr. George, financially bankrupt but morally rich, becomes the protector of Gridley, poor Jo, and finally Sir Leicester (in this last case the benevolence of the poor is actually directed toward the rich). The poor in the Dickens world are the real benevolists. The narrator of *Bleak House* realizes this as he describes two St. Albans brickmaker's wives: "These two women, coarse and shabby and beaten, so united; to see what they could be to another; to see how they felt for one another, how the heart of each to each was softened by the hard trials of their lives. I think the best side of such people is almost hidden from us. What the poor are to the poor is little known, excepting to themselves and GOD" (109).

The poor commit themselves, not just their meager material goods, to those who are even worse off than they. The omniscient narrator of *The Old Curiosity Shop* finds it necessary to intrude in order to place particular emphasis upon the theme of benevolence: "Let me linger in this place, for an instant, to remark that if ever household affections and loves are graceful things, they are graceful in the poor. The ties that bind the wealthy and the proud to home may be forged on earth, but those which link the poor man to his humble hearth are of the truer metal and bear the stamp of Heaven. . . . His household gods are of flesh and blood, with no alloy of silver, gold, or precious stone; he has no property but in the affections of his own heart" (281). The benevolence of the poor is more difficult and, perhaps, less powerful than the benevolence of the rich, but it exists in the Dickens world on a much larger scale than the Father Christmas mode of uninvolved benevolence as exhibited by Abel Garland in this novel and the Cheeryble brothers in *Nicholas Nickleby.*

Little Dorrit, "Dark" Novel?

In *The Pickwick Papers, Oliver Twist,* and *Nicholas Nickleby,* the naturally benevolent man, be he rich or poor, displays that power for improving the world and defeating selfishness and hypocrisy which was so strongly emphasized in the novels of Fielding, Sterne, and Goldsmith. But the poor in the Dickens world—Sam Weller, Newman Noggs in *Nicholas Nickleby,* a succession of "road" characters in *The Old Curiosity Shop,* Mark Tapley in *Martin Chuzzlewit,* the Wooden Midshipman's family in *Dombey and Son*—hardly indulging themselves in any "philosophie de Noël," best embody the Shaftesburian philosophy of natural benevolence. However, does Dickens suddenly, beginning with *Bleak House,* reject his optimistic eighteenth-century view of man in the world and take on a dark, pessimistic view of man? Does he deny the concept of natural goodness and emphasize only the oppressiveness of a world which frustrates the powers for good of the individual? Certainly, the settings have changed. The reader no longer is riding in the open air on the top of a coach with Pickwick and Sam but is sitting in the Marshalsea with William Dorrit or floating down the stinking Thames fishing for corpses with Gaffer Hexam. The settings have changed, but Dickens' world view, his philosophy of man, still remains consistent and optimistic, and the philosophy of benevolence as found in the novels of the eighteenth century is still at work in these later novels. *Little Dorrit*, for example, is reputedly Dickens' darkest novel, yet in *Little Dorrit* Dickens' most sophisticated version of the eighteenth-century philosophy of natural benevolence is articulated and affirmed. William Godwin's *Caleb Williams* and Dickens' *Little Dorrit* possess similar characters and are concerned with similar themes and events, but their greatest similarity lies in Dickens' affirmation of Godwin's view of the individual man's relationship to the world.

In his *Enquiry Concerning Political Justice* Godwin states that the most important concerns of men must be "the question concerning free will and necessity, and the question respecting self-love and benevolence" (362). Godwin's doctrine of Necessity maintains that man is qualified to predict the future according to his own experience of the past. Thus, history can offer instruction to man because "certain temptations and inducements . . . in all ages and climates, introduce a certain series of actions" (369). For Godwin, the only freedom of the human will consists in the fact "[t]hat every choice we make, has been chosen by us, and every act of the mind, been preceded and produced by an act of the mind. This is so true, that, in reality, the ultimate act is not styled free, from any quality of its own, but because the mind, in adopting it, was self-determined, that is, because it was preceded by another act. The ultimate act resulted completely from the determination that was its precursor. . . . All the acts, except the first, were necessary, and followed each other, as inevitably as the links of a chain do, when the first link is drawn forward" (378). In this regard, therefore, man "is in no case, strictly speaking, the beginner of any event or series of events that take place in the universe, but only the vehicle through which certain antecedents operate, which antecedents, if he were supposed not to exist, would cease to have that operation. Action however, in its more simple and obvious sense, is sufficiently real, and exists equally both in mind and matter" (385).

Because of the laws of Necessity which rule the material universe, man has no need for the powers of choice. His path in life, the chain of events of his existence, is already determined for him. Man does, however, still exercise some control over the emotional events of his life, though this control is itself dependent upon past moral experience and past moral action. Godwin emphasizes that "the doctrine of necessity does not overturn the nature of things. Happiness and misery, wisdom and error will still be distinct from each other, and there will still be a correspondence between them. Wherever there is that which may be the means of pleasure or pain to a sensitive being, there is a ground for preference and desire, or on the contrary for neglect and aversion. Benevolence and wisdom will be objects worthy to be desired, selfishness and error worthy to be disliked" (386). Thus, a man can exercise preference in regard to his moral action because he has acted in a similar way according to similar feelings many times before. Also, events in the world occur according to the moral feelings and actions of men. Therefore man's power of emotional preference, which is ruled completely by past experience, influences the movement of historical events.

One of Godwin's applications of his doctrine of Necessity and his concept of the power of personal preference is to political institutions. If an institution is corrupt and oppressive, the nature of man can recognize the necessity of destroying it, and individuals by opposing institutions can become the instruments of Necessity. Thus, the doctrine of Necessity is as much involved with individual action as with institutional or political change.

Godwin intended his novels to be vehicles for the representation of his major philosophical concepts. Therefore, *Caleb Williams,* his most famous novel, which demonstrates the doctrine of Necessity functioning among men, is an event, a moment of translation, in a relentless history of ideas moving toward Dickens. *Caleb Williams* translates dry philosophy into vibrant fiction, thus making philosophical doctrine available to readers who would never pick up the *Enquiry Concerning Political Justice. Caleb Williams,* with its emphasis on Necessity's operation through the actions of individuals, foreshadows the spontaneous combustion of Krook in *Bleak House,* the fall of the house of Clennam in *Little Dorrit,* the need for Necessitarian apocalypse in the corrupt nineteenth-century world.

In both Godwin's *Caleb Williams* and Dickens' *Little Dorrit,* the Godwinian theories of individual man's relationship to his social world are embodied in similar characters, scenes, and situations. In *Caleb Williams* Godwin presents the doctrine of Necessity in a negative and destructive context. The single word used most often to describe Falkland in *Caleb Williams* is "benevolence." The basic conflict of the novel, however, is between benevolence and selfish pride. Falkland, because he has murdered Tyrrel (his first nonbenevolent act), must express a preference between the rule of justice and the social ideal of honor. Justice in this case would be synonymous with benevolence in that Falkland by confessing to the crime would save Mr. Hawkins and his son from the

gallows. However, in all of his past life Falkland has dedicated himself
to the ideal of nobility, and thus he really has no choice in the matter at
all. He must preserve his honor.

Caleb, in his relationship with Falkland, also finds himself caught
between the rule of justice and the rule of honor. However, because of
his low social class, justice is out of reach for Caleb. Finally, at the end
of the novel, Caleb refuses to try any longer to carry out justice upon
Falkland, who is a broken man, but instead gives in to emotional preferences for pity and benevolence: "Shall I trample on a man thus dread-
fully reduced? Shall I point my animosity against one whom the system
of nature has brought down to the grave? It is impossible. There must
have been some dreadful mistake in the train of argument that persuaded me to be the author of this hateful scene." [29] Ironically for
Caleb, honor is synonymous with benevolence as he simply realizes that
he has violated the feudal relationship of love between master and servant upon which his whole life has been based. Thus, Caleb fulfils a
natural and necessary benevolence by wishing to protect his lord in the
end. Better late than never, Caleb bows to the same feelings of benevolent loyalty which later motivate Sam Weller to follow Pickwick into the
debtor's prison.

The great irony of *Caleb Williams* is that both Falkland and Caleb
act according to the dictates of the same set of environmental antecedents. Because of their individual conceptions of the idea of honor, conceptions developed throughout all of their individual past experiences,
Falkland acts *selfishly* to destroy Caleb while Caleb acts *selflessly* to protect Falkland. Caleb's natural impulse to benevolence conquers the artificial nobility of Falkland. In Dickens' *Little Dorrit* the same tensions
are present and the same higher values are affirmed.

The central action of *Caleb Williams* consists of the mental and
physical persecution of the innocent by the guilty. In *Little Dorrit,* as
Clennam leaves the Circumlocution Office after his first encounter with
the administrators of that institution, he meets his former traveling
companion, Mr. Meagles, who introduces him to Daniel Doyce: "Mr.
Clennam, will you do me the favour to look at this man? . . . You
wouldn't suppose this man to be a notorious rascal; would you? . . .
You wouldn't suppose him to be a public offender; would you? . . .
No, but he is. He is a public offender. What has he been guilty of?
Murder, manslaughter, arson, forgery, swindling, housebreaking,
highway robbery, larceny, conspiracy, fraud? . . . He has been ingenious, and he has been trying to turn his ingenuity to his country's service. That makes him a public offender directly, sir" (119). As Meagles'
rhetoric emphasizes, the Circumlocution Office has turned Daniel
Doyce into a criminal guilty of trying to help others. Just as Falkland
persecutes Caleb, the Circumlocution Office takes away Doyce's liveli-

hood and drives him out of society, which he is only trying to improve, to the obscurity of Bleeding Heart Yard. Similarly, other innocents —Mr. Dorrit by Mrs. Clennam, Tattycoram by the spiteful Miss Wade, Pet Meagles by Henry Gowan, and the inmates of Bleeding Heart Yard by Casby—are oppressed by the guilty in *Little Dorrit.*

Another striking similarity between these two novels involves the central characters. Initially both Caleb Williams and Arthur Clennam are motivated by relentless curiosity. In surrendering to his curiosity Clennam, though he is forty years old, is just as naïve as the young Caleb Williams who surrenders to the same impulse and begins to stalk Falkland's secret. Like Caleb Williams, and like so many other Dickens heroes (Richard Carstone in *Bleak House,* Harthouse in *Hard Times,* Sydney Carton, Pip, Harmon/Rokesmith in *Our Mutual Friend*), Clennam becomes both the pursuer and the pursued, driven by some secret wrong which engenders in him an irrational sense of guilt: "The shadow of a supposed act of injustice, which had hung over him since his father's death, was so vague and formless that it might be the result of a reality widely remote from his idea of it" (319). Both Caleb and Clennam share in the guilt even as they are struggling to expose the crime. But, most important, both characters, though innocent, are made to suffer because their existentially benevolent natures drive them to repair an injustice out of the past. They become fugitives, cut off from society, because they have the temerity to say, as Clennam does, " 'I want to know.' " Both must give up their work because of their knowledge or suspicion of the guilt of their employers. Both must constantly live with the shadow of the prison upon them. And both, because of their benevolent natures, must always exist in a state of indecision, because they both will to protect their persecutors even as they are being persecuted.

Both Caleb's and Clennam's lives are a constant search for the moment when the benevolence of their natures can rise out of potentiality and by necessity cure the disease which haunts their past. The only way they can attain this moment is through self-abnegation, and both are willing to pay the price. Clennam desires his imprisonment, as does Caleb Williams who goes to jail rather than say " 'one word of resolute accusation against my patron' " (373). Perhaps the best explanation of the common predicament of Caleb and Clennam is that of Mr. Pancks in *Little Dorrit:* " 'I don't say anything of your making yourself poor to repair a wrong you never committed. That's you. A man must be himself' " (584). The similar actions of these two similar characters are their means of fulfilling their own naturally benevolent natures.

Many points of comparison between the plots and characters of *Caleb Williams* and *Little Dorrit* exist but the greatest similarity between the two novels lies in their similar affirmation of the philosophy of benevolence which reveals itself by means of the doctrine of Necessity. For Godwin, Necessity is a cosmic power for good which operates through individual men in the world. Dickens' social consciousness in *Little Dorrit* displays the manner in which Necessity can operate in the Victorian world if there are people who care enough to allow the natural benevolence of human nature to express itself. Every institution in *Little Dorrit* is subject to Necessity, which operates through the natural benevolence of man.

One of the great social institutions of *Little Dorrit* is Mr. Merdle. He is a little, ratlike man, but he is described by Mr. Dorrit as a national institution: "Mr. Merdle's is a name of—ha—world wide repute. Mr. Merdle's undertakings are immense. They bring him in such vast sums of money, that they are regarded as—hum—national benefits. Mr. Merdle is a man of his time. The name of Merdle is the name of the age" (484). Mr. Dorrit does not realize just how perceptive his words are. Mr. Merdle is only a name. There is nothing of substance in the man or in any of his enterprises. The narrator, through the use of imagery, further hints at the ambiguous difference between the force of Mr. Merdle's name and the substance of the man himself: "He looked far more like a man in possession of his house under a distraint, than a commercial Colossus bestriding his own hearthrug, while the little ships were sailing in to dinner" (558–59). The Colossus image embodies the far-reaching and ruling power of Merdle's commercial enterprises, but it also suggests his transitory existence. Like the great Colossus of Rhodes, which sailors mistakenly felt was a beacon built on so sound a base that it would exist forever, Merdle and his commercial empire will certainly fall. This image also suggests that Merdle is but an idol with feet of common clay, and when the Colossus falls, its feet are found to be of the commonest clay indeed (or perhaps of an even more vulgar material of French derivation). In death his name no longer has any meaning, and he is only "a heavily-made man, with an obtuse head, and coarse, mean, common features." With Merdle's death the great commercial empire which had "set him on his pedestal" comes crashing down because it was based only on "carrion at the bottom of a bath" and "the greatest Forger and the greatest Thief that ever cheated the gallows" (710). Later in Dickens' fiction, the same imagery is used to describe Mr. Podsnap in *Our Mutual Friend*—he stands before the fire "executing a statuette of the Colossus at Rhodes" (115)—who also is a fragile and superficial national institution.

Dickens also deals symbolically with religious institutions in *Little Dorrit*. Mrs. Clennam's house represents the religion operating in the novel and is the tabernacle of that religion. The physical condition of the Clennam house presents clearly Dickens' view of the condition of such religion in the Victorian world. From the beginning of the novel

acute moral insight. Other examples of this childlike fool, Mr. Toots, Mr. Dick, Maggy, and Sloppy, share his moral sensitivity, yet Barnaby, the symbolic heart of his novel, is easily the most thematically meaningful of Dickens' folk-fools. His ambiguous participation in the Gordon Riots, sharing and exposing the rioters' blindness, reveals Dickens' sophisticated understanding of the fool's symbolic nature.

The Holy Innocent classification is obviously the most extensive, including characters from virtually all Dickens' works. Although fools may be "saintly and pure in heart," corrupt "victims of the Eighth Deadly Sin [Folly]," or innocently detached from any moral disputes,[2] the Victorian concept of the wise fool accentuates his moral qualities. As Dickens' friend and literary adviser John Forster observes (*Examiner*, 4 February 1838), reviewing Macready's restoration of the original *Lear,* "The Fool in the tragedy of *Lear* is one of the most wonderful creations of Shakespeare's genius. The picture of his quick and pregnant sarcasm, of his loving devotion, of his acute sensibility, of his despairing mirth, of his heartbroken silence—contrasted with the rigid sublimity of Lear's suffering . . . is the noblest thought that ever entered into the mind and heart of man." [3]

Dickens also praised Macready's production (*Examiner*, 27 October 1849) and acclaimed the Fool "as one of its most affecting and necessary features," noting that "it would be difficult to praise so exquisite and delicate an assumption, too highly." [4] Saint Paul exclaims, "We are fools for Christ's sake" (1 Cor. 4:10), a doctrine that Erasmus' *Praise of Folly* diffused throughout European culture: "To speak briefly, all Christian Religion seems to have a kind of allyance with folly, and in no respect to have any accord with wisedom." [5] Dickens, likewise, recognizing the ironic relationship between "wisdom" and "folly," adopts this Erasmian-Shakespearean paradox and affirms that the "wise doctrine, Every man for himself . . . is an idiot's folly, weighed against a simple heart!" (616).[6] Self-seeking worldly wisdom is mere folly, while the folly of a "simple heart" is the truest wisdom.

With Tom Pinch, however, Dickens also moves beyond the Holy Innocent's simple moral and symbolic roles to explore Tom's isolated social position, frustrated sexuality, and sorrowful awareness of his personal limitations. In the figure of Tom Pinch, the Dickensian Holy Innocent becomes a character as well as a symbol, performing the fool's traditional dramatic functions, yet also endowed with a detailed inner life.

Discussing Touchstone's role in *As You Like It,* John Palmer observes that the fool's "part in the comedy is to shed the light of reality and common sense upon its fanciful figures and diversions," to "see things as they are but without malice," and to "have a keen flair for absurdity in people and things—not least for his own infirmities." [7] Malcolm Andrews, likewise (in his introduction to the Penguin edition of *The Old Curiosity Shop*), suggests that Dick Swiveller fulfills "a kind of Chorus role, a bridge between the reader's reactions and the dramatic action in the novel," restoring "a little equilibrium" (24). Both Dick and Touchstone, in short, are the voice of reason allied with the voice of imagination, performing the fool's classic function of counterbalancing and synthesizing extremes. Touchstone responds to the more extravagant aspects of Rosalind's and Orlando's romantic fervor with understanding and healthy cynicism, while Dick, likewise, is a realist who can casually remark of the divine Nell that she is a "fine girl of her age, but small" (55) and then abruptly dignify a dirty, illegitimate serving-girl with the title "Marchioness." Swiveller is, perhaps, the only truly independent character in the novel, that is, the only major character not blinded by Nell's virtue or intimidated by Quilp's demonic power. As fool, he contributes a necessary synthesis of realism and imagination to a world where these forces are abnormally separated.

The fool often serves as a mirror for nonfools (e.g., Touchstone's response to the melancholy Jaques [2. 7. 12–34]), sharing their wisdom while exposing their folly. Swiveller's thematic relationship with Quilp and Nell—a combination of parody and synthesis—closely parallels this traditional fool's function. Both Quilp and Dick, for example, are perceptive satirists, yet, while Quilp rages angrily, Dick displays a gentle, entertaining vision. Even the "horrible desires to annihilate this Sally Brass" (251) are calmed by several playful feints at Sally's offensive headdress. Dick clearly reflects Quilp's insightful response to the rapacious Brass family, while (in his pseudo violence) parodying and nullifying the dwarf's demonic anger. Like Touchstone, moreover, Dick "uses his folly like a stalking-horse, and under the presentation of that he shoots his wit" (5. 4. 103–4), delightedly enjoying his own satiric humor.

> "What harm!" cried Brass. "Is it no harm to have a constant hallooing and hooting under one's very nose, distracting one from business, and making one grind one's teeth with vexation? Is it no harm to be blinded and choked up, and have the king's highway stopped with a set of screamers and roarers whose throats must be made of—of—"
>
> "Brass," suggested Mr Swiveller. (275)

Like Touchstone or Lear's fool, furthermore, Dick is a comic entertainer, "lighting up the office with scraps of song and merriment, conjuring with inkstands and boxes of wafers, catching three oranges in one hand, balancing stools upon his chin and penknives on his nose, and constantly performing a hundred other feats with equal ingenuity;

for with such unbendings did Richard, in Mr. Brass's absence, relieve the tedium of his confinement" (270). Such clownish performances may seem a relatively minor element in Dick's character, but this light-hearted joviality is an essential facet of his thematic importance. Quilp, for example, is equally eccentric and (indeed) entertaining in his grotesque acrobatics: "Daniel Quilp withdrew into a dismantled skittle-ground behind the public-house, and, throwing himself upon the ground actually screamed and rolled about in uncontrollable delight" (164). In contrast to this perverted, solitary joy, Dick's genial show-manship is expansive and uplifting, an image of Quilp's energy without the dwarf's self-enclosed bitterness. As Dick himself observes, in a passage that Dickens deleted, the purpose of the fool-figure (in this case Punch) is "to hold the mirror up to Nature, show virtue her own image, vice her own deformity" (Penguin, 702). In their celebrated fight scene, as Dick prances around the fallen dwarf in an unconscious parody of Quilp's aggressive malice (99), Dick fulfills that same function.

Although Dick may share his most engaging qualities with Quilp, his thematic-symbolic relationship with Little Nell is equally significant. Dick clearly is not a Holy Innocent figure, yet like Lear's incessantly moralizing fool he displays a perceptive sense of value. Although initially depicted as a profligate young gallant advocating a mercenary ethos (" 'The watchword to the old min is—fork' " [24]), Dick also affirms his belief in compromise rather than conflict, family unity rather than strife. Even in his first appearance, when he is involved with Trent's plot against Nell and her grandfather, he displays the wise fool's customary blend of wisdom in folly. In the midst of his ludicrous account of the relative merits of Jamaica rum, for example, he suddenly advises, "It's a devil of a thing, gentlemen, . . . when relations fall out and disagree. If the wing of friendship should never moult a feather, the wing of relationship should never be clipped, but be always expanded and serene. Why should a grandson and grandfather peg away at each other with mutual wiolence when all might be bliss and concord? Why not jine hands and forget it?" (19). Whereas Quilp, furthermore, is cruelly amused by the Marchioness' loneliness and ignorance, Dick is sympathetically attracted to the neglected girl, earnestly lamenting the fact that "nobody ever came to see her, nobody spoke of her, nobody cared about her" (271). Similarly, Dick is instrumental in the villains' downfall and Kit Nubbles's salvation, and as Brass amazedly observes, "If you'll believe me I've found that fellow, in the commonest little matters of the office that have been trusted to him, blurting out the truth, though expressly cautioned" (465).

Just as Dick both reflects and parodies Quilp's nature, however, so he shares Nell's moral principles while still offering an unconsciously iconoclastic response to her sentimental melodrama. The fool must "hold the mirror up to Nature" without the distorting influence of sentimentality. Unlike the majority of the novel's characters, therefore, who all fall under Nell's morbid spell, Dick (in the passage quoted earlier) remains singularly unimpressed. As he drunkenly exclaims, "Left an infant by my parents, at an early age, . . . cast upon the world in my tenderest period, and thrown upon the mercies of a deluding dwarf" (171), his lot is a subtle burlesque of Nell's somberly melodramatic world. Gabriel Pearson makes this point even more forcefully; discussing Dick's pseudopoetic rhapsody on death (414), he argues that "Dick's own parody poetics and theatricality establish themselves in endemic, neutralizing opposition to Nell's blank-verse elegiacs." [8]

For all this moral strength and wholesome irony, however, Dick is too detached, too thoughtless and self-centered to stand against the Quilpian world. Unlike Sam Weller who masterfully copes with Serjeant Buzfuz, Dick is verbally manhandled by Brass's lawyer until he "retires abashed" (471), while Quilp, likewise, has little difficulty extracting information from the helplessly intoxicated Swiveller (163). Dick is a double fool, a wise fool who sees and understands the truth, and a comic butt duped and used by wiser characters. Dick, however, is also a man "who takes refuge in imagination until he learns that he can actually make a home of it," [9] a man whose thoughtless gaiety and imagination require only strengthening and direction. Through his relationship with the Marchioness, Dick achieves this perfect synthesis of realism and imagination that allows him to abandon his frivolity while retaining both his Quilpian life-energy and his Nell-like virtues of sympathy and truthfulness.

As Garrett Stewart observes, when Dick grants the Marchioness her dignified title (" 'To make it seem more real and pleasant, I shall call you the Marchioness, do you hear?' " [427]), he is doing more than expressing his normally playful character: "This is a romantic daydream in which the 'real' and the 'pleasant' can be willed at once into conjunction; yet at the same time it bespeaks a mature faith in the possibilities of a better world, a faith nurtured in the love of poetry, where the real and the pleasant, truth and beauty, do regularly coincide. Here, domesticated and made comic, is a true Romantic poet's faith in the sustaining power of imagination." [10] This belief in imagination as the pathway to "a better world" where "the real and the pleasant . . . coincide," parallels Enid Welsford's description of the fool as "a creator . . . of spiritual freedom," the man who demonstrates "the pleasing delusion that facts are more flexible than they appear to be," [11] that comedy (or imagination) can remake the world. Robert Goldsmith, on the other hand, observes that the fool is sometimes "too hardheaded to live happily in the forest of romance. . . . His mocking humor enables us to laugh at pretense and vulgar folly, but it cannot open our eyes to the true if transitory loveliness of the Arcadian dream." [12] Dickens, however, literally has it both ways. He transforms the imaginative, frivolous Dick Swiveller and grants him an increased practicality while still sustaining the imaginative, expansive comic world.

When Dick awakes from his feverish sleep, therefore, and poetically designates the Marchioness "a Genie" (475), he preserves and enhances the imaginative "forest of romance." His newly strengthened vision, however, is no longer drunkenly obscured by that "Arcadian dream": " 'This poor little Marchioness has been wearing herself to death!' " (478). Just as Dick grants (or creates) the Marchioness' identity, so she returns the compliment and Dick responds to the metaphoric meaning of his "new" name and to its emotional, human significance as well: " 'Liverer indeed!' said Dick thoughtfully. 'It's well I *am* a liverer. I strongly suspect I should have died, Marchioness, but for you' " (478–79). Dick, moreover, asks Mr. Garland, ' "if you could make the Marchioness yonder, a Marchioness, in real, sober earnest, . . . I'd thank you to get it done off-hand" ' (490). As Stewart points out, " 'Sober' is now the operative marker, placed next to 'real' as a new and finally more satisfying modification." [13] And yet, Dickens notes, "let it be added, to Dick's honour, that, though we have called her Sophronia, he called her the Marchioness from first to last" (552), and though her education "kept him in straitened circumstances for half-a-dozen years, he never slackened in his zeal" (551). The world of the imagination triumphs, not in opposition to the real world, but enhanced and sustained by Dick's new strength of character.

Critical evaluation of the Swiveller-Marchioness relationship has not been universally favorable. Steven Marcus, for example, writes that its "gratifying acrobatic resolution and the assurance it holds out for the future are simply too light and supple for a novel whose unremitting impulse is toward all that lies underground." [14] And yet, as fool, Dick is the "creator of spiritual freedom" who moves beyond the simple evil-energy/virtue-passivity conflict of the novel's main action. If his story is "too light and supple," it also contains much that is painful and harsh–the Marchioness' brutalized, perverted childhood, Dick's own fever and near-death. As William Willeford maintains, "the fool among us is a perpetual link to the light and the life in [the world's] darkness," [15] the wise comic who combines the salient features of both realms to create unity rather than conflict. Nell, therefore, must ascend into an angelic eternity while Quilp dies in darkness, for the extremes remain irreconcilable. Only the imaginative yet "hardheaded" fool is reborn.

Whereas Dick unifies the antagonistic forces of his world, Barnaby Rudge, in contrast, remains fundamentally ambiguous. His limited intelligence and creativity cannot duplicate Swiveller's imaginative syn-

thesis, and yet, in a novel whose moral conflicts are far more involved
than those in *The Old Curiosity Shop,* this ambiguity is a necessary and
valuable facet of his fool-nature.

Neither an entirely credible psychological portrait nor merely a
symbolic character, Barnaby Rudge is one of Dickens' most complex
fool-figures. Although he partakes of the Holy Innocent's simplicity,
goodness, and insight, he is also subtly associated with destructive, demonic forces—Grip, the rioters, his murderous father. This ambiguity
has generated some critical confusion. Jack Lindsay, for example, while
recognizing the influence of the folk-fool, fails to appreciate Barnaby's
role in Dickens' ambivalent vision:

> The folk-fool, who is prophet and liberator, Merlin and Par-
> sifal, is a potent symbol in the medieval world, and so is still
> available for the tragic universe of Shakespeare; but in the
> world of developing industrialism his magic dwindles. . . .
> Dickens conjures him up valiantly in Barnaby, but is unable to
> make him carry all the weight of meaning that the fable de-
> mands. Part of the reason for the novel's weaknesses lies in
> Dickens's ambivalence towards the theme. At his deepest cre-
> ative levels he is drawn with intense sympathy and under-
> standing towards the depiction of a popular uprising, yet at the
> same time he fears such events as merely destructive and
> revengeful.[16]

This analysis is illuminating, yet limited. Asserting that Dickens' refusal
to endorse the rioters' actions unequivocally has seriously weakened the
novel, Lindsay's approach is excessively doctrinaire. His vision of Barnaby is correspondingly narrow. Perhaps Barnaby cannot "carry all the
weight of meaning" demanded by the Arthurian legend (if that is the
"fable" to which Lindsay refers), but he is intricately connected with
Dickens' major theme. *Barnaby Rudge* is undoubtedly ambiguous, yet
does not Barnaby's own ambiguity serve as the perfect vehicle for
Dickens' moral uncertainty? Employing the folk and Shakespearean
traditions of the fool, identifying Barnaby both with the demonic forces
of destruction and with the redemptive power of innocence, Dickens
revitalizes that "dwindling magic."

Barnaby's appearance and costume clearly establish his links with
the fool tradition:

> His dress was of green, clumsily trimmed here and there—ap-
> parently by his own hands—with gaudy lace. . . . A pair of
> tawdry ruffles dangled at his wrists, while his throat was nearly
> bare. He had ornamented his hat with a cluster of peacock's

feathers, but they were limp and broken, and now trailed neg-
ligently down his back. Girt to his side was the steel hilt of an
old sword without blade or scabbard; and some parti-coloured
ends of ribands and poor glass toys completed the ornamental
portion of his attire. The fluttered and confused disposition of
all the motley scraps that formed his dress, bespoke, in a
scarcely less degree than his eager and unsettled manner, the
disorder of his mind, and by a grotesque contrast set off and
heightened the more impressive wildness of his face. (28)

In his primary dramatic functions, likewise, Barnaby is derived from
the conventional literary folk-fool. In contrast to the sane yet often un-
perceptive characters, he possesses an intuitive capacity to grasp essential truth. Gabriel Varden recognizes Mrs. Rudge's anxiety, for example, but only Barnaby (albeit unconsciously) associates her distress
with the events surrounding the Haredale murder (132–35). Barnaby
cannot fully comprehend his mother's sorrowful history, yet his wild
imaginings—connecting her apprehensions with his birthday and
blood-stained wrist—intuitively express the truth. His insight, moreover, is often clairvoyant. As Welsford states, the fool-lunatic has traditionally been regarded as "an awe-inspiring figure whose reason has
ceased to function normally because he has become the mouthpiece of
a spirit, or power external to himself, and so has access to hidden
knowledge—especially to knowledge of the future." [17] Barnaby's devil-
haunted dreams, for example, those "strange creatures crowded up
together neck and heels, to sit upon the bed" (48), and his capacity to
"see" a tumultuous, menacing world lurking beneath the surface of reality, symbolically foretell the demonic energy waiting to be released in
the riots. His "shadowy people," "voices in the air," and "men stalking
in the sky" (81–82) are the perfect poetic metaphors for the tensions
and unrest that will explode in London.

Sir John Chester's response to Barnaby's prophetic fantasies is illuminating. Chester and Barnaby meet at the Maypole where Barnaby,
gazing at the clothes drying on a line, imaginatively perceives a world
of plotting, conspiratorial phantoms lurking beneath prosaic reality—a
divinely inspired fool's insight that succinctly captures Chester's de-
vious character. Barnaby insists, moreover, that Chester himself is intricately involved in this shadowy conspiracy (" 'I say—what is it that
they plot and hatch? Do you know?' " [81]), a remark clearly disconcerting to the fashionable knight: " 'These insane creatures make such very
odd and embarrassing remarks, that they really ought to be hanged for
the comfort of society' " (574). Like the traditional divine idiot, Barnaby does not grasp the truth of his perceptions, but his suprarational
vision intuitively expresses the moral impoverishment of Chester's shal-
low world. More important, Barnaby's natural goodness is not merely

an attack on the "comfort of society," but on its moral blindness as well. His buoyant joyfulness and imagination (" 'You're the dull men. We're the bright ones' " [82]) are a reproach to the fashionable world, an image of its lost values, a symbol of its needed reform. Barnaby, in effect, is both the critic and antithesis of Chester's ethos: " 'Now *do*, Ned, *do* not,' said Mr. Chester, raising his delicate hand imploringly, 'talk in that monstrous manner. About to speak from your heart. Don't you know that the heart is an ingenious part of our formation—the centre of the blood-vessels and all that sort of thing—which has no more to do with what you say or think, than your knees have? How can you be so very vulgar and absurd? These anatomical allusions should be left to gentlemen of the medical profession. They are really not agreeable in society. You quite surprise me, Ned' " (243).

In addition to his function as innocent moral satirist, Barnaby is the center of Dickens' larger thematic structure. Further enhancing Barnaby's role as fool-mystic, Dickens introduces a major theme partly derived from *King Lear*—the question of divine justice.[18] Albany's prayer,

> If that the heavens do not their visible spirits
> Send quickly down to tame these vilde offences,
> It will come,
> Humanity must perforce prey on itself,
> Like monsters of the deep.
>
> (4. 2. 46–50)

is thematically echoed in Barnaby's question about the indifferent stars: " 'If they are angels' eyes, why do they look down here and see good men hurt, and only wink and sparkle all the night?' " (28–29). As James K. Gottshall states, "Dickens saw imaginatively that, however palatable and comforting was the picture of a benign God caring for the pure in heart, it was simply not an accurate picture." [19] The "visible spirits" of heaven do not intercede, and the stars stare down helplessly on the ruins of the Warren (424).

This interpretation, however, is somewhat limited, for Barnaby's fool-function as an innocent child of God significantly lightens this bleak atmosphere. The forces of nature, for example, symbols of a heaven that is indifferent or hostile to others, are wondrous and joyful to Barnaby: "The world to him was full of happiness; in every tree, and plant, and flower, in every bird, and beast, and tiny insect whom a breath of summer wind laid low upon the ground, he had delight" (355). Like Wordsworth's Idiot Boy, Barnaby enjoys an empathetic contact with nature, a contact not merely emotional but moral and religious. Barnaby, in fact, in a world torn by sectarian bitterness, is among the few characters possessing natural religious impulses, and the only character to achieve a spiritually illuminating vision:

> But the moon came slowly up in all her gentle glory, and the stars looked out, and through the small compass of the grated window, as through the narrow crevice of one good deed in a murky life of guilt, the face of Heaven shone bright and merciful. He raised his head; gazed upward at the quiet sky, which seemed to smile upon the earth in sadness, as if the night, more thoughtful than the day, looked down in sorrow on the sufferings and evil deeds of men; and felt its peace sink deep into his heart. He, a poor idiot, caged in his narrow cell, was as much lifted up to God, while gazing on the mild light, as the freest and most favoured man in all the spacious city; and in his ill-remembered prayer, and in the fragment of the childish hymn, with which he sung and crooned himself asleep, there breathed as true a spirit as ever studied homily expressed, or old cathedral arches echoed. (563)

"The thoughts of worldly men," in contrast, "are for ever regulated by a moral law of gravitation, which, like the physical one, holds them down to earth. The bright glory of day, and the silent wonders of a starlit night, appeal to their minds in vain. There are no signs in the sun, or in the moon, or in the stars, for their reading" (217). Unlike these worldly-wise men, who "have quite forgotten such small heavenly constellations as Charity, Forbearance, Universal Love, and Mercy" (217), Barnaby—the favored child of God and archetypal fool-seer—experiences an innocent, imaginative communion with heaven. Gottshall's suggestion that *Barnaby Rudge* is governed by an indifferent cosmos, therefore, acknowledges only part of the star-heaven image pattern. The stars do not descend to redress man's grievances, but man (through his imagination and love) may symbolically ascend. In his mystic insight, his loving heart, his role as a Christian fool, and his misguided (yet fervent) idealism, Barnaby represents those forces of goodness and innocence needed to redeem the Chester-Gashford world. "The fool among us is a perpetual link to the light and the life in that darkness," and although other characters doubt heaven's justice, Barnaby approaches the scaffold hopefully: " 'Hugh, we shall know what makes the stars shine, *now!*' " (595).

In conjunction with his role as fool-seer, Barnaby is also a moral mirror, reflecting the wisdom and folly of others. The country squire's verdict that Barnaby is sane, for example, and John Willet's suggestion that Barnaby "wants imagination" (82), ironically reveal their own imperturbable obtuseness. A similar irony, although far more thematically significant, operates in Barnaby's relationship with Lord Gordon, a figure who, as Lindsay has suggested, is also largely derived from the fool tradition.[20] Their first meeting establishes the symbolic and ironic nature of their association. Gordon's belief in Barnaby's sanity is both a ludicrous and insightful observations, for, although Barnaby cannot comprehend the issues involved in Gordon's campaign, his innocent virtue is precisely the quality needed to make the movement more than mere anarchy. As Gordon states, "those who cling to the truth and support the right cause, are set down as mad" (366). Barnaby and Gordon are mad for blindly embracing a destructive crusade, yet that same madness—their unworldly, "unwise" idealism—belongs, in the world of *Barnaby Rudge,* only to those "who cling to the truth," only to the Holy Innocents. Gordon further exclaims to Barnaby, "I am proud to be the leader of such men as you" (437), a declaration that ironically reveals his limited worldly vision and his perceptive fool-sense.

Despite their moral strengths, however, Barnaby and Gordon are not symbols of an untainted redemptive goodness. As Mrs. Rudge notes, Barnaby is characterized not merely by innocence or "dulness but . . . something infinitely worse, so ghastly and unchild-like in its cunning" (189). The tainted legacy of his father, moreover, symbolically represented by the bloodlike stain on Barnaby's wrist, is another suggestion of corruption: "He twisted his handkerchief round his head, pulled his hat upon his brow, wrapped his coat about him, and stood up before her: so like the original he counterfeited, that the dark figure peering out behind him might have passed for his own shadow" (133). His worshipful attitude to the demonic Grip ("'He's the master, and I'm the man'" [51]), his fascination with the power of gold, and his periodic outbreaks of violence, further qualify his status as a Christian fool. His relationship with Hugh and Dennis—two figures peripherally associated with the fool tradition—also indicates the darker aspects of Barnaby's character.[21] Barnaby cannot comprehend the passions of Hugh's embittered spirit or Dennis' twisted love of punishment, but he becomes their standard-bearer, contributing to the corrupt crusade with equal violence: "Next moment he was back in the stable, dealing blows about him like a madman. Two of the men lay stretched at his feet: the one he had marked, dropped first—he had a thought for that, even in the hot blood and hurry of the struggle. Another blow— another!" (439–40). Gordon's virtue is similarly corrupt. His religious zealotry and clouded understanding release ungovernable forces of destruction; he is the pawn of power-seekers, contributing by his self-delusion to the spreading terror.

Despite these darker characteristics, however, Barnaby and Gordon are too firmly situated within the Pauline-Erasmian tradition to be wholly convincing symbols of evil. Functioning as both the fool-seer and the embodiment of natural moral principle, Barnaby continues to act as a choric voice, intuitively penetrating the atmosphere of fanaticism. He reenters London only to find it "peopled by a legion of devils" (524), while he himself is "full of cares now, and regrets, and dismal recollections; and wishes (quite unknown to him before) that this or that event had never happened, and that the sorrow and suffering of so many people had been spared" (529). Gordon, likewise, despite his deluded madness, also comes to represent the forces of virtue and (paradoxically) of sanity: "He had his mourners. The prisoners bemoaned his loss, and missed him; for though his means were not large, his charity was great, and in bestowing alms among them he considered the necessities of all alike, and knew no distinction of sect or creed. There are wise men in the highways of the world who may learn something, even from this poor crazy lord who died in Newgate" (629). Despite their contributions to the riots' horror, Barnaby and Gordon retain an innocent moral sensibility. Their folly leads them into violence, yet, as fools, they represent the forces antagonistic to violence, the forces, in fact, which redeem the world from violence.

Barnaby Rudge, therefore, clearly carries "all the weight of meaning that [Dickens'] fable demands." He is the Holy Innocent, the fool-seer, the social critic, and the moral touchstone who reveals the wisdom and folly of others. As the traditional clairvoyant fool, he foretells and elucidates the forces of destruction that underlie his society. He is the standard-bearer for the rioters—innocent, unenlightened, yearning, and demonic—and he is their antithesis. Dickens recognizes both the idealism and terror of this "popular uprising," tacitly approving its life-energy while damning its excesses. Barnaby, the ambiguous folk-fool, is the symbolic embodiment of this contradictory response.

Barnaby's involvement with the riots, finally, although leaving unimpaired "his love of freedom and interest in all that moved or grew," effects a subtle change in his fool-nature: "But he recovered by degrees: and although he could never separate his condemnation and escape from the idea of a terrific dream, he became, in other respects, more rational. Dating from the time of his recovery, he had a better memory and greater steadiness of purpose; but a dark cloud overhung his whole previous existence, and never cleared away" (633). He retains his innocence and affection, but the more spiritual, mystical qualities vanish; unlike Swiveller, Barnaby cannot unify conflicting extremes to be reborn.

Having entered the violent urban world, therefore, the fool-seer disappears from Dickens' novels, to be succeeded by fool-figures like Tom Pinch, a far more realistic, equally innocent, yet totally unmagical character. Those few critics who acknowledge Pinch's links with the fool tradition regard him as a peripheral figure in the novel, and accentuate his pathos and passivity. Lindsay, for example, suggests that Tom represents "the Fool as the socially exploited Innocent unaware of the facts and of his own strength," [22] and J. Hillis Miller writes that Tom "may, like the innocent good fool of Erasmus, be rewarded in heaven, . . . but from the point of view of life in this world, the real arena of Dickens' novels, his life is, after all, a negative affair." [23] Michael Steig, on the other hand, suggests that Tom "is the most fully developed character in the work, as he is the only one with a discernible inner life, and the only one whose psychological development is presented in detail." [24] Steig does not refer to the fool tradition, but his analysis, presenting a quasi-Oedipal interpretation of Tom's relationship with Mary and Pecksniff, illustrates the fool's sexual frustration. Tom is, in effect, both central and peripheral; as Holy Innocent he occupies a leading position in *Martin Chuzzlewit's* moral structure, while as socially (and sexually) isolated fool he remains a solitary, unassimilated figure. Dickens clearly is extending his use and understanding of the fool tradition, yet in attempting this detailed psychological analysis of the Holy Innocent convention he encounters grave (perhaps insurmountable) difficulties.

Before considering these interpretive problems, it is necessary to examine Tom's major fool-functions. Although not endowed with the same consistently clairvoyant power as Barnaby, for example, he accurately foretells Martin's experience in America, prophesying that "some trial and adversity just now will only serve to make you [Martin and Mary] more attached to each other in better days" (98). Unconscious truth-telling, the fool's traditional capacity to deflate pretension, is another function Tom shares with the folk and Shakespearean model. His innocent rejoinder to Martin's self-aggrandizing account of his relationship with Mary and his uncle, for example, is humourously devastating (and precise):

> "Now you must bear in mind, Pinch, that I am not only desperately fond of her (for though she is poor, her beauty and intellect would reflect great credit on anybody, I don't care of what pretensions, who might become her husband), but that a chief ingredient in my composition is a most determined—"
> "Obstinacy," suggested Tom in perfect good faith. But the suggestion was not so well received as he had expected. (95)

Tom is not a mental defective like Barnaby, but he clearly lacks Swiveller's comic intelligence. He responds to Martin's self-praise "in perfect good faith," without any awareness of the explicit satire. When Sampson Brass, in contrast, raged against those "screamers and roarers whose throats must be made of—of—," Dick's response ("Brass") was consciously satiric. Tom's major fool-functions, in effect, despite his undoubted intelligence, are closer to Barnaby's simpleminded innocence than Dick's penetrating wit. Even his most significant and pervasive fool-function, namely, as a moral touchstone, requires little active intelligence. Lest this seem too slighting, however, it should also be noted that Tom is Dickens' most consistent and perfect example of the touchstone motif. As Dickens himself observes,

> No slight circumstance, perhaps, could have better illustrated the difference of character between John Westlock and Martin Chuzzlewit, than the manner in which each of the young men contemplated Tom Pinch. . . . There was a certain amount of jocularity in the looks of both, no doubt, but there all resemblance ceased. The old pupil could not do enough to show Tom how cordially he felt towards him, and his friendly regard seemed of a graver and more thoughtful kind than before. The new one, on the other hand, had no impulse but to laugh at the recollection of Tom's extreme absurdity; and mingled with his amusement there was something slighting and contemptuous, indicative, as it appeared, of his opinion that Mr. Pinch was much too far gone in simplicity to be admitted as the friend, on serious and equal terms, of any rational man. (203–4)

Although other Dickensian fools act as touchstones, none equals Tom's capacity to reveal another's moral strengths and weaknesses. Old Martin, for example, "disgusted by what in his suspicious nature he considered a shameless and fulsome puff of Mr. Pecksniff," regards Tom as "a deceitful, servile, miserable fawner," and yet cannot help but feel some misgivings, "for he had felt kindly towards Tom at first, and had been interested by his seeming simplicity" (390). Merry's view of Tom as the "ugliest, awkwardest, frightfullest being, you can imagine" (132) indicates her callous lack of perception, while Jonas Chuzzlewit's self-blinded malice is revealed when he ludicrously interprets Tom's guileless character in terms of his own mistrustful cunning: " 'I've heard something of you, my friend, and your meek ways; and I recommend you to forget 'em till I am married to one of Pecksniff's gals, and not to curry favour among my relations, but to leave the course clear' " (391). Dickens, moreover, employs a character's changing attitudes toward Tom to illustrate moral development. Young Martin's patronizing contempt is gradually transformed (through that "trial and adversity" which Tom foretold) to a kindly, respectful appreciation (528), while old Martin, who eventually transcends his "suspicious nature," reveals his moral growth through his recognition of Tom's innate virtue: "And when he spoke of Tom, he said God bless him; and the tears were in his eyes; for he said that Tom, mistrusted and disliked by him at first, had come like summer rain upon his heart; and had disposed it to believe in better things" (808–9). Tom, therefore, as old Martin's praise implies, not only reveals moral strengths and failings, but is an active agent of redemptive innocence, a moral force (like Barnaby) that counterbalances the prevailing social-moral corruption. In a novel whose "main object . . . [is] to show how Selfishness propagates itself" (Preface), the Holy Innocent's selflessness is an important countertheme.

In addition to these traditional fool-functions, Tom also reveals Dickens' efforts to explore the Holy Innocent's inner life and psychological development. Tom experiences the most radical transformation in *Martin Chuzzlewit*, for in the loss of his faith in Pecksniff, the very cornerstone of his world is shattered: "His compass was broken, his chart destroyed, his chronometer had stopped, his masts were gone by the board; his anchor was adrift, ten thousand leagues away" (494). Emerging from this confusion, without descending into misanthropic pessimism, Tom learns that falseness and villainy are widespread, that "there are more Pecksniffs than one" (570). Swiveller, of course, also gains a stronger moral character, but for the Holy Innocent to gain this awareness of human corruption and still preserve his moral simplicity, represents a considerable advance in Dickens' development of the fool tradition. Tom emerges as a unique Holy Innocent figure—a fool who has overcome the limitations of naïveté without surrendering the moral power of innocence. In contrast to his previous gullibility, his response to Ruth's boorish employer is an admirable blend of innocent integrity and worldly knowledge (571–74).

For an author to explore the inner life of a fool, however, especially the Holy Innocent, is a difficult and risky task. When perfect innocence enters the realistic novel, it can easily become (like Little Nell) stilted and unbelievable, a mere literary device rather than a viable character. Alternatively, in exploring the fool's psychological growth and deeper desires, the novelist may undermine his own primary intention, subverting the fool's principal moral functions. Barnaby's ambiguity was necessary to the thematic structure of *Barnaby Rudge*, but Tom Pinch can display such contradictory impulses only at the expense of his major fool-functions. And yet, in his relationship with Mary and Martin, Tom reveals definitely less holy and less innocent impulses— impulses toward sexuality, anger, and aggression.

One passage in particular clearly reveals this countertendency in Tom's character: "She touched his organ, and from that bright epoch, even it, the old companion of his happiest hours, incapable as he had thought of elevation, began a new and deified existence" (395). Although this sexual pun is undoubtedly inadvertent, as Steig observes, "Dickens was aware at some secondary level of consciousness that he has presented Tom as entering a belated (or second?) puberty," [25] a sexual response inimical to the pure Holy Innocent. Tom's response to

Martin's unconsciously cruel condescension, likewise, suggests powerful emotions raging beneath his placid surface—

> "In honour of old times," said Martin, "and of her having heard you play the organ in this damp little church down here—for nothing too—we will have one in the house. I shall build an architectural music-room on a plan of my own, . . . and many's the summer evening she and I will sit and listen to you, Tom; be sure of that!"
>
> It may have required a stronger effort on Tom Pinch's part to leave the seat on which he sat, and shake his friend by both hands, with nothing but serenity and grateful feeling painted on his face; it may have required a stronger effort to perform this simple act with a pure heart, than to achieve many and many a deed to which the doubtful trumpet blown by Fame has lustily resounded. (193–94)

The potential violence and anger aroused in Tom by Martin's denial of Pinch's manhood are implicitly suggested.

Dickens could successfully present such characters as Sam Weller and Dick Swiveller with equal measures of sensuality and moral sensitivity, for the intelligent, comic fool has the creative imagination to reconcile these forces. The Holy Innocent, in contrast, must remain angelically pure to discharge his symbolic fool-functions; inchoate feelings of sexuality and aggression subvert this primary role. Frustrated in his one serious love affair and forced to spend a celibate life in his sister's husband's household, Tom would likely experience some dissatisfaction—if not complete embitterment. Such, however, is not a quality of the loving, contented Holy Innocent, and, "since Dickens cannot tell *us* with any conviction" that Tom remains happy and fulfilled, "he must preach to Tom about what his heart should be—and of course it must not be resentful, jealous, or envious": "Thy life is tranquil, calm, and happy, Tom. In the soft strain which ever and again comes stealing back upon the ear, the memory of thine old love may find a voice perhaps; but it is a pleasant, softened, whispering memory, like that in which we sometimes hold the dead, and does not pain or grieve thee, God be thanked!" (836). Denied any active outlet for his energy or desires (especially those potentially disruptive impulses), Tom must be safely relegated to a loving and untroublesome celibacy in which, Dickens insists, there is no pain or grief, "God be thanked."

As a traditional fool-figure, therefore, Tom is entirely successful; like Dick and Barnaby, he counterbalances the prevailing vices of his society, symbolically representing the redemptive innocence needed to revivify its stagnant moral sense. As a Holy Innocent who has gained a stronger, more insightful perception, Tom represents Dickens' increasingly sophisticated understanding of the fool-tradition. And yet, as a psychologically believable Holy Innocent whose sexuality and emotional energies have been forcibly subdued, Tom, at the novel's end, must play his futilely elevated organ in solitude.

Inexplicably, no major critical study of the fool tradition examines (or mentions) Dickens' novels, and yet his wise fools are among the most complex and innovative representations of this classic figure. Adopting and altering the folk and Shakespearean models, Dickens creates a multifaceted character and symbol, capable of carrying impressive thematic weight, of heightening the pathos and humor, of illuminating moral faults, of qualifying and parodying sentimentality. Although many novelists employ the fool in one or more of his different guises, Dickens is perhaps the only major writer (after Shakespeare) to recognize and present the fool in all his diverse functions. The fool, finally, remains one of Dickens' most recurrent character types. Micawber and Jenny Wren, for example, are subtle variations on the street-wise and imaginative Sam Weller, Dick Swiveller, and Mark Tapley. Barnaby Rudge—the clairvoyant-defective—reappears in the lesser figures of Mr. Toots, Mr. Dick, Maggy, and Mr. F's Aunt, while Tom Pinch's successors include the vast number of Holy Innocents (Florence, Cuttle, Traddles, Pocket, Gargery, Twemlow, and many others). In one sense, it might be argued that Dickens' vision of the fool degenerates; the clearly defined personifications of the tradition are superceded by somewhat more diffuse examples. On the other hand, the fool may be said to gain importance, becoming more pervasive and spreading over the entire social spectrum. While there are few major fool-figures in such works as *Bleak House, Little Dorrit,* or *Our Mutual Friend,* there are many characters who perform part of the fool's traditional symbolic, moral, and satiric functions, counterbalancing those who are simply foolish in their moral perversity. Feste observes, "Foolery, sir, does walk about the orb like the sun; it shines everywhere" (3. 1. 37–38). And Charles Dickens, likewise, who saw the "foolery" of greed and heartlessness reigning over Victorian society, also saw the wise fool as the truest remedy.

David D. Marcus

SYMBOLISM AND MENTAL PROCESS
IN *DOMBEY AND SON*

DICKENS' SYMBOLS resist efforts to formulate them into coherent patterns. Within an individual novel, a symbolic image or motif will commonly possess several contradictory or seemingly unrelated interpretations so that it becomes impossible to select one of those interpretations as definitive or to reconcile their variety by taking them cumulatively. So far, only John Holloway, in his provocative essay on *The Old Curiosity Shop,* has discussed this problem in any depth; after tracing several of the symbols through this very early novel, he suggests that the apparent confusion is itself a deliberate technique: "It is surely clear that one who attempts, systematically, to elicit augmentations of meaning from all these complex matters will not get far. Dickens seems almost at pains to invest whatever could look like a symbol with a dialectical, self-contradictory potentiality; and this is to say that what we find in the book is what Carlyle told us to look for: 'In a Symbol there is concealment and yet revelation . . . by Silence and Speech acting together.' " [1] Holloway's and Carlyle's emphasis on self-contradiction provides a necessary starting point for an understanding of Dickens' peculiar use of symbols, a use that is yet more complex than the embodiment of opposites. As I shall demonstrate by examining the sea and railroad imagery of *Dombey and Son,* Dickens employs symbolism as a method of representing dramatically the act of perception, of showing the interaction of the mind and the world around it. I would, of course, be greatly overstating my case to claim that *Dombey* represents all that is to be found in all of the symbols in all of Dickens' novels; but the issues that this study raises do have wider implications, particularly for the works that follow. The constant repetition of the sea and railroad imagery in *Dombey* does exemplify a technique that Dickens will often use in later novels: the fog in *Bleak House,* the prison in *Little Dorrit,* the river in *Our Mutual Friend.*

[57

In general, critics have dealt with this technique by either emphasizing one meaning from among the many or by identifying patterns among several occurrences. From this point of view, symbols function to establish the moral hierarchies that are supposedly Dickens' answer to the social and individual problems that his novels pose. For example, J. Hillis Miller recognizes that the sea is used in different ways but nevertheless claims that above all else it "is the symbol of that realm beyond this earth where the seemingly inescapable separation between people will be transcended and the reciprocity of love will be possible." [2] Using a different approach, William Axton points out that the motif of the ocean and its waves, like the railroad, "involves in its extensive repetitions overtones of permanence, alternatively of the inescapable conditions of mortality and of those eternal values which transcend death, destruction, and suffering." [3] These viewpoints offer important insights, but they also create as serious a problem as they solve. For both of these critics suggest that Dickens offers a permanent moral center in the midst of the flux of experience whereas in fact Dickens' moral solutions are almost invariably the least satisfying aspect of his art, and his moral paragons—Florence Dombey, Esther Summerson, Tom Pinch—are typically his least interesting and most ineffectual characters.

My discussion of Dickens' symbolism will address itself directly to this vexing dilemma. For I shall argue that the sea and railroad images are one method of demonstrating to the reader the subjectivity of the relationship of *every* character's mind to the external realities that he or she encounters.[4] From this point of view, Dickens' interest lies in dramatizing the way in which the mind automatically imparts meaning to whatever it perceives; both Florence's goodness and her father's emotional desiccation derive support through this process. Thus Dickens' moral concerns are expressed on a much more sophisticated plane than has been generally recognized; the novel becomes for its readers an exploration of human limitations, an opportunity to see the process of seeing and to understand that the individual's moral nature asserts itself not so much in conscious acts but in the unconscious ways that he sees himself and others. By allowing the reader to view a wide variety of responses to common objects, the sea and railroad imagery as they "appear symbolically, in a multitude of permutations" [5] provide standards that heighten the reader's awareness of the idiosyncratic nature of any one character's response. As I shall demonstrate after my discussion of these symbolic devices, the principle on which Dickens builds his symbols is precisely the principle on which he builds the novel's dramatic conflicts.

Dickens' use of the sea in Chapter xli provides an extraordinarily concentrated example of symbols and their multiple meanings. Before it is even interpreted by any of the novel's characters, the sea, by the very terms in which the narrator describes it, assumes a profoundly ambivalent nature, a mysteriousness which encompasses—with the self-contradiction noted by Holloway and Carlyle—the opposites of the knowable and the unknowable: [6] "All is going on as it was wont. The waves are hoarse with repetition of their mystery; the dust lies piled upon the shore; the sea-birds soar and hover; the winds and clouds go forth upon their trackless flight; the white arms beckon, in the moonlight, to the invisible country far away." [7] On the one hand, this passage describes a world of physical processes whose meaning, if any, explicitly remains a "mystery" inaccessible to man. As the first sentence points out, everything is proceeding as usual, and every detail of the scene has a naturalistic explanation: the "white arms" are sails upon the water, the "invisible country" is France. On the other hand, the terms of the description inherently give life to the inanimate: the waves are "hoarse" and the "white arms beckon." Moreover, the passage contains an analogy between the physical world and the movement of human life toward death; its imagery had been associated earlier in the novel with the approaching death of Paul Dombey (xii, 167–68; xvi, 221–26) and here foreshadows the impending death of Mrs. Skewton whose illness and rapid deterioration have caused the trip to Brighton where this chapter takes place. That analogy—surely what we must regard as a symbolic meaning—does not explain the mysteriousness of the sea; it merely recasts it by seeing it in terms of that which is mysterious in human life. Thus the description presents simultaneously two opposed ways of seeing. From one point of view, the external world exists apart from man and is inexplicable. From another point of view there is an attempt to conceptualize that world in human terms, to use the ways that men have of knowing themselves as a way of knowing it.

This process that takes place within the narrator's description has at least as much importance as the particular meaning that arises out of it; for as the sea passes through the consciousness of each of the characters in this chapter, the same reshaping of the external world into human terms occurs. The meanings that attach to it function as distorting mirrors that allow the reader to see the assumptions through which people know themselves and unconsciously give form to their experience.

In the paragraph that follows the narrator's description, Florence listens to the sound of the waves telling her of her dead brother: "she hears in the wild low murmur of the sea, his little story told again, his very words repeated; and finds that all her life and hopes, and griefs, since—in the solitary house, and in the pageant it has changed to—have a portion in the burden of the marvellous song" (577). Like the narrator, Florence perceives the sea in human terms, but the sharp contrast

of tone that distinguishes her description from that of the authorial
voice clearly locates the source of her vision within herself. Through
their metaphors, both of them give a degree of life to the scene; but
where the narrator hears a "hoarse" sound and mere "repetition,"
Florence hears a "wild low murmur" that becomes a "marvellous song."
There is surely distance between the two, a point that receives further
support from the overt content of the sea's music: what Florence hears
is the story of her own life. The sea itself remains incomprehensible;
the marvellousness of its song certainly implies mystery, and Florence
sees her life as having only a "portion" in its message. Florence's perception ultimately reveals to the reader a way in which she makes liv-
able a world that is almost totally unresponsive to her; she sees with a
principle of harmony that offers her consolation in the midst of the
emotional deprivation that the death of her brother and the coldness of
her father have made her lot.

In a comic vein, a similar pattern repeats itself with Mr. Toots. In
the next paragraph, he hears in the sound of the waves a "requiem" for
Paul and a "madrigal" in praise of Florence. Like both the narrator and
Florence, he perceives the sea in terms of the human condition, and
like Florence, he harmonizes the scene into musical terms. The sea
does not offer him any way of transcending his limitations, and in fact
he hears the waves "saying something of a time when he was sensible of
being brighter and not addle-brained" (577). Toots's tendency to harmonize whatever he perceives functions in much the same way as
Florence's habit of mind: it enables him to accept the disparity between
what he desires and what the world offers him, and it softens the
harshness of that reality. If the sea reminds him of the ultimate human
disappointment of death and of his personal disappointments as well, it
also whispers to him a "kind thought" that allows him to approach
Florence and make known to her his presence in Brighton.

Not all of the characters live with so sharp an awareness of the
human condition, and within this chapter the sea also mirrors these
narrower conceptions of the self and the world. Florence and Toots
pay a visit to Doctor Blimber's school, and as they depart after chatting
with some of the pupils who had known them and Paul, they hear the
Doctor tell his charges to resume their studies: "For that and little else
is what the Doctor hears the sea say, or has heard it saying all his life"
(580). Similarly, Mr. Feeder, Doctor Blimber's assistant, walks on the
beach wondering whether, when he marries Cornelia Blimber, the Doctor will retire, and he "plainly hears the waves informing him, as he
loiters along, that Doctor Blimber will give up the business" (583). Both
Doctor Blimber and Mr. Feeder live so immersed in their daily concerns that they are incapable of perceiving anything else. As Miller
points out, Dickens uses the term "habit" as a metaphor for this type of

circumscribed vision, "the unconscious repetition of the same narrow judgments, feelings, and view of things, a repetition which eventually blinds one to all the world, even to the world of habit itself." [8] Miller notes that such characters turn the world into a mirror of themselves, a point that I have argued has a much wider application in this novel. In the context of all of the sea's messages, Doctor Blimber's and Mr. Feeder's perceptions give the reader yet another way of seeing the internal principles that characters use to organize all that they encounter. Unlike Florence, Toots, and the narrator, they have no sense of themselves as a part of a human condition or of a world of process larger than themselves and beyond their comprehension. For these two, their immediate concerns and daily activities define the boundaries of their capacity to know.

Mrs. Skewton provides a far different and much grimmer example. Florence, Toots, Dr. Blimber, and Mr. Feeder are all unaware of the ways in which they impose themselves upon the world, but Mrs. Skewton has self-consciously created a role for herself, one designed to exclude any recognition of her vulnerability to age and death. At her first appearance in the novel, we learn that she sits in a single unvarying position "in which she had been taken in a barouche, some fifty years before, by a then fashionable artist" (288). At age seventy, she is a patchwork of cosmetics—false teeth, false curls, false complexion—desperately trying to maintain an appearance of youth. She is sent to Brighton in hopes that she might recover from the stroke that has reduced her to a figure of grotesque senility, but her condition progressively deteriorates to the point where she is no longer able to walk at all, and she is pushed through the town in her chair, "painted and patched for the sun to mock." In this state of mind, she too hears her own version of the water's message: "Such is the figure that is often wheeled down to the margin of the sea, and stationed there; but on which no wind can blow freshness, and for which the murmur of the ocean has no soothing word. She lies and listens to it by the hour; but its speech is dark and gloomy to her, and a dread is on her face, and when her eyes wander over the expanse, they see but a broad stretch of desolation between earth and heaven" (584).

The earth need not be so devoid of comfort in the face of mortality. The death of little Paul, however sentimental, stands in contrast to Mrs. Skewton's despair, and as we have seen in this chapter, Florence and Toots live with a consciousness of death that consoles as well as saddens them. But Mrs. Skewton lives in terror of any such awareness: the casual mention of the word "die" in one of Major Bagstock's courtly compliments reduces her to near-hysteria (572), and as her illness worsens, the memory of that incident continues to haunt her (584). Because she has never been willing to acknowledge that her life too is subject to forces beyond her control, because she has purposefully avoided any recognition that she is aging and will die, she finds herself over-whelmed by her own emptiness which she sees reflected in the external world. There is no humane principle within her, no sustaining sense of relatedness to the incomprehensible that might soften her fate; instead, Mrs. Skewton can only experience "a broad stretch of desolation be-tween earth and heaven" because her mind has never bridged the gap between the two.

The juxtapositions within this chapter represent a particularly in-tense example of a process that occurs throughout the novel. Dickens strives to locate the source of meaning in the mind of the perceiver by never allowing his readers to settle into a single meaning. Alternate constructions of the same reality are rarely far apart. In the opening of the novel, the sea figures in the description of Mr. Dombey's vision of the cosmic importance of Dombey and Son: "The earth was made for Dombey and Son to trade in, and the sun and moon were made to give them light. Rivers and seas were formed to float their ships; rainbows gave them promise of fair weather; winds blew for or against their en-terprises; stars and planets circled in their orbits, to preserve inviolate a system of which they were at the center" (2). But a few pages later, the narrator gives a very different meaning to the sea in describing the death of Mrs. Dombey who "drifted out upon the dark and unknown sea that rolls round all the world" (10). Like Mrs. Skewton, Mr. Dom-bey lives within assumptions that purposefully exclude any sense of the human condition, and the two meanings of the seas in this chapter remind us of his limited field of vision.

If other characters are more humane, they are no less subjective. At Doctor Blimber's academy, young Paul looks at the sails on the water and interprets their movement as a motion beckoning to him; but Dickens places against this symbolic vision the mind of Toots who, simultaneously looking at the same scene, sees the sails as either Smugglers or Preventives (167–68). Dickens forcibly points out to the reader that the supposed beckoning exists only as an event in the inner space of Paul's mind. Much later in the novel, Florence sails to China with her new husband, and as the ship leaves England, the sea speaks to her "of love, eternal and illimitable, not bounded by the confines of this world, or by the end of time, but ranging still, beyond the sea, beyond the sky, to the invisible country far away!" (811). Miller claims that this love is a direct, unmediated feeling that comes to man through the "divine sea." [9] Miller's interpretation is surely correct in relation to Florence's perception of the sea; but as if to remind us that her mean-ing is only one possible way of thinking about the sea, Dickens immedi-ately uses the metaphor of a ship sailing through the stormy waters of circumstance as a description of the course of events that ultimately bankrupts the firm of Dombey and Son (812). Meaning is never fixed but exists only as a reflection of man's ability to impart significance to the world around him.

Like the sea, the railroad demonstrates this same malleability of human vision. In perhaps the most famous example in the novel, Mr. Dombey rides in a train toward Leamington after the death of his son and sees the railroad as "a type of the triumphant monster, Death" (280). Even more clearly than in his use of the sea, Dickens makes Dombey's perception of the railroad a measure of the perceiving mind: "He found a likeness to his misfortune everywhere" [10] (282). As the narrative voice renders Mr. Dombey's experience of the journey, it pointedly intersperses reminders that there are alternative ways of seeing these same events. The trip reaches its "fitting end" in the midst of a scene of poverty and misery: "As Mr. Dombey looks out of his carriage window, it is never in his thoughts that the monster who has brought him there has let the light of day in on these things: not made or caused them" (281–82). And again, he finds himself troubled at the thought of Florence's face: "Because he knew full well, in his own breast, as he stood there, tinging the scene of transition before him with the morbid colours of his own mind, and making it a ruin and a picture of decay, instead of hopeful change, and promise of better things, that life had quite as much to do with his complainings as death" (282). Dickens makes evident the disparity between the shifting scene with its multitude of possible interpretations and Mr. Dombey's static perception that can apply only "morbid colours" to all things.

The use of the railroad develops in both individual and social terms this contrast between a human stasis and an environment that is never stable. The sea has an existence totally independent of man, and its movements appear as repetitions of its own incomprehensible and eternal rhythms; but men have created the railroad, and it functions in several ways as an agent of change. Its construction has transformed the landscape, and its operation has reshaped man's sense of both time and distance. With considerable justification, Steven Marcus sees the railroad as symbolic of the changing world.[11] Moreover, Dickens was writing *Dombey and Son* in the years 1846–48 and was therefore addressing himself, as Humphry House points out, to an audience that had seen these developments take place within a very short span of its own experience.[12] And yet, when Dickens represents attitudes toward the railroad's impact on society, he depicts only the skepticism that had preceded its operation and the acceptance that followed, polar states of mind that reflect profoundly changed realities but that very conspicuously lack the sense of change itself.

The history of Staggs' Gardens illustrates on a social level this temporal discontinuity that characterizes attitudes toward change. In Dickens' first description of the neighborhood, he tells us that it has just undergone the "first shock of a great earthquake," the reduction of a great part of the area to rubble to make way for the construction of the railroad (63). But with the single exception of Mr. Toodle, whose belief in the coming change has been represented earlier in the novel (18), the residents view the place for all its squalor and for all the visible signs of its impending transformation "as a sacred grove not to be withered by railroads" (64). Within the very few years of Paul Dombey's lifetime, Staggs' Gardens "had vanished from the earth" (217). The skeptical chimney sweeper who had earlier led the jeering against the railroad has now become a prosperous sweeper of railroad chimneys. As Steven Marcus points out, the new neighborhood represents the "culture of the railroad." [13] That culture appears for us not only in the many physical changes that the railroad has caused but in the state of mind and style of life that people have assimilated: "Wonderful Members of Parliament, who, little more than twenty years before, had made themselves merry with the wild railroad theories of engineers, and given them the liveliest rubs in cross-examination, went down into the north with their watches in their hands, and sent on messages before by the electric telegraph, to say that they were coming" (218–19). The adjective "wonderful" carries several possible meanings. Perhaps these Parliamentary travelers are full of wonder at the speed of the new railroad and telegraph; perhaps they are amazing in their routine use of an innovation that was once the subject of their jibes; certainly Dickens is using the word as an expression of their inflated grandeur. For however fascinated by the speed of the new railroad these legislators may be, their amazement is not at all coupled with any potentially humiliating awareness of their own lack of vision.

Dickens is using these contrasting descriptions of Staggs' Gardens to make a satirical point, one that extends into a social and historical principle his concern with the subjectivity of man's relationship to the external world. Just as the "morbid colours" of Mr. Dombey's mind have blinded him to any optimistic possibilities for his own life, their own habit of mind has blinded the residents of Staggs' Gardens and the once skeptical members of Parliament to the possibility of their world becoming anything other than what it is. The medium of satire sharpens into dramatic irony the reader's awareness of the disparity between human vision and that which it seeks to grasp; but in quieter forms, the perception of that distance is constantly available to us, allowing us to witness the action as a drama of consciousness.

Thus Carker's fevered journey through France and England to his eventual death on the railroad tracks portrays for us a change in his perception of himself. Accustomed to manipulating others—his position as Mr. Dombey's manager certainly functions as a metaphor for his character—Carker unexpectedly confronts the failure of his schemes: Edith refuses to become his mistress, and his onetime benefactor now pursues him. He begins to experience a new feeling, "The dread of being hunted in a strange remote place, where the laws might not protect him—the novelty of the feeling that it *was* strange and remote, originating in his being left alone so suddenly amid the ruins of his plans" (767–68). Other characters either refuse to recognize forces that are unresponsive to their will or soften their recognition of them by humanizing the harshness of life's disappointments; but Carker is jarred into so sudden an acknowledgment of his own limitations that it shatters his self-image and destroys his ability to act: "To have his confidence in his own knavery so shattered at a blow—to be within his own knowledge such a miserable tool—was like being paralysed" (770).

Carker's paralysis occurs because the boundaries that his mind had unconsciously imposed on reality disappear along with his conception of himself. Stylistically, Dickens renders Carker's perception through a three-page series of mostly incomplete sentences that convey a profusion of objects sweeping through a consciousness no longer able to arrange experience even sequentially: "It was a fevered vision of things past and present all confounded together; of his life and journey blended into one. Of being madly hurried somewhere, whither he must go. Of old scenes starting up among the novelties through which he traveled. Of musing and brooding over what was past and distant, and seeming to take no notice of the actual objects he encountered, but with a wearisome exhausting consciousness of being bewildered by them, and having their images all crowded in his hot brain after they were gone" (773). He returns to England in the hope that he will be able to "recover the command of himself," but still his thoughts "wandered where they would, and dragged him after them" (775). His experience since the beginning of his flight remains a jumble "constantly before him all at once" (775). His ability to order his experience continues to dissolve until the final moments of his life: "the past, present, and future, all floated confusedly before him, and he had lost all power of looking steadily at any one of them" (777). Lacking any principle of selectivity, Carker's mind is unable either to direct its own energies or to make sense out of the raw data that his senses provide. Unprotected by any firm idea of himself, Carker feels himself overwhelmed by the otherness of a world that he can only experience as confusion.

His vision of the train as a "fiery devil" drawing him toward destruction externalizes this process of internal dissolution. The railroad acts as a locus for the mental conflict that has been taking place within Carker since the beginning of his journey. As he flees the scene of his humiliation, he experiences a feeling that he cannot directly relate to his immediate situation: "Some other terror came upon him quite removed from this of being pursued, suddenly, like an electric shock, as he was creeping through the streets. Some visionary terror, unintelligible and inexplicable, associated with a trembling of the ground,—a rush and sweep of something through the air, like Death upon the wing. He shrunk, as if to let the thing go by. It was not gone, it never had been there, yet what a startling horror it had left behind" (767). Moments of this terror strike him throughout his flight, and as he sits "drinking and brooding" at an inn, he specifically attaches the experience to the passing of the train: "For now, indeed, it was no fancy. The ground shook, the house rattled, the fierce impetuous rush was in the air!" (776). Carker struggles against his own attraction to death, but his struggle is hopeless even before the encounter with Mr. Dombey that sends him staggering onto the tracks in front of the train: "He was marked off from the living world, and going down into his grave" (778). In taking Carker's life, the railroad functions as an instrument of his consciousness, a consciousness that seeks to escape from its inability to satisfy even the simple human need for rest.

The relationship that Carker's mind forms between itself and the train typifies Dickens' use of the railroad and the sea: in slightly different ways, they both function as external locations for internal dramas. These repeated images do not in themselves possess symbolic meanings but rather, through the constant variations in their significance, demonstrate for the reader the process by which men create and then impose those meanings on all they encounter. Symbolism in *Dombey and Son* thus provides a model of human perception that has broad application throughout the novel. All vision becomes symbolic in the sense that men see not only objects but one another in terms of themselves and their own needs. By allowing the reader to see that symbolic meaning is a creation of the perceiving mind and not a quality inherent in the object itself, Dickens creates a perspective on the action of the novel that allows us to see the limitations of each character's view of the others. That perspective reveals the individual turning others into extensions of himself by "interpreting" them in terms of his own internalized assumptions much as each character "interprets" the sea or the railroad.

Thus the principle of symbolism also functions as the principle of social interaction in this novel. The effects of this process extend far beyond the simple errors that we attribute to subjectivity, for the main action of the novel—the relationship of Florence and her father— demonstrates not misunderstanding but the impossibility of any understanding. This inability to know others appears most clearly in Mr. Dombey, and it characterizes not only his relationship to his daughter but all of his ties to other people. As Steven Marcus notes, "His great passion is to possess people exclusively and totally, and he is resentful, in fact terrified, of any response except absolute submission." [14] Dombey's obsessed mind reshapes experience into its own image in a constant struggle to avoid recognition of anything or anybody that he cannot control. Even a direct confrontation with a hostile reality does no good; when Susan Nipper forces him to listen to her impassioned lecture on his neglect of Florence, Dombey reacts with anger and dismisses her from his household and his mind (613–16). Carker, the one character in the novel who understands Dombey's grotesquely warped perspective, tells Edith that her husband is "the slave of his own greatness, and goes yoked to his own triumphal car like a beast of burden, with no idea on earth but that it is behind him and is to be drawn on, over everything" (628). He is "so prone to pervert even facts to his own view" that he has willfully misunderstood Edith's response to an earlier warning about her behavior (629). However self-serving Carker's descriptions of Dombey may be, they are also accurate. Dombey's pride goes far beyond the arrogance of wealth and social position; it is a state of mind in which Dombey himself is trapped.

His attitude toward Florence reflects this inner struggle, an attempt to maintain the equilibrium of the closed system within which he lives. Dombey sees his daughter reflexively: his aversion to her arises out of a fear of her unwitting ability to touch upon those aspects of his own personality that he is unwilling to acknowledge. Shortly after the funeral of his wife, Dombey remembers the deathbed embrace of Florence and her mother, and his own response to that scene, a feeling of being "Quite shut out":

> Unable to exclude these things from his remembrance, or to keep his mind free from such imperfect shapes of the meaning with which they were fraught, as were able to make themselves visible to him through the mist of his pride, his previous feeling of indifference towards little Florence changed into an uneasiness of an extraordinary kind. He almost felt as if she watched and distrusted him. As if she held the clue to something secret in his breast, of the nature of which he was hardly informed himself. As if she had an innate knowledge of one jarring and discordant string within him, and her very breath could sound it. (29)

Dombey constantly perceives Florence's behavior as a threat to the structure of reality that he has created for himself. Dickens contrasts Paul's very loving response to his sister with his unenthusiastic response to his father: "If Mr. Dombey in his insolence of wealth, had ever made an enemy, hard to appease and cruelly vindictive in his hate, even such an enemy might have received the pang that wrung his proud heart then, as compensation for his injury" (149). Again, this pattern repeats itself when Dombey, feigning sleep, watches Florence and Edith together: "He hardly knew his wife. She was so changed. It was not merely that her smile was new to him—though that he had never seen; but her manner, the tone of her voice, the light of her eyes, the interest, and confidence, and winning wish to please, expressed in all—this was not Edith" (504). Like the disappointments that death brings to Dombey, Florence also reminds him that people cannot be transformed into the objects that Dombey would have them become. His rejection of Florence is a part of his struggle against self-knowledge, an attempt to force experience into a mold that allows him to evade the more painful human dimensions within himself by dehumanizing others. Just as the meanings of the sea and the railroad in fact portray the minds that perceive them, Dombey's view of his daughter gives an external dramatic form to his internal battle and shows the reader the process of the perceiver unconsciously distorting his surroundings into an image of himself.

This same process occurs more subtly but no less strongly within Florence herself. As we have seen, Florence, unlike her father, recognizes that the individual will does not lie at the center of all things, that a disparity exists between her inner needs and what the external world offers her. In her relationship to her father, she attempts to explain that disparity by creating an image of her father that, like her father's image of her, supports the assumptions that she imposes on reality. The result is simply a less egotistical, more humane distortion that preserves for her the possibility of gaining her father's love. Thus, after the death of her brother, she visits the home of Sir Barnet Skettles with an unspoken desire to observe other children with their parents: "Florence sought to learn their secret; sought to find out what it was she had missed; what simple art they knew, and she knew not; how she could be taught by them to show her father that she loved him, and to win his love again" (343). There is, of course, no secret, no simple art. As if to emphasize to the reader the self-delusion that underlies Florence's search, Dickens immediately juxtaposes her view against a more realistic appraisal of Mr. Dombey's behavior. As Florence walks in the garden, she overhears a conversation between an orphaned child and the aunt who is her guardian. The child asks why Florence's father is so inattentive to her, and the aunt explains the situation: "She would love him dearly if he would suffer her, but he will not—through no fault of hers; and she is greatly to be loved and pitied by all gentle hearts" (345). Florence is deeply hurt for the moment by what she accidentally hears, but it has as little lasting impact on her as Susan Nipper's lecture will have on her father; she again retreats into a fantasy whose admirable feature is its unwillingness to accept any version of reality which does not offer at least the potential for parental love. Once again, Florence's attempts to win her father's love actually dramatize an internal struggle to maintain her own vision.

Dickens quite frequently points out to the reader the disparity between Florence's vision and the realities that contradict it, realities that she either cannot know or refuses to accept. Shortly after she overhears the conversation between the aunt and her niece, Florence imagines that if she were fatally ill, her father would be reconciled to her (350); although she cannot know it, the reader can juxtapose against this imaginary deathbed scene her father's growing hatred of her, the resentment he feels because she lives and Paul is dead (282–83). When Edith returns from her wedding trip, Florence begs her new mother to teach her the way to her father's love (506); but Florence's request is at best pitifully ironic in light of the economic and social motives behind the marriage of Edith and Mr. Dombey, motives that the omniscient narrator has developed for us at length but that remain hidden from Florence. As the distance that separates Edith and her husband increases, Florence responds by retreating yet further into an inner world that allows her to maintain an equal affection for both of them: "As shadows of her fond imagination, she could give them equal place in her own bosom, and wrong them with no doubts" (652). When her father strikes her, "she saw him murdering that fond idea to which she had held in spite of him" (666). Yet that "fond idea" never quite dies. At the end of the novel, Florence returns to her now bankrupt and suicidal father to beg his forgiveness as though she had been in the wrong: "I am penitent. I know my fault. I know my duty better now" (843). Florence has left her father's house, but she cannot free herself from the habit of mind that has been both her refuge and her prison.

This form of self-deception occurs among the novel's minor characters as well. Captain Cuttle listens to Walter tell of his impending transfer to the West Indies as an indication of Mr. Dombey's dislike for him, but the Captain is unwilling to believe what he hears: "He had arranged the future life and adventures of Walter so very differently, and so entirely to his own satisfaction; he had felicitated himself so often on the sagacity and foresight displayed in that arrangement, and had found it so complete and perfect in all its parts; that to suffer it to go to pieces all at once, and even to assist in breaking it up, required a great effort of his resolution" (212). Predictably, the Captain deliberates for a bit and decides "that there was some mistake here; that it was undoubtedly much more likely to be Walter's mistake than his" (213). Similarly, Major Bagstock, that apoplectic voyeur, carries on a merely Platonic relationship with his neighbor, Miss Tox, but inflates it grandiosely in his own mind; the Major "was mightily proud of awakening an interest in Miss Tox, and tickled his vanity with the fiction that she was a splendid woman, who had her eye on him" (84). In the wake of

Mr. Dombey's second marriage, Miss Tox finds herself an outcast from the Dombey household, but she does not rid herself of concern for her former associates for she "really had got into the habit of considering Dombey and Son as the pivot on which the world in general turned" (533). Like Florence and her father, these characters dramatize an intense need to see the world as an extension of their inner lives even in the face of disappointment and contradiction.

Symbolism, then, becomes a broadly applicable term in this novel, a term that serves as a principle of both mind and action. The sea and the railroad allow the reader to juxtapose the variety of meanings that characters' minds impose on their experience; the action of the novel allows the reader to see the conflict of these mutually exclusive realities as they unknowingly encounter one another. Thus the reader's point of view becomes inherently ironic: what the characters see as reality, the audience sees as solipsism. But the self-enclosure that Miller terms the center of *Dombey and Son* is as much a symptom as a cause: [15] it exists as a result of the mind's continuous effort to define and protect itself by functioning selectively and preventing an onrush of unmediated experience of the kind that overwhelms Carker and terrorizes Mrs. Skewton. There is, of course, a moral distinction between those like Florence who accept the human condition and all the pain that it brings them and those like Mr. Dombey who fight against any sense of life's finite nature; but the narrator maintains his and our distance from both of them. Both visions depend on distortions of the external world. I would, therefore, redefine what Holloway means when he discusses the dualism of symbols; for although they are dualistic, they are not a dialectic that resolves its two parts in a synthesis. Symbols present the reader with a simultaneous awareness that their meanings are both false and necessary, and these qualities remain in constant tension. If they place implicit barriers between human beings and severely limit the possibilities for our knowledge of one another, they also assert the existence of a form of consciousness that is uniquely human in its constant effort to reshape into an accommodating form the world around us.

In both *Dombey* and the novels that follow, Dickens' view of consciousness becomes in itself a moral problem. As the final conversion of Mr. Dombey makes excessively clear, there can be no doubt about what values Dickens would wish to triumph, but his exploration of mental process raises an impossible barrier against our accepting so unequivocal a moral vision: can any values be accepted as true if all meaning is solely the result of the mind's highly selective mediation? In his late novels, Dickens' interest will shift from the problems of intimate relationships that he treats in *Dombey* and again in *David Copperfield* back to the institutions, the ideologies, the customs of his society. His analysis of his culture will continue to focus on the assumptions with which men see, particularly the states of mind that the society instills in its members and that are for Dickens the most enduring forms of slavery: Richard Carstone's Chancery-tormented consciousness; Thomas Grad-grind's unidimensional Utilitarianism; the prison that William Dorrit must always carry within him; the blind, class-conscious fury of the French Revolution that is merely an inversion of the old order; Pip's great expectations; Eugene Wrayburn's aimlessness. *Dombey and Son* is not as wide-ranging as these late novels, but in its concentration on the workings of the mind, it inaugurates a moral attitude toward experience that will remain at the core of Dickens' writing to the end of his career. For, as the split between Dickens and Florence indicates and as the split between Dickens and Esther Summerson will even more dramatically illustrate, the narrator and the reader identify with a knowledge that is far broader than the knowledge of Dickens' sentimental heroines. The experience of reading the novel offers an awareness of human limitations, of the boundaries that the conditions of existence impose on every person, and in this awareness and not in any simple admonition resides the basis of moral knowledge.

Robert E. Lougy

REMEMBRANCES OF DEATH
PAST AND FUTURE:
A READING OF *DAVID COPPERFIELD*

A Traveller I am,
Whose tale is only of himself.
Wordsworth, *The Prelude*, III

But if ever I meet with a Boojum, that day,
In a moment (of this I am sure),
I shall softly and suddenly vanish away,
    And the notion I cannot endure.
    Lewis Carroll, *The Hunting of the Snark*

THE BAKER in Carroll's *The Hunting of the Snark* is a strange reflection of the identity and the quest of the Romantic artist. The Baker's life and story hang suspended in a delicate balance; he is a hunter in pursuit of an elusive and unknown prey that he can discover only at the cost of his own annihilation. And indeed, as the poem ends, the Baker's triumph is signaled, not by means of a vivid narrative of battle, but by the simultaneous ending of his story and his life. The Baker simply vanishes, his story interrupted by the destiny he must fulfill. For a brief but heroic moment his art and his life merge into song before being engulfed by silence. The song remains unfinished because that which he sings is true. We should not mourn the Baker's death, however; rather we should rejoice and join in his own exultation, for his is a death that is not met with sorrow or surprise, but with gleeful awareness and victorious laughter—

In the midst of the words he was trying to say,
    In the midst of his laughter and glee,
He had softly and suddenly vanished away—
    For the Snark *was* a Boojum, you see.

72]

The silence that descends upon the artist-hero arises out of a harmony between the demands of his art and the demands of his soul; his song could have been completed only if there remained a dissonance between his art and his life. The Baker also shares with his Romantic predecessors the ambivalent rewards of language and memory, for if they permit him to tell his tale and to announce his victory, they also draw him unwillingly on into his mission and preclude the postponement of his fate—

> "I said it [the prediction of his fate] in Hebrew—I said it in Dutch—
>   I said it in German and Greek:
> But I wholly forgot (and it vexes me much)
>   That English is what you speak!"

Twenty-six years before Carroll celebrated the Baker's victory, another nineteenth-century hero, David Copperfield, embarked upon a journey, guided by a memory and language he hoped were true, in pursuit of an object even more elusive than the Boojum, namely, a fuller comprehension of the "I" whose story he tells. Like the Baker's voyage, David's journey too is marked by madness, anxiety, and death; unlike the Baker, however, David lives to complete his tale and to find happiness and fulfillment. When we accompany him to his tale's end, we find "everything as it used to be, in the happy time." The conclusion presents us with domains—those of the Wickfield residence and David's own home—that are sanctifying and enriching, meant to complement and to complete the inner life of the hero who has returned to them.

There seems, however, to be a profound dissonance at the end of the novel between David's story and his life, in spite of the novel's attempt to make us see the circle it draws as complete and whole.[1] We have heard and seen too much; the images we bring away from the novel seem to clash, almost violently oppose one another: a warm and love-filled parlor juxtaposed with the graveyard in which David's father is buried; David's boyhood home falling into decay and inhabited by a lunatic who stares out at the graveyard from David's own room; a storm whose real threat comes from within rather than from without, from the past and future rather than from the present. These images, and many others, require us to qualify our responses to the novel and make it difficult for us to trust in the sufficiency of its final spaces.

David Copperfield's haunting and compelling beauty arises from its struggle to deny for as long as possible that final stasis that awaits it. In this respect it embodies that irony which Roland Barthes attributes to the best of modern works, the irony of a work of art denying its own artfulness, of postponing the moment when its vision will be compromised or terminated by its form. Barthes suggests that "the Novel is a

Death; it transforms life into destiny, a memory into a useful act, duration into an orientated and meaningful time"; but, at the same time,
the greatest works (and *Copperfield* must certainly be included here)
protest against this death, compelling us to look behind the fictive mask
they wear.[2] In *David Copperfield* the narrator travels forward into a past
he is trying to redeem and to make whole. And while he may seem to
end where he began, he does not, for the journey calls forth images
that assume a reality of their own. They remain alive within the novel
to reveal why the narrator returns to them and to thwart his attempts
to forget or repress them.

To begin the novel is to initiate an act that is but partially free,
since the language and the alternative structures that the novelist may
draw upon have been inherited from a past which he can protest
against, but which he may not deny. We immediately see this protest:
on the title page the novel is described as "The Personal History, Adventures, Experience, & Observation of David Copperfield the
Younger of Blunderstone Rookery (Which he never meant to be Published on any Account)." At its very inception, then, the novel an-
nounces its own artlessness; we are asked to believe that it is not a novel
we are reading but rather a private manuscript to which, contrary to its
creator's wishes, we have gained access. And within the narrative itself,
this initial declaration is sustained: the document is indeed not so much
a work of art as the expression of a mind reflecting or confessing itself
on paper. "I search my breast," David writes, "and I commit its secrets,
if I know them, without any reservations to this paper" (646). He later
makes this point again: "In fulfillment of the compact I have made with
myself, to reflect my mind on this paper, I again examine it, closely,
and bring its secrets to the light" (697). Or still again: "I feel as if it
were not for me to record, even though this manuscript is intended for
no eyes but mine, how hard I worked" (606). The word "novel" is assiduously avoided; *David Copperfield* is not a novel but, variously, a
manuscript, a paper, a document, a number of pages. What we find,
then, when we consider the creation of *David Copperfield,* is a novelist
(Dickens) writing a novel about a novelist (Copperfield) writing a novel,
who all the while denies that he is writing a novel at all.[3] On the one
hand, Dickens thrusts before us his denial of the novel tradition, but,
on the other hand, he must surely recognize that the denial itself is a
part of the very tradition he is trying to refute. More importantly, however, Dickens acknowledges the traditional mythos of the novel in the
first sentence: "Whether I shall turn out to be the hero of my own life,
or whether that station will be held by anybody else, these pages must
show." This initial statement serves to define and, to a certain extent, to
limit the nature of the exploration undertaken. However, it is a liberat-
ing gesture also: it allows the narrator to free himself from the spaces

seen at the novel's conclusion, even while attesting to the fact that the narrator is still haunted or perplexed by certain images that he must confront and attempt to comprehend.

David Copperfield is a novel about David's past, but it is also a novel about his present and future and the needs which compel him to go back through memory in search of answers to allay his fears and satisfy his desires.[4] He is driven forward into the past by his need "to reflect" his mind onto paper and by the hope that he may "cancel this mistaken past" (818), even while knowing that it cannot be canceled but only forgotten, reshaped, or confronted. And the past is frequently forgotten by being remembered in such a way that its terror and unintelligibility are contained, reshaped within a written memory that deprives it of its terror by giving it structure and coherence. Thus while *David Copperfield* is a novel of remembering, it is also a novel of forgetting encouraged by the very structures that the narrator's memory clings to, in particular to the structures of a past tranquilized by an inherited vocabulary and by the narrative form of the novel itself. It is in part for this reason that the artful rendering of his quest is repeatedly denied; he sees the possibilities of self-deception and illusion that are inherent in the form.

At the end of *David Copperfield* the hero disappears, enclosed within conventions that assimilate the individual. He is freed from anxiety and fear and is caught up within a public mode of fulfillment and its prevailing categories of success and happiness. As a successful novelist, a loving husband and a happy father, David moves into such categories and, in so far as he remains there, he bestows a silence upon that figure whose liberation is possible only through the gesture of language. Thus, when the novel's first sentence allows David to break free, the battle commences again; and the pattern of his journey reflects that pattern of nineteenth-century heroism in which the hero is destined to leave self-created spaces which he finds too small, only to return to them again in order to find momentary poise and protection.

— 2 —

The choice in phantasy comes to be to suffocate to death inside, or to risk exposing oneself to whatever terrors there may be outside.—R. D. Laing, *Self and Others*

Anticipation of one's own uttermost and ownmost possibility is coming back understandingly to one's ownmost "been."—M. Heidegger, *Being and Time*

When David Copperfield begins his imaginative quest, he embarks from circumstances which epitomize those goals of success, comfort,

and love for which he has striven: "I had advanced in fame and fortune, my domestic joy was perfect, I had been married ten happy years.
Agnes and I were sitting by the fire, in our house in London, one night
in spring, and three of our children were playing in the room" (866).
Nevertheless, it is a step he does take; and since it is one that contains
certain risks, we have to wonder what compels him to do so. The question implicit in the novel's first sentence may shape the direction of the
quest, but does not, in itself, give impetus to it. Since everything that
David has attained would seem to mitigate against such a journey, we
have to think of him as he is for so much of the novel: the hero ridden
by demons and compelled by memories he can neither comprehend
nor dispel, haunted by images both of his past and his future. By contrast, the present seems to be almost completely absent in *David Copperfield;* it seems to be so completely occupied or concealed by the narrator
that it plays little part in the novel. Yet it is from the vantage of the
present that David looks, looking into the past not for its own sake but
in order to perceive the directions of his own possibilities. As David's
aunt observes, "It's in vain, Trot, to recall the past, unless it works some
influence upon the present" (347). And to this observation we may well
add "and unless it works some influence upon the future as well."
David looks to his past in order to understand what he will become and
to incorporate into himself the meaning of those images which torment
him. The knowledge he seeks is the knowledge of his own death—not a
general and abstract knowledge of the fact that all men must die, but
rather that immediately personal comprehension that only he can die
his own death, the certainty of which is as much a part of what he is as
of what he will be.

There is also another kind of death anticipated in the novel: at
times Dickens seems to envision that end of which Wordsworth, that
other great traveler into the past, spoke of when he wrote of those
poets who in their youth "begin in gladness,/ But thereof come in the
end despondency and madness" ("Resolution and Independence").
While one can hardly describe David's youth (at least that of his post-
Murdstone period) as being one that began in gladness, yet when the
novel concludes David is still a fairly young man whose past is seen as
purposeful, fruitful, and intelligible. But its success and continuity are
conceived of within public modes or myths of fulfillment, in terms of
what Heidegger has called the "they-self." What calls one forth out of
lostness in this "they-self" is anxiety, the state of mind that exists when
one is summoned to himself by his recognition of an alien voice that is
his own, by an awareness that he exists in a world in which he is "not-
at-home," and finally, and most crucially, by his anxious anticipation of
his own death, a death which is "one's ownmost, which is non-rela-
tional, and which is not to be outstripped" (*BT,* 294).[5] But since this

anxiety is filled with terror for the one who experiences it, he attempts to evade it by fleeing back into the "they-self," wherein such anxiety is tranquilized, understood inauthentically, and concealed. Flight, however, is ultimately unsuccessful; it ultimately protects one neither from his own voice nor from his subsequent moods or states of mind.

This voice is familiar to readers of nineteenth-century British literature; variously identified, it haunts the Romantic artist. And while Wordsworth is able to respond, albeit ambivalently, to such an anxiety in "Resolution and Independence" by perceiving in the leech-gatherer the image of a freedom toward death and a resoluteness that he himself desires, the Romantic artist is certain to confront it again. It is this voice that calls to David from beyond those spaces—the "they-self" again—to which he has fled. In going back, as he says, to begin at the beginning, he returns to the parlor with its images of warmth, delicious smells, and the protective, comforting figures of his mother and Peggotty. Yet not all of David's childhood images are reassuring; when he looks into his memory he is again threatened and beset by geese and other fowl of a "menacing and ferocious manner" waddling after him "with their long necks outstretched" (14). Especially disconcerting is the image of his father's grave which continues to haunt and perplex the narrator: "There is something strange to me, even now, in the reflection that he [David's father] never saw me; and something stranger yet in the shadowy remembrance that I have of my first childish associations with his white gravestone in the churchyard, and of the indefinable compassion I used to feel for it lying out alone there in the dark night, when our little parlour was warm and bright with fire and candle, and the doors of our house were—almost cruelly, it seemed to me sometimes—bolted and locked against it" (2).

Tormented by an ambivalence, David feels compassion for his father, lying alone in the cold night; but he is also guiltily grateful to be protected from the outside and from his father's grave, from any unnatural disruption of the order of things: "One Sunday night my mother reads to Peggotty and me in there, how Lazarus was raised from the dead. And I am so frightened that they are afterwards obliged to take me out of bed, and show me the quiet churchyard out of the bedroom window, with all the dead lying in their graves at rest, below the solemn moon" (14).

Though death is momentarily stilled here, the images of safe and enclosed spaces being violated or threatened with violation by outside forces do recur later in the novel. One has only to think of the Murdstones' occupation of Blunderstone Rookery, of Steerforth's violation of Peggotty's ship-home, of the mysterious stranger threatening Betsey Trotwood, and of the intrusion of King Charles' head into the troubled psychic spaces of Mr. Dick. At times, attempts are made to conceal or

evade such images, as during one short dialogue between David and
Mr. Omer, in which the deaths of David's mother and his infant
brother are alluded to: "With a pretty little party laid along with the
other party. And you quite a small party then, yourself. Dear, dear!"
Although the drift of Omer's meaning is rather oblique, David's response suggests that he immediately comprehends it: "I changed the
subject by referring to Emily." Shortly after this dialogue, Omer develops his point more fully: "When a man is drawing on to a time of
life, where the two ends of life meet; when he finds himself, however
hearty he is, being wheeled about for the second time, in a speeches of
go-cart; he should be over-rejoiced to do a kindness if he can. . . . And
I don't speak of myself, particular, . . . because, sir, the way I look at it
is, that we are all drawing on to the bottom of the hill, whatever age we
are, on account of time never standing still for a single moment"
(734–35). This observation is less threatening to David than the earlier
one; speaking not so much of David's death as of the inevitable death
of all men, it contains a universal and nonpersonal kind of truth.

Even though this generalization of death has a tranquilizing influence, those images harbored within the folds of David's memory forbid
any lasting peace. At one point in the novel David speaks of the winds
"going by me like a restless memory" (844); and, finally, it is this dis-
quiet blowing from out of his past that compels David upon his journey
to reclaim those images carried upon it. *David Copperfield*'s readers have
frequently been perplexed by its ending, and perhaps for the reason
that the images that agitate David's memory are eventually contained,
but only temporarily and by means of a literary form that does not sufficiently reflect David's interiority. Early in the novel David fears the intrusion of such images (his anxiety about his father's grave, for example), but at the same time he feels apprehensive about the
consequences or implications of closing off such images altogether.
Like those thoughts that haunt Wordsworth, David's greatest fears
come toward him from a future that he can comprehend only by going
into his past. And when he is confronted with these images, he can neither deny them nor contain them: "I trembled, and turned white.
Something—I don't know what, or how—connected with the grave in the
churchyard, and the raising of the dead, seemed to strike me like an
unwholesome wind" (42).

Few nineteenth-century heroes are as haunted as David or as possessed by an imagination that so fully penetrates the present reality of
things and anticipates the consequences of time and mutability upon
them; in *David Copperfield* time always threatens to destroy the dream,
the memory, the ideal. Even sanctified space is disfigured or destroyed:
"It pained me to think of the dear old place as altogether abandoned;
of the weeds growing tall in the garden, and the fallen leaves lying

thick and wet upon the paths. I imagined how the winds of winter would howl round it, how the cold rain would beat upon the window-glass, how the moon would make ghosts on the walls of the empty rooms, watching their solitude all night" (248). These image clusters are later developed further—

> For my own part, my occupation in my solitary pilgrimages was to recall every yard of the old road as I went along it, and to haunt the old spots, of which I never tired. I haunted them, as my memory had often done, and lingered among them as my younger thoughts had lingered when I was far away. The grave beneath the tree, where both my parents lay—on which I had looked out, when it was my father's only, with such curious feelings of compassion. . . . —I walked near, by the hour. It lay a little off the churchyard path, in a quiet corner, not so far removed but I could read the names upon the stone as I walked to and fro, startled by the sound of the church-bell when it struck the hour, for it was like a departed voice to me. My reflections at these times were always associated with the figure I was to make in life, and the distinguished things I was to do. My echoing footsteps went to no other tune, but were as constant to that as if I had come home to build my castles in the air at a living mother's side.
>   There were great changes in my old home. The ragged nests, so long deserted by the rooks, were gone; and the trees were lopped and topped out of their remembered shapes. The garden had run wild, and half the windows of the house were shut up. It was occupied, but only by a poor lunatic gentleman, and the people who took care of him. He was always sitting at my little window, looking out into the churchyard; and I wondered whether his rambling thoughts ever went upon any of the fancies that used to occupy mine, on the rosy mornings when I peeped out of that same little window in my night-clothes, and saw the sheep quietly feeding in the light of the rising sun. (319–20)

The first sentence of this passage could almost serve as the epigraph of the novel, for, although *David Copperfield* is many things, it is in large part a solitary pilgrimage, one in which the narrator both haunts and is haunted by the "old spots" along the road he has traveled. In lingering among these spots and reviving his memories of the young boy who once walked within them, David attempts to impose his own need for continuity and identity upon the flux and mutability of the natural world. In many respects, the changes described in the passage above are similar to those experienced throughout the novel: fairly standard images of mutability, such as the weed-filled garden and the uncared-

for and deserted home. What is unique, however, about this passage—
and evidence of the way in which Dickens so often transcends those
images available to him—is the reference within it to the "poor lunatic
gentleman" who now occupies David's old room and looks out of the
same window through which David himself had so often gazed long
ago. It is difficult, in terms of the plot alone, to account for the presence of this figure. He has not appeared before and he is developed no
further within the novel. We are neither told who he is nor how he
came to occupy David's room. Neither his past nor his future is revealed to us. We see him again only once, during Barkis' funeral: "I
walked over to Blunderstone early in the morning, and was in the
churchyard when it came, attended only by Peggotty and her brother.
The mad gentleman looked on, out of my little window" (447).

It is fitting, however, that Dickens gives us so little information
about the old man. His image alone suffices; it serves to recall David
not so much to his past as to beckon him to his future, or at least to its
possibilities, possibilities that stand in sharp contrast to his reflections
within the same passage "on the figure I was to make in life, and the
distinguished things I was to do." When David first sees the old gentleman, he wonders what fancies might occupy his mind, and whether
they might not resemble those David had had as a boy when he looked
through the same window. When we return to the particular fancies
that David has in mind (12), however, there appears to be a profound
dislocation within his memory. What was compelling for the child
David was not the images of sheep feeding quietly in the morning light,
but rather those night images which they were temporarily dispelling:
images of the grave and of his father rising like Lazarus from the dead.
Only after those night images had been stilled were David's anxieties
lessened and the boundaries between the interior and the exterior reinforced. And when we reflect upon the nature of the fancies that the
"mad gentleman" might have had (given what we see of madness
throughout the novel), it is difficult to believe that his fancies were of
"sheep quietly feeding in the light of the rising sun."

But we are not told what his fancies were, nor is it really important
for us to know. What is important is that the image helps to define and
give shape to David's response, one that suggests flight from the
image's true significance by means of a memory that mystifies the past
and thereby bestows coherence and serenity upon it. The "poor lunatic
gentleman" threatens David because David sees in him a vision of his
own possibilities—the Romantic artist's fear of sinking into despondency and madness—and David flees from him toward the vision of a
serene and distinguished future that is not threatening. But even
though these projected images of the past and future are sources of
solace for David, the image of the silently mad figure continues to intrude upon them throughout his imaginative journey.

The very next scene carries forward the exploration of moods and states of mind that David has just embarked on. David comes upon Steerforth "lost in meditations" and "sitting thoughtfully before the fire" (321). This scene is one of the few in the novel in which Dickens attempts to reveal the inner depths of the elusive character of Steerforth, and it also serves to reflect, through a narrative prism, David's own quest for a father. These aspects of *David Copperfield* have been examined before,[6] so I wish to look at this scene somewhat differently. The real explorer of self in the novel is David, yet here it is Steerforth who appears in reverie and introspection. The introduction of a meditative side to Steerforth's character is unexpected and not reflected in any visible transformation of his choices or actions. After this scene he remains elusive and opaque; indeed he becomes almost nonexistent after he runs away with Emily.

Why, then, does Dickens include this particular scene at this point in the novel?—clearly because it allows him to amplify those moods or resonances within David that he has begun to explore in the scene immediately preceding. Dickens is, however, unable to project David himself into a situation like Steerforth's, not only because of his first-person narrative technique, but more importantly because of the disparity throughout the novel between David and that adventure (or plot) in which his interiority can find expression and definition.[7] Thus he projects David outside of himself and allows us to view David seeing himself, so to speak. Steerforth in front of the fire and before his mind's eye is David before his pen and paper, beset by memories, by his own presence, and by a disconcerting fluidity between fantasy and reality: "I have been," Steerforth tells David, "a nightmare to myself, just now—must have had one, I think. At odd dull times, nursery tales come up in the memory, unrecognised for what they are" (322).[8] Like Steerforth, David is his own nightmare, carrying with him a history and a future that, through reflecting his mind on paper, he is trying to contain and comprehend. He is that "lunatic gentleman" in the window gazing down upon himself, and in as much as he is engaged in re-creating himself, he is his own father, "a reproachful ghost," giving rise to strange and haunting images within his "caverns of memory." And just as Steerforth is thrown into a reverie by being confronted with himself—"I strolled in here and found the place deserted. That set me thinking, and you found me thinking" (323)—so, too, it is when David is least protected from himself, when the night images have replaced those of the day, that he is most thrown in upon himself.

Like those other scenes in the novel in which Dickens seems to be drawing upon his deepest artistic impulses, this particular one contains within it a poetic logic that enriches and enhances the work. Woven throughout, in fact, are certain images that create a matrix of meaning which, while it frequently complements the plot, stands above or beyond the narrative logic of the novel. Contained in this scene, for example, are reverberations or echoes that send us back not only to the preceding episode but back to David's earliest remembered childhood as well. When Steerforth observes that "I believe I have been confounding myself with the bad boy who 'didn't care,' and became food for lions" (322), we are reminded of David's earliest anxieties and night fears, "as a man environed by wild beasts might dream of lions" (14). And David's intrusion upon the reverie and solitude of Steerforth, like a "reproachful ghost," looks forward as well as backward, for it is the drawing of David toward himself that accounts for the energy behind his quest and the directions that the quest takes. The pattern begun here will finally reach its culmination in the "Tempest" chapter, for it is there that David sees himself looking back at him in the reflection of the window, "a haggard face from the black void." The demarcation between the outside and the inside, so precarious through much of the novel, finally breaks down and David's own image converges, in a moment filled with inexplicable fear and terror, with those of his father and the old lunatic gentleman.

But this confrontation with Steerforth does more than give Dickens room to explore David's depths more fully and to amplify his fears, anxieties, and isolation. Steerforth's protest that "I have never learned the art of binding myself to any of the wheels on which the Ixions of these days are turning around" (321) also reproves David's own earlier speculations about the figure he was to make in life and the distinguished things he was to do. As such it qualifies both this avenue of public redemption and the novel's ending. When the scene ends, Steerforth disappears not only from David's life but virtually from the novel as well. But by means of his actions after his departure, Steerforth brings his own mother and David's "mad gentleman" into the center of an image that stands in ironic ironic relief against those images within which the hero will ultimately find protection and comfort, for Mrs. Steerforth and the old gentleman have achieved within the silent enclosures of their madness a protection from an outside world that contains for David a past and future filled with terror and a reality in conflict with his dreams.

— 3 —

"I suppose history never lies, does it?" said Mr. Dick, with a gleam of hope.
"Oh dear, no, sir!" I replied, most decisively. I was ingenuous and young, and I thought so.—*David Copperfield*

If enclosure within the silence of one's own mind is the particular form of madness that Dickens identifies in the mad gentleman and, later, in Steerforth's mother, there is another form of madness that also haunted the nineteenth-century artist, that of Arnold's Empedocles, wandering for eternity as a naked, restless mind, trapped in a prison of selfhood and separated forever from the world about him. This is the image of Childe Roland and Tennyson's Merlin as well; it is also the image of King Charles, haunting the psychic spaces of both Mr. Dick and the novel's hero. On the title page there is a dreaming or meditating infant in the center of the illustration; he appears to be both the creator and the prisoner of the structured chaos around him. In his dreams he is the child playing near the crib and the child who has imaginatively tamed death by converting the grave and tombstone into a make-believe coach. But, as we follow the illustration, we see that this child—the artist in the midst of his own created images—also appears to be an old man being led to the grave and, finally, he who lies in the grave. Like this child, David too is an artist surrounded by his own created images, but his journey stops short of the grave and is resolved in such a way that he can tell his tale.

There is, however, another artist in *Copperfield* who is haunted by images, and his Memorial, unlike David's, remains unfinished. I am, of course, speaking of Mr. Dick. A descendant of the long tradition in Western literature of the fool as saint and the madman as sage, he is also the Romantic artist, the man haunted by images that come to him out of the past and prevent the completion of his creation, whether the work be Mr. Dick's Memorial, Wordsworth's *The Recluse,* Coleridge's *Biographia Literaria,* or Keats' "Hyperion." Like the Romantic artist, Mr. Dick still possesses the spontaneity and joyous freedom of childhood: "How often have I seen him, intent upon a match of marbles or peg-top, looking on with a face of unutterable interest, and hardly breathing at the critical times! . . . How many winter days have I seen him, standing blue-nosed, in the snow and east wind, looking at the boys going down the long slide, and clapping his worsted gloves in rapture!" (251).

The Romantic artist, however, is not a child, but rather a man who has that capacity Coleridge identified in Wordsworth, the capacity to "carry on the feelings of childhood into the powers of manhood; to combine the child's sense of wonder and novelty with the appearances, which every day for perhaps forty years had rendered familiar." [9] It is this same ability that David rightfully identifies in himself: "I believe the power of observation in numbers of very young children to be quite wonderful for its closeness and accuracy. Indeed, I think that most grown men who are remarkable in this respect, may with greater propriety be said not to have lost the faculty, than to have acquired it; the rather, as I generally observe such men to retain a certain freshness, and gentleness, and capacity for being pleased, which are also an inheritance they have preserved from their childhood" (13).

If Mr. Dick is mad, his madness or unreason is radically different

from that which finally encloses Mrs. Steerforth. While her madness
imprisons her within a dominant will that has gone astray and has
turned back upon itself to rend and immobilize, Mr. Dick's madness
protects and comforts him. Maintaining him in a state of grace in a
world without God, it enables him to remain innocent and wise and,
through his actions, to define the limits of reason and to transcend
those limits: " 'A poor fellow with a craze, sir,' said Mr. Dick, 'a simple-
ton, a weak-minded person—present company, you know!' striking
himself again, 'may do what wonderful people may not do. I'll bring
them [Dr. Strong and Annie] together, boy. They'll not mind what *I*
do, if it's wrong. I'm only Mr. Dick. And who minds Dick? Whoo!' He
blew a slight, contemptuous breath, as if he blew himself away" (654).
King Charles' image causes Mr. Dick to doubt historical time with its
clear delineation of the past and present, and, as David himself comes
to realize, Mr. Dick's intuition is correct: history is a lie, a fiction creating a duration with continuity and coherence, telling us of a past in
which the buried images of yesterday do not intrude upon the consciousness of the living.

As Betsey Trotwood suggests, Mr. Dick's struggle arises from a
profound disturbance within himself created by the clash of the ideal
with the real, between the love and compassion that should exist and
the unkindness and cruelty he knows from experience do exist:
" 'That's [King Charles' image] his allegorical way of expressing it. He
connects his illness with great disturbance and agitation, naturally, and
that's the figure, or the simile, or whatever it's called, which he chooses
to use. And why shouldn't he, if he thinks proper?' " She goes on to
add, however, that " 'It's not a business-like way of speaking . . . nor a
worldly way. I am aware of that; and that's the reason why I insist upon
it, that there shan't be a word about it in his Memorial' " (205). The
public fear of madness demands that madness be hidden, concealed
within a wall of silence and anonymity that will protect the outside
world from it, even though this world itself is, as Mr. Dick observes,
"mad as Bedlam, boy!" (202). Madness in the nineteenth-century novel
is frequently viewed not as a contained disruption within the psychic
spaces of the inflicted but as a perpetual threat to the moral, economic,
and ethical foundations of society. As metaphor, it is often a moral
rather than a medical judgment, the consequences of excessive sexuality (Rochester's wife in *Jane Eyre*) or debauchery (*Vanity Fair*'s Steyne
family). And if madness is defined, in part, as either the willful or in-
voluntary separation of an individual from the productive forces of society, then the cure for such madness would include the incorporation
of the individual into productivity; therapy, consequently, must be
directed toward such inclusion. If the transgression is too grievous and
the violation too great, the individual is consigned to a state of nonexis-

tence (confinement taken to its logical extreme), destined to suffer and to offer penance to a world that demands it, even while denying the penitent any hope of salvation or forgiveness. Once Emily runs away with Steerforth, for example, she virtually ceases to exist in the novel (except to allow Mr. Peggotty and Rosa Dartle to fulfill their various destinies).[10] Indeed, in several scenes—the confrontation of Emily and Rosa Dartle, and the departure of the emigrants—Dickens has to undergo artistic contortions in order to keep Emily concealed and quiet.

The ship on which the Peggottys sail is one containing emigrating paupers and transported criminals, mutual transgressors against the state and society. The image of such a ship captured the consciousness of the nineteenth century in much the same way the *Narrenschiff* captured the mind of the Middle Ages. But this latter-day vessel promised to society-at-large not the isolation of its insane but the exclusion of its poor and its outlaws. To its passengers it offered a new world, yet one that could only remind them of a past they could hope neither to expiate nor to forget. In a new land that was at the same time a moral construct, they would be forced, if they wished to survive, to cultivate the very virtues (labor, economy, and thrift) that would have prevented their downfall in the first place.

These same virtues, however, that are reinforced by the threat of transportation are undermined or threatened by Mr. Dick's metaphor, for it calls into being that chaos and nothingness that are barely concealed by the public myths of fulfillment, by David's dreams of the "figure I was to make in life" (320). Mr. Dick's metaphor is, finally, too threatening; if allowed to exist, it would throw into jeopardy not only those public virtues but also the meaning of David's journey that is established by the conclusion of the novel. The significance of Mr. Dick's Memorial lies precisely in the fact that it cannot be completed, only terminated. Its fulfillment is always ahead of it; in order to be true to itself, it must acknowledge, by its incompletion, those images that prevent its satisfactory conclusion. Like the Baker's Song, the only authentic completion of the Memorial would coincide with the conclusion of his life. But this, of course, could not be in *David Copperfield*. Thus it is that the intrusion of the demonic and its concomitant recognition of a reality to which reason is blind can be held off only at the cost of a silence that descends upon and envelops the artist. The final containment of King Charles' image is accomplished by the mindless copying of other people's words, an act antithetical to language and discourse: " 'But these writings, you know, that I speak of, are already drawn up and finished,' said Traddles, after a little consideration. 'Mr. Dick has nothing to do with them' " (508). This therapy does have its rewards: it puts shillings into Mr. Dick's pocket and, more importantly, it includes him within the world of productivity and consumption: "He earned by the following Saturday night ten shillings and nine pence; and never, while I live, shall I forget his going about to all the shops in the neighbourhood to change this treasure into sixpences, or his bringing them to my aunt arranged in the form of a heart upon a waiter, with tears of joy and pride in his eyes" (529). Mr. Dick's initial frenetic activity—"he was like a man playing the kettledrums, and constantly divided his attention between the two"—does not last, and the poise he finally attains seems to be a permanent one: "finding this (the division of his attention) confused and fatigued him, and having his copy before his eyes, he soon sat at it in an orderly business-like manner, and postponed the Memorial until a more convenient time" (528). The virtues of prudence and orderliness prevail, and we must assume that the "more convenient time" will be forever postponed, permanently consigned to the realm of the unbusinesslike and the unworldly. During the final pages of the novel we are again told of the success of this treatment: "My aunt informed me how he incessantly occupied himself in copying everything he could lay his hands on, and kept King Charles the First at a respectful distance by that semblance of employment" (836).

Several complex impulses seem to be operating within Dickens' description of Mr. Dick's transformation. First of all, King Charles' head is not gotten rid of, only kept at "a respectful distance" by writing with which Mr. Dick "has nothing to do." His redemption must be perpetually earned by means of an activity that Melville perceived quite differently in "Bartleby the Scrivener." The activity in both cases is identical; what differs is the moral or ethical construction within which each is set. And yet Melville is neither more compassionate than Dickens nor more aware of the madness and death impulse that lie barely beneath the surface of society's structures of normalcy and sanity. When Dickens binds Mr. Dick to Ixion's wheel, he does so gently and with compassion; it is an act whose moral and humane impulses we have to recognize and respect, one that sincerely wishes to bestow happiness and a restored sense of purpose and identity upon Mr. Dick. But it is also an act that is an image of a dream or desire that Dickens shared with his age, the fulfillment of which exacts a certain price, namely, a departure by the end of the novel from what Mr. Dick was to what, given the impulses behind his transformation, he should have been. It is difficult to reconcile the Mr. Dick we see throughout most of the novel, an individual filled with gaiety, spontaneity, and a great capacity for love, with the one Betsey Trotwood describes late in the novel as being saved from "pining in monotonous restraint" (638) by the mindless copying of other people's words. His "semblance of employment" is an extreme image of Marx's "alienated labor," and there is no indication in the novel that it helps to rid him of his unreason. What it does is to make unreason respectable by enclosing it within an activity whose alienation is evidenced in the choreography of the act itself—of Mr. Dick and King Charles kept apart and isolated by a work wholly disassociated from the one who performs it. Madness is not cured; it is simply given another name.

— *4* —

> That in the face of which one has anxiety is characterized by the fact that what threatens it is *nowhere*. Anxiety "does not know" what that in the face of which it is anxious is. . . . Therefore that which threatens cannot bring itself close from a definite direction within what is close by; it is already "there," and yet nowhere; it is so close that it is oppressive and stifles one's breath, and yet it is nowhere.—M. Heidegger, *Being and Time*

> I fell into a dull slumber before the fire, without losing my consciousness, either because of the uproar out of doors, or of the place in which I was. Both became overshadowed by a new and indefinable lethargy that bound me in my chair—my whole frame thrilled with objectless and unintelligible fear.—*David Copperfield*

In Mr. Dick, the artist-as-child is killed, assimilated within a social and ethical vision that cannot accommodate either idleness or the demonic, yet it is not too surprising that the demonic will arise again in the novel, for its creator's own life suggests that he too was demon-ridden.[11] The profound dissonance between interiority and adventure within a world that cannot reflect or fulfill that interior finds its extreme example in Mr. Dick, almost as if Dickens perceived in Mr. Dick's destiny the redemption and the silence of his novel's hero, an artist haunted by images less easily dispelled, one whose memorial is less easily concluded. But if *David Copperfield* concludes by enclosing its hero within a series of images inadequate to the search he has been waging, this conclusion occurs only after one of the most significant struggles waged in nineteenth-century British fiction.

It seems to me that the supreme moment of the struggle takes place in the "Tempest" chapter (lv). In it David confronts directly those image-ridden winds that compel him on his journey. The language of this chapter seems disproportionate at times to the narrative action— the account of the deaths of Ham and Steerforth occupies only the last several paragraphs of the chapter—until we realize that while these deaths are required and anticipated by the plot, they occupy a subordinate position within the chapter. The chapter moves primarily toward a recognition of his own death that David can no longer conceal or evade; it gathers within itself all those images that David has confronted during his solitary pilgrimage and reveals them with an almost visionary translucency. The chapter's very beginning suggests that the depth it touches lies beyond those that can be accounted for by the plot alone, even by events so momentous as the deaths of Ham and Steerforth: "I now approach an event in my life, so indelible, so awful, so bound by an infinite variety of ties to all that has preceded it in these pages, that, from the beginning of my narrative, I have seen it growing larger and larger as I advanced, like a great tower in a plain, and throwing its fore-cast shadow even on the incidents of my childish days" (784).

Whatever it is that David now approaches, he realizes that the whole narrative has been shaped and defined by it, that, even when David returns to his "childish days," he returns to a landscape shadowed by images from it. It is not an event of which he speaks, for it cannot be isolated by time or placed within a duration whose continuity it helps to establish. On the contrary, it stands before David now and has always stood before him; even as he writes of it, it exists for him as something that keeps slipping out of the actual into dreams, and then back into the actual again. It is not elicited, but, like the Ancient Mariner's curse (one that similarly compels the Mariner to tell his tale), it comes forth unbeckoned and unwelcome: "For years after it occurred, I dreamed of it often. I have started up so vividly impressed by it, that its fury has yet seemed raging in my quiet room, in the still night. I dream of it sometimes, though at lengthened and uncertain intervals, to this hour. I have an association between it and a stormy wind, or the lightest mention of a sea-shore, as strong as any of which my mind is conscious. As plainly as I behold what happened, I will try to write it down. I do not recall it, but see it done; for it happens again before me" (784).

In its almost surreal rendering of nightmare, horror, and anxiety, this chapter is reminiscent less of other nineteenth-century fiction than of the age's poetry, in particular of Browning's "Childe Roland to the Dark Tower Came," an account of a nightmare journey that resembles David's. David tells his tale in order to put together those pieces of the net that are still disconnected; he journeys forth through memory in order to find the thread that runs through the "I" whose tale he is telling (21). The particular terror of the "Tempest" lies in the fact that it not only threatens the success of the journey, but threatens its very validity. The storm that breaks over Yarmouth and the ocean that threatens to pull the structures of the town back into itself represent the potential triumph of formlessness over form, of death over life. They portend the victory of a consciousless force pulling all alien matter back into itself: "As the receding wave swept back with a hoarse roar, it seemed to scoop out deep caves in the beach, as if its purpose were to undermine the earth. . . . Undulating hills were changed to valleys, undulating valleys (with a solitary storm-bird sometimes skimming through them) were lifted up to hills; masses of water shivered and shook the beach with a booming sound; every shape tumultuously rolled on, as soon as made, to change its shape and place, and beat another shape and place away; the ideal shore on the horizon, with its towers and buidings, rose and fell; the clouds fell fast and thick; I seemed to see a rending and upheaving of all nature" (788).

Within this chapter, images come forth out of David's early childhood to haunt him and to create anxieties for which he cannot find a discernible object or an identifiable cause. In speaking of the impact that this experience still has for him—"its fury has yet seemed raging in my quiet room, in the still night"—David uses a metaphor that isolates and defines those memories whose echoes reverberate most strongly within this chapter, and in turn gather their resonances from it; the memories evoked by this episode are primarily those of protected spaces violated by disruptions from within and without, and of those of the night and darkness throwing the certainty and comfort of the day into doubt. Images, at times fragmented and broken, of memories that are called forth include those of David's revisiting of Peggotty's ship-home after his own home had been broken up, of listening to the wind and "fancying . . . that it moaned of those who were gone" (143), of Little Em'ly's challenging of the sea and his own fear of death by drowning, of himself in his childhood bedroom fearful of the intrusion of his father's ghost. All these images, like the storm itself, come to David, carrying impulses that are still within him as he tells his story. The direction of this chapter and the energies that lie behind it are extremely complex. Part of its problem (by which I do not mean fault or weakness) arises from Dickens' own awareness that his creation is ultimately inaccessible. He writes it, gives it being, but still he seems to comprehend it only partially. Perhaps realizing his inability to account fully for the scene, he chooses instead to allow it to come forth in all its complexity and ambivalence.

Indications of the inadequate correlation between the novel's narrated plot and the resonances of this chapter are found quite early. We discover that David is exhausted, restless, and in a mood that has an intense hold over him: "I was very much depressed in spirits; very solitary; and felt an uneasiness in Ham's not being there, disproportionate to the occasion. I was seriously affected, without knowing how much, by late events; and my long exposure to the fierce wind had confused me. There was that jumble in my thoughts and recollections, that I had lost the clear arrangement of time and distance. . . . So to speak, there was in these respects a curious inattention in my mind. Yet it was busy, too, with all the remembrances the place naturally awakened; and they were particularly distinct and vivid" (789). Confused and jumbled by his "long exposure to the fierce wind," David feels disoriented in time and space. He may not know or be able to identify the sources of his uneasiness, but he is able to identify what the sources are not—his language carefully modifies and qualifies his experiences: his uneasiness was "disproportionate to the occasion," and when he writes of his apprehension, he observes that "*I was persuaded* that I had an apprehension of his returning from Lowestoft by sea, and being lost" (789). His anxiety is such that he cannot dispel it; and, as when the boat-builder laughs at his concern for Ham's safety, his search for external sources of consolation fail. After failing to find reassurance, David retires to his room, and the description which follows is critical.

> The howl and the roar, the rattling of the doors and windows, the rumbling in the chimneys, the apparent rocking of the very house that sheltered me, and the prodigious tumult of the sea, were more fearful than in the morning. But there was now a great darkness besides; and that invested the storm with new terrors, real and fanciful.
>
> I could not eat, I could not sit still, I could not continue steadfast to anything. Something within me, faintly answering to the storm without, tossed up the depths of my memory and made a tumult in them. Yet, in all the hurry of my thoughts, wild running with the thundering sea,—the storm and my uneasiness regarding Ham were always in the foreground. . . .
>
> I fell into a dull slumber before the fire, without losing my consciousness, either of the uproar out of doors, or of the place in which I was. Both became overshadowed by a new and indefinable horror; and when I awoke—or rather when I shook off the lethargy that bound me in my chair—my whole frame thrilled with objectless and unintelligible fear. (789–90)

These passages are among the greatest descriptions of dread, of nothingness and death, to be found in nineteenth-century literature. Dickens obviously does not have the vocabulary that Heidegger and Sartre have given to our age, but, being Dickens, he does not need it. In any event, it is when the search for a cause proportionate to the mood ceases, when the narrator allows the horror and unintelligibility of the scene to define themselves, that we see a language fully capable of carrying its own weight and making its own connections. It is when "great darkness" descends over the hero that we see the interior and exterior in a momentary poise or harmony ("something within me, faintly answering to the storm without"); the terrors that are invested upon the storm by the darkness arise from a violent shaking not only of "the very house that sheltered me," but of all those conceptual structures and fond hopes that David has created for his protection and comfort. The fear that he experiences is "objectless and unintelligible"; it reveals David to himself with unparalleled clarity and prescience. And when the order and coherence within which he has protected the "I" of the tale collapse, David confronts directly and without evasion those images which, even still, he does not fully understand. The history of which David writes—indeed, the very reasons behind his writing—are shaped and compelled by this episode, one that stands both in front of him and behind him: "I have seen it growing larger and larger as I advanced, like a great tower in a plain, and throwing its fore-cast shadow even on the incidents of my childish days" (784).

Those images that David has carried throughout, those that have agitated his memory like a restless wind—the lunatic's peering face and his father's grave-enshrouded image—reappear, this time becoming fused within David's imagination with his own self-reflected image: "I got up several times, and looked out; but could see nothing, except the reflection in the window-pane of the faint candle I had left burning, and of my own haggard face looking in at me from the black void" (604). Unlike his earlier confrontations with these images, David can no longer evade their full significance or diminish the terror of their meaning by mystifying the past or by reshaping his memory in the service of forgetting. The ordered delineation between the past and the present, the interior and the exterior, life and death, break down; and the images of David, of the lunatic gentleman, and of David's father merge into an experience that speaks to David of "despondency and madness," nothingness and death. As he enters the kitchen of the hotel where he is staying, a young girl screams, "supposing [him] to be a spirit"; but her screams are drowned out by David's own screams, albeit screams muffled by fear and dread and thus finding their proper voice in the deafening sounds of the wind and ocean.

For one who has anticipated his own death as profoundly as David does in this chapter, it becomes a tranquilizing experience to write of the deaths of others, even of those deeply loved, in so far as it restores once again a narrative that contains order and coherence. Images without intelligibility become transformed into a history in which the boundaries between the dream and the actual, between life and death, are given definition and projected outside of oneself. Thus it is that the ostensible conclusion to this chapter—the description of the deaths of Ham and Steerforth—really begins and ends in less than two pages. A strange serenity seems to pervade the chapter's concluding paragraph: "And on that part of it [the shore] where she and I had looked for shells, two children—on that part of it where some lighter fragments of the old boat, blown down last night, had been scattered by the wind— among the ruins of the home he had wronged—I saw him lying with his head upon his arm, as I had often seen him lie at school" (795). The images themselves are, of course, not necessarily consoling, suggesting, as they do, images of childhood and youth broken and scattered like the old ship-home. Yet, unlike the earlier images of the chapter, these are controlled and nonthreatening. They suggest a death or dissolution that can be both comprehended and confronted; memory can accommodate them and impose upon them a sad but quiet serenity, one that encloses the narrator and those who have died within a vision in which the narrator can silence that terror of separation and discontinuity that lies behind much of the power and beauty of the chapter.

— 5 —

> So was it with me then, and so will be
> With Poets ever. Mighty is the charm
> Of those abstractions to a mind beset
> With images, and haunted by itself.
> Wordsworth, *The Prelude*, VI

After the "Tempest" chapter where does the nineteenth-century novel, and *David Copperfield* in particular, go? In what ways can it cope with a knowledge found in the realms of darkness and dreams, and how can it translate that knowledge into the language and structure of the novel? Except for isolated scenes and episodes, the outside world of *David Copperfield* does not seem large enough to accommodate the soul of the mature narrator or to allow it full expression. The soul is contained within the circle of its own knowledge, a knowledge that is destined to be falsified or forgotten once the hero enters into the world of social convention and orthodox values, however admirable they might be. In order to complete his own Memorial, and to return once again to those spaces from which he has departed when he began his imaginative "solitary pilgrimage," he must once again confront those images, but he must also finally deny or forget them. There is not, in spite of a courageous search for one, a permanent correspondence or identity between the center of the circle (the narrator's memory and imagination) and its periphery, that social landscape he traverses. The hero must either move away from himself by fleeing into that periphery and an ultimately inadequate consolation (evidenced by his need to take flight once again) or by assimilating the world into his own private vision, by forcing the ideal upon the real and by projecting himself as the hero of an extremely precarious vision.

This vision is precarious because it is threatened by time. Youth in *David Copperfield* can triumph over time only by means of an early death, by a violent crashing-out from the oncoming world which those left behind still must face. The hero as youth, whether the inarticulated heroism of a Ham or the demon-ridden heroism of a Steerforth, can retain his heroism only by moving outside of time, by becoming the image that David retains of Steerforth "fast asleep, lying, easily, with his hand upon his arm, as I had often seen him lie at school" (437). To remain behind, on the other hand, is to face one's own future coming toward one, a future whose possibilities are conjured up by the image of the "poor lunatic gentleman" in David's old room. Fairly late in the novel, David reflects upon impressions that "slumbered, and half awoke, and slept again, in the innermost recesses of my mind" (698), and here Dickens posits a type of heroism which he will explore more fully in *Great Expectations*. In this construction, the hero possesses what Lukács has described as "virile maturity," the capacity to realize both that the ideal and the real can never coincide, and that he must still continue to search for precisely such a coincidence.[12]

> What I missed, I still regarded—I always regarded—as something that had been a dream of my youthful fancy; that was incapable of realisation; that I was now discovering to be so, with some natural pain, as all men did. But that it would have been better for me if my wife could have helped me more, and shared the many thoughts in which I had no partner; and that this might have been; I knew.
>
> Because these two irreconcilable conclusions; the one, that what I felt was general and unavoidable; the other, that it was particular to me, and might have been different; I balanced curiously, with no distinct sense of their opposition to each other. When I thought of the airy dreams of youth that are incapable of realisation, I thought of the better state preceding manhood that I had outgrown. And then the contented days with Agnes, in the dear old house, arose before me, like spectres of the dead, that might have some renewal in another world, but never more could be reanimated here. (697)

The "irreconcilable conclusions" within this passage extend beyond a solitary clash between the general and the particular; what we see here is a clash between the ideal and the real, of that which should be with that which is. As David realizes, what he perceives are equal but opposing truths incapable of resolution or synthesis. This passage also contains evidence of a tension arising from a mind at odds with the direction of its own movement, one engaged in the process of self-revelation while also attempting to conceal or mitigate the implications of the revelation. In this case David's recognition of these mutually exclusive and irreconcilable positions is muted, as it were, by a mode of perception that helps to muffle or alleviate the pain he feels. He moves toward a mystified past and a mystified future—toward the past's "better state preceding manhood" and the future's promise of a repetition of the mystified past, "of the contented days with Agnes in the dear old house . . . that might have some renewal in another world, but never more could be reanimated here." [13] The directions of this passage suggest the real and enduring threat that time poses to the man who journeys forth in order to redeem it. This threat is disarmed, however, by the movement toward a vision that is almost static, one that conceives of a reality beyond time and also beyond humanity. Because the above passage is both honest and courageous, it elicits our admiration, but at the same time it also elicits sadness, for, by the end of the novel, the tensions evident in it have disappeared, absorbed within a vision that conceals the natural pain David shares with all men.

If *David Copperfield* fails to find a world that can adequately reflect its hero's depths, Dickens' struggle to envision such a world makes his novel a magnificent work, one whose power is evidenced in that at times faltering, at times prophetic, structure into which his vision unfolds. The movement of the novel is at odds with itself: while the journey undertaken is essentially an imaginative one, one that moves with greatest energy when the region being traversed is that of a man beset and haunted by images that compel him on his journey, it is within the public order and its social structures that the novel must attempt to define and reveal David's interior. *David Copperfield* suggests only partial awareness of the widening chasm that developed in nineteenth-century fiction between the public and private vision; after all, a good part of the novel is concerned with what David should do and what he wants to do.[14] At the same time, the tensions within it that arise from his inability to find self-definition within the public modes of fulfillment (the only appropriate livelihood for him is that of the artist, for it is private and yet makes possible public communication and rewards) tend to thrust the narrator further into himself. The circus and Coketown have not yet been cast asunder; one can still, with some effort, find it possible for work and play, prudence and spontaneity, to exist side by side. Wemmick is certainly anticipated by Traddles, but Walworth can still reside, though surreptitiously, for Traddles within the city limits.

The demonic or irrational forces that are in part responsible for the confusion of Mr. Dick and David also help one to withstand or subvert that world of reason and domination understood so well by Miss Mowcher. Traddles acknowledges, through the skeletons he is forever drawing, those demons that accompany him and keep his hair unruly. When Traddles enters public life, he maintains his concealed garden of Eros, a hidden and private enclosure whose "domestic arrangements are, to say the truth, quite unprofessional" (825). Within this enclosure Traddles, his wife, and her sisters engage in kissing, romping, and playing at "Puss in the Corner." They stand out in "that withered

Gray's Inn" as much as if "the Sultan's famous family had been admitted on the roll of attorneys, and had brought the talking bird, the singing tree, and the golden water into Gray's Inn Hall" (830). Admittedly, Eros has been transformed in this scene into the cherubic Cupid that adorned so many Victorian valentines, yet the implications of the scene—the contrast established between work and play, between sexuality and the "withered Gray's Inn"—verify Steven Marcus' observations of how Dickens and other great nineteenth-century artists humanized and amplified those metaphors that are more vividly and less complexly seen in Victorian pornography.[15]

The history of Traddles is further evidence of the difficulty Dickens encountered in translating David's interior drama and conflict into action and adventure. Death, exile, emigration, or a perpetually maintained duality and deception (as in Traddles' case) more in the cause of survival than subversion seem frequently to be the avenues whereby the novel's perception is converted into action. In fact, among the major characters of the novel only Mr. Peggotty can express and fulfill himself through action. Led through suffering and wandering on a journey that embodies his own mythic capacities, Mr. Peggotty transcends and transforms the world through which he travels. Like the classic heroes whose pattern he repeats, he is preceded by his own legend during a journey that sanctifies and transfigures the world: as David writes, "everything seemed, to my imagination, to be hushed in reverence for him, as he resumed his solitary journey through the snow" (589). Peggotty's search transcends the limits of an individual mission and almost assumes the stature of a religious pilgrimage.

> "By little and little, when I come to a new village or that, among the poor people, I found they know'd about me. They would set me down at their cottage doors, and give me whatnot fur to eat and drink, and show me wheer to sleep; and many a woman, Mas'r Davy, as had a daughter of about Em'ly's age, I've found a-waiting for me, at Our Saviour's Cross, outside the village, fur to do me sim'lar kindnesses. Some has had daughters as was dead. And God only knows how good them mothers was to me!" . . .
> "They would often put their children—partic'lar their little girls," said Mr. Peggotty, "upon my knee; and many a time you might have seen me sitting at their doors, when night was coming on, a'most as if they'd been my Darling's children. Oh, my Darling!" (584–85)

These passages, however, also reveal how close Dickens came to losing control over the figure of Peggotty, finding it difficult, undoubtedly, to translate an almost perfect goodness into dialogue and action. This same precariousness also suggests the hold this figure had on Dickens' imagination: throughout the novel Peggotty's fulfillment, and even his suffering, stands out against the fulfillment, and the suffering, of the novel's hero.

There are indications toward the later part of the novel that Dickens is trying to depict within the narrative a correspondence between recognition and action on David's part, but it is finally a correspondence forced upon the novel. In the final denouement of Uriah Heep, for example, an action that results from the combined efforts of Traddles and Micawber, Dickens brings David into the scene and gives him an active participation far in excess of his actual role by having Uriah direct his anger against David instead of against the real agents of his fall: " 'Why, there's Copperfield, mother,' he angrily retorted, pointing his lean finger at me, against whom all his animosity was levelled, as the prime mover in the discovery; and I did not undeceive him; 'there's Copperfield, would have given you a hundred pounds to say less than you've blurted out!' " (755). Throughout the scene David is a passive, indeed bewildered, spectator, not knowing even when arriving at Micawber's office what was going to happen or what had been done; yet, in trying to bring David actively into it (even at the cost of duplicity on David's part) and to pit him against his old adversary, Dickens gives him a role of active participation with which his hero is uncomfortable. In fact, in the final exchange between the two, Uriah seems almost to emerge the victor, penetrating in his remarks to the canker of hypocrisy within the body politic that Dickens would examine again: " 'They used to teach me at school (the same school where I picked up so much umbleness), from nine o'clock to eleven, that labour was a curse; and from eleven o'clock to one, that it was a blessing and a cheerfulness, and a dignity, and I don't know what all, eh? Won't umbleness go down? I shouldn't have got round my gentleman partner without it, I think' " (760). This speech is not answered by David: its truth does not permit refutation; it can only be ignored.

In Chapter lvii ("Absence") Dickens continues to seek for a language and a metaphor capable of defining and amplifying David's pilgrimage. However, neither the language nor the metaphor suffices, for they are borrowed from a tradition whose sources of strength Dickens can no longer draw upon. David's journey into Switzerland and into the isolation which finally leads to a renewed integration with mankind is in one respect absolutely correct as metaphor. At the same time, however, it finally belies those truths that it brings forth. The chapter's early descriptions capture with great power that psychic landscape into which David has been cast, a landscape corresponding to the hero's own moods and reflections: "It was a long and gloomy night that gathered on me, haunted by the ghosts of many hopes, of many dear re-

membrances, many errors, many unavailing sorrows and regrets"
(813). Traveling through "a ruined blank and waste, lying wide around
me, unbroken, to the dark horizon" (813), David approaches, albeit
unwittingly and unwillingly, an intimation of man's place in this world,
one that will be further defined in Dickens' later novels, such as *Great
Expectations* and *Our Mutual Friend*. In this chapter, as in the "Tempest"
chapter, we see the hero confronting himself without illusion: "I
roamed from place to place, carrying my burden with me everywhere.
I felt its whole weight now; and I drooped beneath it, and I said in my
heart that it could never be lightened" (813).

But the unbroken horizon and the unsheltered spaces are too
threatening; their vastness and lack of definition are too frightening.
The hero is in danger of exploding, of disappearing into a world un-
marked by those literary and social demarcations established by his
predecessors. When Dickens confronts the deepest (and, I think, the
truest) impulses of his imagination, he discovers in them that terror of
discontinuity and separation which Geoffrey Hartman finds in Wordsworth.[16] The images from *David Copperfield* that remain with us—the
graveyard, the lunatic gentleman, the entire "Tempest" episode—are
those that give expression, or at least recognition, to such impulses. It is
fitting that it is in *Copperfield*, the most Wordsworthian of Dickens'
novels, that we see the hero seeking an affirmation of continuity in Nature; it finally provides him, however, with even less solace than it
provided his imaginative predecessor. Like the poet, David is unsuccessful in discovering in Nature a reprieve from the primacy of his own
imagination. In the novel the natural world is devoid of rectifying powers or transcendental immanence: in it, Nature stands in a distant relationship to man: "I had found sublimity and wonder in the dread
heights and precipices [of the Alps], in the roaring torrents, and the
wastes of ice and snow; but as yet, I had found nothing else" (814).
Even this "sublimity and wonder" seems a feeble descriptive phrase,
more like emotions David should have felt than emotions verified by
the scene. Thus David's description of Nature several paragraphs later
is unexpected and unwarranted, the sudden intrusion (and equally
sudden disappearance) of Nature as an instrumentality within a work
from which it has been conspicuously absent: "All at once, in this serenity, great Nature spoke to me; and soothed me to lay my weary head
upon the grass, and weep as I had not wept yet, since Dora died! . . . I
resorted humbly whither Agnes had commended me; I sought out Nature, never sought in vain; and I admitted to my breast the human interest I had lately shrunk from" (815–16).

It is difficult to believe in the above passages; Dickens has not
earned the right to draw so heavily upon such a metaphor, and the fact
that he would do so suggests the intensity of his search for a language

or a metaphor that could viably accommodate and define his hero. Dickens could have waged such a struggle for only so long before sensing that there was no metaphor capable of adequately resolving the dissonances within his hero; in one respect the "Absence" chapter signals David's escape from the burdens of selfhood. It initiates his reintegration with mankind and leads rather quickly to his marriage with Agnes. The tensions within the novel seem to disappear and David moves toward a world quite different from the one he had known before. He moves out of one tormented by anxieties and into one in which the recalcitrant self and the outer world are harmoniously wedded—until, that is, the self emerges again to pursue the forever elusive image of complete reconciliation.

The form of the romance emerges victorious and absorbs into itself that Romantic artist whose quest must remain internal, waging within himself a battle whose outcome will determine the death or survival of the imagination. Once *David Copperfield* assumes its final form, it fulfills both its own destiny and its own death. The hero is absorbed into a social vision of fulfillment as well as into his own silence. The tensions between the ideal and the real have apparently disappeared, and we are presented with an artistic vision (enclosed within the metaphor of domesticity) of a world within which man is no longer alienated. Yet David still lives within that world he has previously presented to us. Thus, in order for the novel's final vision to be realized, he must become increasingly more alienated from that deeper voice and vision he has heard and seen. When David enters those spaces where "everything was as it used to be, in the happy time" (838), where Agnes has been busy "in keeping everything as it used to be when we were children" (840), we witness the silencing of a profound imagination.

Once the tensions within the novel disappear, it comes fairly rapidly to its conclusion, with a final vision whose loss of complexity is seen in the humorous, but easy, transition into comparatively orthodox social and moral satire (Heep and Littimer in prison, and the dialogue between David and Mr. Chillip about the Murdstones). Neither is really required, but they do suggest Dickens' attempt, partly successful, to give renewed vitality to a work he perhaps sensed was moving too rapidly toward closure. But Dickens is too honest and perceptive an artist to bury the images of his novel for long; thus we see them reappear, transformed but identifiable, in his following novels: in the winds that travel from David to *Bleak House* (there to trouble and perplex Mr. Jarndyce), in the widening chasm seen between public and private myths of fulfillment in the dual narrative structure of *Bleak House* and in the circus and Coketown of *Hard Times,* in the progressively increasing distance between the interior and the exterior that we find in *Little Dorrit* and *Great Expectations.*

But if *David Copperfield* promises its hero a gratification that will become more tenuous or suspect in Dickens' later novels, we see even here what is perhaps Dickens' final uneasiness about the novel's conclusion (his own admission, although obliquely presented) that the spaces he has created may not be able to fulfill all that they promise. The passages I have in mind occur at the end of the novel and concern the changed Julia Mills.

> But Julia keeps no diary in these days; never sings Affection's Dirge; eternally quarrels with the old Scotch Croesus, who is a sort of yellow bear with a tanned hide. Julia is steeped in money to the throat, and talks and thinks of nothing else. I liked her better in the Desert of Sahara. Or perhaps this *is* the Desert of Sahara. For, though Julia has a stately house, and mighty company, and sumptuous dinners every day, I see no green growth near her; nothing that can ever come to fruit or flower. . . . When society is the name for such hollow gentlemen and ladies, Julia, and when its breeding is professed indifference to everything that can advance or can retard mankind, I think we must have lost ourselves in the same Desert of Sahara, and had better find the way out. (875–76)

The crucial questions in this passage—the location and precise configuration of the Desert of Sahara—remain only ambiguously answered. When we reflect on the passage, we can see the antithesis established— between the Desert on the one hand and the green and fecund garden on the other—is precarious and problematic. We are to read it, most certainly, as the observation of a man who himself lives within the "green growth," participating in a world wherein things do indeed "come to fruit or flower." There is no self-irony intended, nor are we justified in regarding the passage in such a light, but we should be aware of the inherent fragility of the landscape out of which the hero makes his judgments: if the hero has come full circle to the point from which he began his narrative, in so doing he has woven about him a sphere that is vulnerable to destruction. Julia Mills' silence echoes the silence both of Mr. Dick and the silence that will soon envelop David. Each is absorbed into a world that will dispel the images of which he or she wrote and spoke. Their voices, however, die quietly and painlessly; they can still speak, if only of things that conceal the very loss they have incurred. And if for now the Desert of Sahara is confined to that part of society that is dead and deadening, it cannot be held off for long by the warmth and love of the immediate world-garden that surrounds David. It will eventually encroach on this gentle fortress until the final images of the novel are turned inside out and the garden located on the perimeters of civilization. When the Desert has achieved ultimate success, it transforms the landscape into one which death has triumphed over life. Madness becomes the image of reason having satiated its own appetite, and David's virtues of earnestness, industry, and thrift become the signposts of a world controlled and ravaged by Small-weeds and Bounderbys. But while there are indications of latent doubt at the end of *David Copperfield,* they are presented in such a way that the conclusion is not seriously disturbed or violated. These doubts are, however, destined to reappear and demand a new confrontation in the novels that follow.

At the end of *David Copperfield,* the narrator's final voice seems to bespeak an alienation from the self that he has sought, found, and then lost. The hero seeks protection within an enclosure that finds its final image in the green and fruitful garden. But this garden has been created by the alienation of the hero and its existence depends on the perpetuity of certain assumptions, which, while they may appear solid and substantial in the light of day, are threatened by those images of the dark, images that tell of a history that does lie, of a past that does not contain its dead, and of a future that promises only the terror (and the joy) of becoming what one is.

It is appropriate, finally, that *David Copperfield* is a novel about a novelist writing a novel while denying that he is writing a novel at all. For it is a novel about the novel, one that contains its genre's history and also prefigures its genre's future. It is a novel that speaks of alienation while attesting to its own alienation. On the one hand it seeks solace and protection within the structures of its form, while on the other hand it expresses the limits and weakness of the form and engages in rebellion against them. Struggling with a tradition that provides it with an ambivalent comfort, it must borrow the vocabulary and structures of that tradition in order to wage battle against it. Dickens gazes deeply into the inner regions of the self and hears from within image-haunted winds, but what he sees and hears sends him back toward the protection of definition and form. There he must deny, or attempt to deny, those demonic voices that sing of freedom and its terrors. The world of *David Copperfield* is richly inhabited by those heroes of whom the young and lonely David has read: "Roderick Random, Peregrine Pickle, Humphrey Clinker, Tom Jones, the Vicar of Wakefield, Don Quixote, Gil Blas, and Robinson Crusoe, . . . they, and the Arabian Nights, and the Tales of the Genii" (55). But these heroes and the worlds they move in are not David's, even though they posit values and beliefs that will endure. For the landscape of *David Copperfield* is one that explores regions previously unexplored in English fiction. The rich tradition of the novel that Dickens drew upon was able to help him explore the landscape and could provide him with support and comfort, but it was capable of only partially demarcating the world through which his hero traverses. And even though we do see a movement back into the tradition, the realm into which David journeys beckons forth to those novels that are yet to come, just as surely as David himself is beckoned forth by his image-ridden memory.

Frank Edmund Smith

PERVERTED BALANCE:
EXPRESSIVE FORM IN *HARD TIMES*

DURING MOST of the time since its publication, *Hard Times* has been viewed as a social document, exposing to some the vices of the factory system and to others the evils of trade unionism. With some exceptions the ideological readings of the novel have given over to appreciation of its artistry. The interrelation of theme and form has become the crux of contemporary critical appraisals of Charles Dickens' brief novel. Since F. R. Leavis suggested almost thirty years ago that the moral fable form underscores the "comprehensive vision" of social abuses,[1] critics have further attempted to link the novel's structure with its ideas. In a brief discussion J. Hillis Miller indicates a structure of opposing symbols that dramatizes the conflict between organized society and personalized love.[2] Monroe Engel finds in the total symbolism the key to the union of form and meaning.[3] Earle Davis, contending that *Hard Times* should be read as art, has argued that the work is structured into three plot sequences that all focus on the theme of practicality.[4]

That an artistic understanding of the novel has become the norm is best demonstrated by Robert Lougy, who calls *Hard Times* "radical literature" and supports his thesis not by an external ideology laid on the novel but through an examination of its image patterns.[5] In a 1969 essay David Sonstroem opens with a brief summary of two lines of argument about *Hard Times* (both lines involve essentially artistic judgments) and attempts to reconcile them by sharing both views: "I find *Hard Times* to be a truly impressive achievement of meaningful symbolic structuring, but weak dramatically, because the personalities of certain characters do not support their full symbolic charge." [6] Then he argues for the novel's success and failure by examining the polar structure of its controlling metaphors: fact and fancy.

The above critics have deepened our understanding of *Hard Times* but in doing so have held to a kind of theme-form dialectic that struggles to identify adequately the experience of the novel. Looking at *Hard Times* as a unified work of art, I would like to suggest an understanding of the novel that transforms this dualistic theme-form depiction into a holistic, organic description of the novel. Although Dickens writes didactically in order to teach the reader the danger of life's extremes, it is the form which this message assumes that communicates such extremes. Not merely the lesson that Dickens preaches but the formalization of the materials with which he presents it creates the reader's experience. The real drama of *Hard Times* is the shaping of its own form as a reflection of its materials.

Alice Kelley finds something like this occurring in *Bleak House*. She catalogues the many Bleak Houses of the novel, and in the final, unfortunately brief, segment of her essay she draws an analogy between Bleak House itself and the larger world of that novel: "In Dickens's description of the architectural structure of John Jarndyce's Bleak House, another astonishing level of symbol is revealed; for the shape of the plot and the fate of many of the characters are paralleled by the actual physical makeup of the house." [7]

A monistic view of *Hard Times,* then, sees the gross structure of that novel as expressive form, that is, the shape of the novel is a picture of its materials. The novel is not a collection of things poured into a plot but a process of relationships between words, images, symbols, events, and characters. The concern of the novel is order, and all of its materials convey the idea of order and disorder. The "message" of these materials is formally expressed by the novel's total structure. A contrapuntal substructure of repetitive forms supports the superstructure. The form of the narrative is balance. The form of its supporting structures is also balance, but a balance that is precarious, confused, disorderly.

Hard Times is a novel of perverted balance. Within the almost perfectly balanced gross structure Dickens has created a complement of grotesquely balanced minor forms. He devises a world in which everything has been so carefully arranged in such an evil way that time must prove the balance false and reconstruct a true stability: "Time went on in Coketown like its own machinery: so much material wrought up, so much fuel consumed, so many powers worn out, so much money made. . . . It brought its varying seasons even into that wilderness of smoke and brick, and made the only stand that ever *was* made in the place against its direful uniformity" (90).

The almost trite sectioning of the novel demonstrates Dickens' self-conscious concern with structure. "Sowing," "Reaping," and "Garnering," he has entitled the major divisions. One sort of balance is achieved in the first part of *Hard Times* as the evil seeds of fact are planted and nurtured, but in time the certitude of the Gradgrinds and the Bounderbys that their view of life conforms to truth is confuted by the very nature that they ignore. The fulcrum of reaping pivots the novel's course in the center, and the new balance of good—for hope is also planted in the first part—is derived in the final separation of the wheat from the chaff.

In the pivotal chapter of the novel, when Bounderby dismisses Stephen, Dickens provides a statement of the expressive form as seen through the eyes of Bounderby: " 'Now it's clear to me,' said Mr. Bounderby, 'that you are one of those chaps who have always got a grievance. And you go about, sowing it and raising crops. That's the business of *your* life, my friend' " (152). It is ironic, of course, that Bounderby and the people like him have been sowing, but after this point they begin to dine on their own bitter fruits. Again, Dickens makes a single statement of meaning and form when Louisa comes home to see her dying mother. By this time, all the evil that had grown to the point of Stephen's dismissal has begun to be reaped and to be recognized for what it is, but the seeds have been planted and must be harvested: "[Louisa's] remembrances of home and childhood were remembrances of the drying up of every spring and fountain in her young heart as it gushed out. The golden waters were not there. They were flowing for the fertilization of the land where grapes are gathered from thorns, and figs from thistles" (197).

It is apparent from the first page of *Hard Times* that some sort of order—a balance—is the essential experience for the reader. Thomas Gradgrind demands that facts compose the essence of every person: " 'Plant nothing else, and root out everything else' " (1). Only in this way can one order his life to be useful. Thomas Gradgrind has done just this to his life. He has achieved a cold, rational, perfect balance: "A man of realities. A man of facts and calculations. A man who proceeds upon the principle that two and two are four, and nothing over. . . . With a rule and a pair of scales, and the multiplication table always in his pocket, Sir, ready to weigh and measure any parcel of human nature, and tell you exactly what it comes to" (3). His own human nature, in fact, has been weighed and measured to a calculated ordering: "His character was not unkind, all things considered; it might have been a very kind one indeed, if he had only made some round mistake in the arithmetic that balanced it, years ago" (27). Gradgrind demands just this sort of balance of everyone else. The normal human balance of fact and fancy has been perverted to cold calculation, and the other arm of the scale of natural order is left to swing wildly—achieving equilibrium only through a kind of madness. We shall see the fruit of Gradgrind's unnatural balance later when we consider the strange balance that stabilizes between his children.

The very town is balanced in a mad way. Dickens describes it as perfectly arranged into square block buildings, straight streets, eighteen red square churches, and exactly-alike-everydays: "All the public inscriptions in the town were painted alike, in severe characters of black and white. The jail might have been the infirmary, the infirmary might have been the jail, the town-hall might have been either, or both, or anything else, for anything that appeared to the contrary in the graces of their construction" (23). The perversion of this overcalculation becomes revealed in the ironic fantasy appearance of the town to outsiders: "The lights in the great factories, which looked, when they were illuminated, like Fairy palaces—or the travelers by express-train said so—were all extinguished" (64). Morning's light exposes the town's (and the novel's) mad balance of unyielding fact and unbelievable fantasy: "The Fairy palaces burst into illumination, before pale morning showed the monstrous serpents of smoke trailing themselves over Coketown" (69). One might equate this night and day portrait of Coketown with the psychological model of the human unconscious and conscious mind. That which is repressed from the conscious, perhaps too awful to recognize, is forced down to the unconscious there to compensate—balance—by way of dreams, fantasies, illusions. We will find this sort of dreadful balancing act going on in the psyches of some of the characters.

The people of Coketown have been weighed, calculated, and made so artificial that they, too, have become a fantasy and are reduced to only that part of themselves which is purely functional: " 'the Hands,'—a race who would have found more favor with some people, if Providence had seen fit to make them only hands, or, like the lower creatures of the seashore, only hands and stomachs" (63). In this orderly imbalance that informs *Hard Times,* when fact becomes too extreme, the need for equilibrium sometimes places an extreme fancy on the other side of the scales to effect a warped order. Or, as Dickens says, comparing M'Choakumchild's facts to the boiling oil that Morgiana poured on the Forty Thieves: "When from thy boiling store, thou shalt fill each jar brimful by-and-by, dost thou think that thou wilt always kill outright the robber Fancy lurking within—or sometimes only maim him and distort him?" (8). Dickens speaks of the possibility that the fancy of the working people, long suppressed, is "struggling on in convulsions." And, he compares the macrocosm to the microcosm: "Is it possible, I wonder, that there was any analogy between the case of the Coketown population and the case of the little Gradgrinds?" (24).

There is, in fact, analogy running through every level of *Hard Times.* The foregoing provides an introduction to the expression of balance throughout the novel. Patterns of balance can be observed reflecting each other through the entire dynamic of the action. This paper can not hope to demonstrate all of them, and it need not. We can take as a given several other studies of *Hard Times* that, in the course of developing their own theses, explicate the motif of balance. The Sonstroem essay that was mentioned earlier does just that. His elaborate detailing of image clusters that oppose fact to fancy clearly demonstrates that Dickens has created a pattern of balanced metaphors. And, these basic metaphors—fact and fancy—are central to the argument of this paper. Robert Green, who links the style to the purpose of the novel, carefully examines the prose and discovers, among other devices, balanced phrasing. He shows that the style used to describe the people of fact differs from that used to describe the people of fancy.[8] Finally, George Bornstein finds two agricultural patterns—miscultivated field and corrupted garden, and he implies in his thesis the balance inherent in *Hard Times:* "[Dickens] idealizes neither the chaotic growth of a wholly natural forest nor the ordered mechanism of a wholly artificial city, but the ordered growth, the blend of pattern with spontaneity, exemplified by the cultivated field or garden." [9] Although these critics do not talk about balance as I am using it here, their analyses do suggest the many levels of balance that occur in *Hard Times.* Given that, I choose to develop at length one particular pattern of balances that informs the substructure as an analogue of the gross structure, that is, the series of symbiotic relationships that occur between the male and female characters. Each of these relationships is a perverted balance held in tension by the extremes of the characters involved. The centrifugal force that they generate, each at the end of a balance beam, keeps them in a semblance of order, united by some perverse attraction.

The Sissy-Bitzer relationship is the leitmotif of the other couplings and, in fact, envelopes the novel. One might consider this the least formalized of all the relationships—the other couples at least live together—yet critics since Leavis have drawn attention to the scene in which Sissy and Bitzer are revealed in the same shaft of sunlight. That sunbeam contrasts Sissy's dark, earthy, natural color with that of the anemic Bitzer, who looks "as though, if he were cut, he would bleed white" (5). The balance set up between these extreme personalities, though it fades out of the action during the middle of the narrative, introduces the balanced pairings and concludes them.

From the opening of the novel the disease of fact is placed in conflict with the healer fancy, a healthy sort of fancy, represented in the general by the circus,[10] which draws the Gradgrind children briefly away from their "ologies," and in the specific by Sissy Jupe. Though Sissy knows the real pain of abandonment, this "fact" does not preclude her capacity to appreciate fancy, nor does she use her imagination for simplistic escape from reality. Entered in the Gradgrind school, she immediately comes into conflict with the imbalanced system of Coketown and its young representative Bitzer. Sissy, who, as Leavis notes, knows what a horse really is, is forced to accept Bitzer's definition that devitalizes the animal. All of her healthy fancy that understands the way things really are and, therefore, admits of representations of horses and flowers on the wall or floor, is squelched in the name of fact. But, Dickens tells us, it is this overrationalization of life that imposes false understandings, not the view of the world that allows imagination, for such a balanced sight can blend both literal and figurative perceptions of reality.

Constantly, in the first chapters of the novel, we see the world of Coketown facts cut off from possible salvation. Tom and Louisa peek in at the circus, hoping to discover the human qualities which they lack, but their father takes them back to their rocks and minerals. When Gradgrind and Bounderby go looking for Sissy to rid their town of her humanizing influence, they find her being chased by the inhuman Bitzer. Sissy, brought to the balanced Gradgrind home—"a calculated, cast up, balanced, and proved house. Six windows on this side of the door, six on that side; a total of twelve in this wing, a total of twelve in the other wing; four-and-twenty carried over to the back wings" (10)—is forbidden to discuss her past with the Gradgrind children and is constantly attacked with facts. Because of Sissy's thoroughly developed humanity, she is unable to understand facts freed from their relation to people, as we clearly see in her problems with statistics. Waiting for the letter from her father (the letter that never comes), Sissy exhibits the undying hope of the fully human person, a hope that Gradgrind's philosophy cannot comprehend: "Mr. Gradgrind . . . remark[ed], when she was gone, that if Jupe had been properly trained from an early age she would have demonstrated to herself on sound principles the baselessness of these fantastic hopes. Yet it did seem (though not to him, for he saw nothing of it) as if fantastic hope could take as strong a hold as Fact" (12). Sissy's hope is planted, like the seed of some exotic flower, in the furrows of the novel. Though we see little of her, her positive influence will blossom forth just as the gross structure of the novel teeters off balance. She will tip the scales back to normal.

Balanced against her normalcy, Bitzer, the polar opposite of Sissy, lives, more than anyone else in the novel, in the coldness of unadulterated fact. He never gets excited; he has no interests or desires that involve feeling. We learn that Bitzer has sent his aged mother to the poorhouse and that he has no intention of ever marrying. As he says, " 'I have only one to feed, and that's the person I most like to feed' " (118). Sterile, neutral, zombielike, Bitzer watches, calculates, bides his time, becomes a perfect factual success. Like Sissy, to whom he has been tied by that beam of sunlight, Bitzer's personality will be proved by time. In the climactic scene they are brought together again in the circus ring, and their opposing realities are tested.

The balanced coupling most evidently like that of Sissy and Bitzer is the crooked order established between Stephen Blackpool and his wife. Although Blackpool, like Sissy, is certainly an ideal Dickensian character—all good, almost natural man—he is forced by an artificial social system to remain married to a drunken, corrupted wife, thus frustrating the potential good of a relationship between himself and another complete person, Rachael. The psychic pain engendered by this imbalance manifests itself in a startling dream that Dickens describes at length but ambiguously. In the dream Stephen first comes to a full recognition of his entrapment with his wife and sees fully the "condemnation upon him, that he was never, in this world or the next, through all the unimaginable ages of eternity, to look on Rachael's face or hear her voice." Becoming a hopeless wanderer, he is the "subject of a nameless, horrible dread," "doomed to seek" "one particular shape which everything took" (86) Like a man possessed, every object he sees in the dream transforms into that dread shape. Filled with shame and guilt, the single purpose of his life becomes to prevent anyone else from recognizing that shape. As the dream resolves to reality and he finds himself once more within his own room, he recognizes that shape in the poison bottle beside his wife's bed. Spellbound, he does nothing as the figure in the bed pours the poison into a cup and prepares to drink. Rachael awakes in time to prevent the death, but Stephen confesses in the following scene that from the moment he had seen the poison bottle he had contemplated murder and suicide. The conscious mind of the good person, forced to live an unwholesome life, may reject ugly solutions, but the repression ferments in the unconscious and compensates for reason's control with nightmare schemes, finally forcing the consciousness to admit its potential for evil. This dark compensation is the outgrowth of violations against nature. Stephen Blackpool is natural man balanced desperately against the corruption of society. He and Rachael are the only two people in the novel who have both the nature and the potential opportunity for a truly balanced relationship. But, they cannot realize this natural order because the system imposed by the fact-toters—the artificers—demands statistics before humanity. The contrived order of the social system, as represented by Gradgrind and Bounderby, cannot allow a creative order to exist because it would expose the establishment and the lives balanced on it as fraudulent.

Gradgrind's own marriage is just such a fraudulent balance. Mr. and Mrs. Gradgrind foolishly attempt a self-completion by uniting a complete fact with a complete fiction. The hard-fact Gradgrind, looking for equilibrium, chose a wife as unlike him as can be—a nothing, almost an imbecile. "In truth, Mrs. Gradgrind's stock of facts in general was woefully defective; but Mr. Gradgrind in raising her to her high matrimonial position, had been influenced by two reasons. Firstly, she was most satisfactory as a question of figures; and, secondly, she had 'no nonsense' about her. By nonsense he meant fancy; and truly it is probable she was as free from any alloy of that nature, as any human being not arrived at the perfection of an absolute idiot, ever was" (17–18). Gradgrind's principal conduct with his wife is intimidation. He treats her like a cipher. She becomes increasingly befuddled and finally takes to her room, an emotional invalid, long before she dies. When she learns that Louisa is to be married, her first concern is for her daughter's health for, as she says (with implications for her own compensation), her own head began to split as soon as she was married. In their own baroque way, the Gradgrinds are a perfectly complementary match, but their children, the extensions of themselves, grow up to be inadequate human beings. Again, Dickens affirms, as he did in *David Copperfield,* that a successful marriage is the union of two complete humans. The awkward balance of two insufficient people trying to make each other whole destroys rather than creates.

The fruit of the Gradgrind marriage, Tom and Louisa, share an unnatural brother-sister relationship that strongly reenforces the underlying perverted balance of *Hard Times.* Fact does not take as complete a hold on them as it does, for example, on Bitzer. Rather than erasing their human natures completely, their forced devotion to facts has turned them just a little awry. They are very much aware that they lack something, and in their struggle to become whole their natures become perverted. What happens to Tom is fairly clear. He becomes a self-pitying, sneaking "whelp," who disgusts even the pragmatic Harthouse. Dickens often calls him "unnatural." Tom is aware of what his father's system has done to him, and, because he has no experience of love or human feelings, he has every intention of using the system to get even: " 'I wish I could collect all the Facts we hear so much about,' said Tom, spitefully setting his teeth, 'and all the Figures, and all the people who found them out: and I wish I could put a thousand barrels of gunpowder under them, and blow them all up together! However, when I go to live with old Bounderby, I'll have my revenge' " (52). The calculated coldness of Tom's education has taught him just how to manipulate people while erasing any possible scruple for doing it. With no compunctions he prostitutes Louisa, first to Bounderby for his own self-advancement, then to Harthouse for self-gratification. Like Bitzer, Tom is totally egocentric: "He was becoming that not unprecedented triumph of calculation which is usually at work on number one" (62). Also, like Bitzer, he is not interested in the normal male complement of a wife. Yet, because his fancy has not been totally killed, as Bitzer's has, the struggle of this starved faculty for nourishment of some kind gradually throws him out of control. Dickens tells us that he has adopted some sort of unnamed "perversions," which lead him into debt. He is a "monster" whose strangled imagination is visited by the ghost of "groveling sensualities." Although the exact nature of his depravity is left ambiguous, Louisa confirms Harthouse's suspicion that Tom gambles and loses. Having been governed all of his life, Tom is incapable of governing himself. Living with Bounderby, he goes out of control, becomes imbalanced.

Louisa is a much more complex person than Tom. Her desire for fancy has been even less extinguished by fact, but the very strength of her starved imagination causes her to be even more out of balance. It is Louisa who is always cut short in wondering. Her curiosity leads Tom to the circus. The passions that Louisa has been forced to control lie buried deep but must be expressed in some way, so she stares into the fire and sees things. We rarely see Louisa when she is not looking at fire. She spends long hours gazing into the flames in her own home, and when she steps outside, she sees the lurid red of Coketown and tries to discover in it the secret that time will reveal about her womanhood. When her father tells her of Bounderby's proposal of marriage without love, Louisa, looking at the smokestacks of town, says: " 'There seems to be nothing there but languid and monotonous smoke. Yet when the night comes, Fire bursts out, Father!' " (100). We see clearly the festering turbulence in Louisa which she herself can only dimly imagine. Her father's answer, " 'Of course I know that, Louisa. I do not see the application of the remark,' " is characteristic of the gulf of unfeeling that surrounds her impoverished sensibilities and forces them to imbalance. The fire that rages within compensates the cold, controlled indifference without. Here is one more example of the repression-fantasy motif that we have already noted in the town itself and in the personality of Stephen Blackpool. The power of the symbol of Louisa's repression is best evidenced in its capacity to communicate even through others. As she strolls in the garden with Harthouse, who has begun to tap her underlying sympathies, Sparsit peers at her so intently that Bounderby asks, " 'What's the matter, ma'am? . . . you don't see a Fire, do you?' " (188). Then, when she returns home to Sissy, her resentment that she could not be the total person Sissy expected her to be causes "a dull anger" to smoulder "within her like an unwholesome fire. All closely imprisoned forces rend and destroy. The air that would be healthful to the earth, the water that would enrich it, the heat that would ripen it, tear it when caged up" (224).

Searching desperately for any kind of person-oriented feeling, Louisa fixes her uncontrolled emotions on Tom. Unfeelingly, he takes advantage of the situation, and their resulting relationship takes on a strongly sexual cast.[11] Louisa marries Bounderby, a man she is very conscious of not loving, to prove her love for her brother. She knows that to love she must give herself, but she does not have the human

judgment to control the self-sacrifice. Thus, she prostitutes herself in
her misguided desire to love. Giving herself sexually for Tom is highly
suggestive of giving herself sexually to Tom. A catalogue of scenes and
developing actions will further indicate the extent of the sexual implications that Dickens gives their relationship.

Tom seems to anticipate and hope for Louisa's marriage to Bounderby years before the event. Tom tells Louisa that he has plans to
"smooth" and "manage" Bounderby by threatening him with the dis-
favor of his "little pet," Louisa. He makes other comments of a similar
nature. When Tom becomes aware that Bounderby's offer of marriage
is at hand, he presses her to do him favors by giving her favors to
Bounderby. "With her hand upon her brother's shoulder, Louisa still
stood looking at the fire. Her brother glanced at her face with greater
interest than usual, and, encircling her waist with his arm, drew her
coaxingly to him" (94). Knowing how exactingly Dickens uses detail, it
is clear that the physical contact between brother and sister in this scene
(in which one wishes to lead the other into a sexual relationship) is not
accidental. After the wedding, Tom expresses enthusiasm over his sister's cooperation and the prospects for his success. Her response is to
cling "to him as she should have clung to some far better nature" (109).
When Louisa, at last, returns to her father, she tells him that she has
married Bounderby solely for Tom's sake: " 'I had a hope of being
pleasant and useful to Tom. I made that wild escape into something
visionary, and have slowly found out how wild it was. But Tom had
been the subject of all the little tenderness of my life' " (217). Louisa's
natural emotions have been so perverted that they can find expression
only in her brother. Harthouse notices this when Tom walks into the
room in which the normally sad Louisa is dining. "A beautiful smile.
Mr. James Harthouse might not have thought so much of it, but that
he had wondered so long at her impassive face. She put out her
hand—a pretty little soft hand; and her fingers closed upon her brother's, as if she would have carried them to her lips" (130–31). The scene
most suggestive of an incestuous relationship between brother and sister takes place after the robbery when Louisa, suspecting Tom's guilt,
goes to his room at night. Again, Dickens' explicit description (from
which I have selected passages) cannot be ignored.

> Then she arose, put on a loose robe, and went out of her
> room in the dark, and up the staircase to her brother's room.
> His door being shut, she softly opened it and spoke to him,
> approaching his bed with a noiseless step.
> She kneeled down beside it, passed her arm over his neck,
> and drew his face to her. . . .
> "My dear brother:" she laid her head down on his pillow,

and her hair flowed over him as if she would hide him from every one but herself: "is there nothing that you have to tell me? Is there nothing you can tell me if you will? You can tell me nothing that will change me. . . .

"As you lie here alone, my dear, in the melancholy night, so you must lie somewhere one night, when even I, if I am living then, shall have left you. As I am here beside you, barefoot, unclothed, undistinguishable in darkness, so must I lie through all the night of my decay, until I am dust. . . ."

"You may be certain"; in the energy of her love she took him to her bosom as if he were a child; "that I will not reproach you." (189)

The above scene emphasizes Louisa's near-nakedness and depicts a considerable physical intimacy. Tom and Louisa's relationship is certainly not literally incestuous, but neither is it completely healthy. Louisa's warped fancy has so fixated all of her stunted emotions on Tom that Harthouse immediately recognizes this and attempts to seduce her through the "whelp." He succeeds, by pretending to befriend Tom—even offering to Louisa to give money to Tom—in transferring Louisa's feelings for her brother to him. Providing the necessary information to Louisa's intended seducer, Tom callously informs him that he used Louisa to get in with Bounderby, and explains away the apparent insensitivity of his actions by thrice remarking that she had never had any lover anyway. Dickens concludes that Tom should have drowned himself for what he revealed that night. One can trace this seduction by association via Louisa's rare smile. Harthouse begins to wish for, then to plan, that the face that smiles so sweetly for Tom will smile for him. Finally, after instructing Tom to be "more loving and agreeable" to his sister, "there was a smile upon Louisa's face that day, for some one else!" (178). Louisa's emotional identification of Harthouse with Tom plus the fascination in her untrained heart for a handsome, attentive stranger leads her to agree to an assignation with him. Coming to her senses in time, Louisa reveals her troubled feelings to her father, who later tells Bounderby: " 'I think there are—Bounderby, you will be surprised to hear me say this—I think there are qualities in Louisa, which—which have been harshly neglected, and—and a little perverted' " (241). The final scene between Tom and Louisa demonstrates that neither of them has understood the nature of the love that they professed to share. For Louisa it was destructive giving; for Tom it was heartless taking:

"O Tom, Tom, do we end so, after all my love!"
"After all your love!" he returned, obdurately. "Pretty love! Leaving old Bounderby to himself, and packing my best friend

Mr. Harthouse off, and going home just when I was in the greatest danger. Pretty love that! . . . You have regularly given me up. You never cared for me." (285)

Tom is too self-serving, Louisa too blind, to realize, as the reader does, that Tom has been, in effect, pimping his sister in return for position, influence, money, and self-gratification.

The perverted relationship that achieves a kind of balance between the askew, incomplete personalities of Tom and Louisa is the major, but not the final, mad equilibrium in this novel that condemns artificial order. We come, at last, in the pursuit of the coupling motif to the symbiotic relationship between Mrs. Sparsit and Mr. Bounderby, the novel's substratum comic analogue of the gross structure. Sparsit and Bounderby use each other to maintain their self-deluding fantasies. Insecure about their social roles, they both create wholly or partially fictitious histories to disguise the persons that they really are. Mrs. Sparsit is so incomplete as a person that she bases her reality on her relationship to the upper-class Powler family. She lives on Bounderby's "stipend," manages his house, and pretends to be humble. She engages in elaborate rituals of deference to him—surrendering the best place at the fire when he enters, eating the poorest food at his table until he, inevitably, insists that she partake of the best food and wine. In her condition of genteel poverty, she needs the middle-class factory owner Bounderby as a contrast by which she can feel noble.

Bounderby, on the other hand, needs her to balance off his carefully constructed persona. He has composed for general consumption a totally false lower-class history of himself. This history allows him to exercise to the utmost his pride as the self-made man. Sparsit is for him a mantle piece that he can show off in support of his ego. "If Bounderby had been a Conqueror, and Mrs. Sparsit a captive Princess whom he took about as a feature in his state-processions, he could not have made a greater flourish with her than he habitually did" (43). The deference that he demands others pay Sparsit because of her "family" he easily channels to himself. Sparsit, jealous of the support which Bounderby's presence gives her illusions, tries to wreck his marriage. To keep her ego inflated, she attempts to replace Louisa by exhibiting an overconcern for Bounderby's health and comfort. Constantly, she calls Louisa "Miss Gradgrind." She suffers the extremes of a storm to rid herself of Louisa's threat. Finally, she tracks down and drags back Mrs. Pegler to prove that she is indispensable to Bounderby. Bounderby, not to be outdone when it comes to self-inflation, never misses a chance to remind Sparsit that she is a "lady born" who is now in his employ. He demeans her by his constant exhortation to visitors that they pay her respect for her origin, regardless of her present position. He seems to say to Harthouse, " 'I am the proprietor of this female, and she's worth your attention, I think' " (184). Bounderby supports his fictitious self on the relationship that he imagines between himself and Sparsit. As he tells Gradgrind: " 'You know my origin; and you know that for a good many years of my life I didn't want a shoeing-horn, in consequence of not having a shoe. Yet you may believe it or not, as you think proper, that there are ladies—born ladies—belonging to families—Families!— who next to worship the ground I walk on' " (243). By this time, that lady has long taken to calling him, when alone with his portrait, a "noodle." When, because she has humiliated him, he decides to break the connection with Sparsit, he discovers the "crowning glory" in being able to say to others, " 'She was a woman of family, and wanted to stick to me, but I wouldn't have it, and got rid of her' " (294).

When Louisa becomes entrapped in the Bounderby-Sparsit relationship, she proves the balance faulty. Indeed, Mrs. Sparsit's staircase is an extraordinary symbol [12] of repressed sexuality projected on the source of her frustration. It is the final, and perhaps the most obviously constructed, link in the pattern of repression-fantasy motifs that occurs in one element or character of most of these perverted balances. That Mrs. Sparsit is jealous of the position from which she has been removed by Louisa, there can be no doubt. Bounderby, in fact, anticipates a highly emotional response when he informs Sparsit of his impending marriage, and, after much hesitation, he communicates that message armed with powerful smelling salts. Much to his surprise, Sparsit takes the news with icy calm and the beginnings of a knowing pity that she refines into a patronizing contempt as time passes. After nine years as his housekeeper, Sparsit might have expected to become Bounderby's wife herself. Certainly, she cannot be pleased at being replaced as mistress of his home, a position that afforded her prestige and security, in addition to a relationship that had been so carefully constructed that her personality artfully dovetailed with his. Can any husband and wife expect their personalities to mesh more completely? Yet, Sparsit barely responds to the news that promises to divest her of all this. She, too, has repressed her natural emotions, but, though buried, they do not die. They surface in a twisted sexual assault on Louisa. In a manner very like that of Tom, she directs events, so far as she can, to insinuate Louisa into a sexual relationship for her own ends. She describes Louisa to Harthouse, arousing his interest. Then, from her intimate knowledge of his personality, she manipulates Bounderby so that, as Dickens says, "the Sparsit action upon Mr. Bounderby threw Louisa and James Harthouse more together" (195). Shortly after this, her normally unpoetic nature fancies an "allegory" of "a mighty Staircase with a dark pit of shame and ruin at the bottom" (201). At the top of those imaginary stairs she places Louisa, watching with her bright, penetrating eyes as her prey takes the steps to her fall. Through two chapters Dickens shapes this elaborate symbol of the feverishly compensating mind of Sparsit. Not content to be a mere spectator at the playing out of her own projection, Sparsit ludicrously pursues Louisa through the woods, in the rain and on the railroad until, exaltingly, she sees her fall from the lowest stair and plunge "down the precipice." In comic triumph she crashes in on Bounderby in his hotel and, displaying the emotion she has trapped inside so long, passes out, giving Bounderby, now, the opportunity to use salts to revive her. The passion with which Sparsit pursues Louisa's destruction expresses externally the forces that have been damned up within her. So, the fallen woman imagery of Dickens' oblique Victorian allusion to sexual repression demonstrates once more the contortions that artificial social contracts can twist into nature. In the Sparsit-Bounderby coupling, we learn that two inflated, empty people, carefully balancing their egos against each other, cannot support a third, especially when her humanity is out of order. Nature exposes the artificers, forcing them to separate.

These relationships of strange and perverted order are the fruit that has grown out of the artificial seed sown in society by the exaggeration of half of the expression of human life—facts. We watch these orderings prove false in the course of the novel as artificial society destroys itself and its members. The structure of *Hard Times* exposes unnatural order in the first section; artifice destroys in "Reaping"; and it is itself destroyed in the final third as nature reestablishes a healthy balance. The personification of nature is the circus and its extension in Coketown, Sissy Jupe. When the circus comes to Coketown, the evil of the place overcomes its salvific powers, but it leaves Sissy Jupe who, as Leavis notes, has growing potency through the novel.[13] The world in which Sissy is placed is so out of order that at first her goodness is powerless against it, but it cannot make her one of its own. The attempts of Gradgrind to order Sissy under his system fail because she is a whole person: "Somehow or other, he had become possessed by an idea that there was something in this girl which could hardly be set forth in a tabular form. . . . He was not sure that if he had been required, for example, to tick her off into columns in a parliamentary return, he would have quite known how to divide her" (92). Unable to operate actively against all the evil that is growing in the world of *Hard Times*, Sissy drops out of the narrative to prepare a better world with fresh materials—the little Gradgrinds. We last see Sissy in Chapter xv, of Part I when, with a look, she expresses her disapproval of the Louisa-Bounderby marriage. From that point the evil that has been planted begins to grow rapidly. Harthouse enters the novel and attempts to seduce Louisa. Blackpool is gradually heaped with more and more injustice from his unnatural marriage and even from his fellows, who have become corrupted by a society of hard, unforgiving facts. Mrs. Sparsit commences her plotting, and Tom gets into debt.

The evil builds until halfway through the novel (Part II, Chapter v—the eleventh of the twenty *Household Words* installments) Stephen is fired. The unnatural order into which Stephen does not fit expels him. This is the fulcrum point in the balance of the gross structure of *Hard Times*. From this point the evil is unleashed and must fulfill its ugly promise, but also the goodness of nature begins to expand through the narrative so that by the end of the novel both the materials and the structure have balanced to a formal expression of meaning. In the following scenes Stephen leaves town, but not before Louisa has gone to his home and met humanity: "For the first time in her life Louisa had come into one of the dwellings of the Coketown Hands; for the first time in her life she was face to face with anything like individuality in connexion with them" (157). Both Sparsit and Harthouse now begin their attempts to destroy Louisa, but before they can accomplish their goals, the bank robbery is discovered. Significantly, one of the few good people in the novel is accused of the robbery. This is the final imbalance of the Coketown world. Also significantly, Tom has stolen the money through his balance books. As he explains to Bounderby one night when he gets home late from the bank, " 'When you were my age, . . .' you hadn't a wrong balance to get right' " (131). Ironically, they all have wrong balances to get right, and stunted nature tries feverishly to restore equilibrium as they all fall down Mrs. Sparsit's staircase. Before the bottom is reached, however, Louisa visits her dying mother. Once again (Part II, Chapter ix) Sissy enters the overt narrative. Some time has passed since we last saw her. Her appearance is brief, but we learn that she has worked a change for the good in the Gradgrind household, and thus the future does hold promise for the younger Gradgrinds. Louisa sees likenesses between herself and her younger sister, but there is also a difference that she cannot name: "Louisa had relinquished the hand: had thought that her sister's was a better and brighter face than hers had ever been: had seen in it, not without a rising feeling of resentment, even in that place and that time, something of the gentleness of the other face in the room [Sissy's]; the sweet face with the trusting eyes, made paler than watching and sympathy made it, by the rich dark hair" (199). Mrs. Gradgrind also senses the difference between the two sisters and attributes it to the younger sister's having got something more than the Gradgrindian education that Louisa had undergone. Mrs. Gradgrind attempts to identify the source of the pain that she feels somewhere in the room. Not finding it, she says, " 'You learnt a great deal, Louisa. . . . But there is something—not an Ology at all—that your father has missed, or forgotten. . . . I have often sat with Sissy near me, and thought about it. I shall never get its name now. But your father may' " (199).

As Sissy's goodness begins to operate in the novel, it confutes the expanding evil. Louisa gains strength by it to spurn Harthouse and return home. From this time in the novel, good becomes active. Mr. Gradgrind does begin to see what he has missed in his multitude of "ologies." At the beginning of Part III Sissy herself fully reenters the action of the novel, and the restoration of lost balance becomes the full-time work of the plot. Sissy's power to effect change by subtly altering the perception of life is even recognized by Gradgrind: " 'It is always you, my child!' " (277). Sissy makes Harthouse leave town, and she joins the other symbol of goodness, Rachael, to find Stephen and to restore his name. They find him. This natural man has been shattered by the explosion of evil, but in death he helps to restore balance by suggesting the real culprit—Tom. He tells Rachael what he has learned about total human understanding properly ordering the world: " 'In my pain an' trouble . . . I ha' seen more clear, and ha' made it my dyin prayer that aw th' world may on'y coom toogether more, an' get a better unnerstan'in o' one another, than when I were in 't my own weak seln' " (273). Meanwhile, both Bounderby and Sparsit have been exposed as frauds and have wrenched apart.

At the beginning of *Hard Times* the circus had come to Coketown, but its example of the natural life—the balance of joy against pain, fancy against fact—was powerless before the accumulated weight of Gradgrind-Bounderby reason. By the end, the novel has expressed the consequences of such a life, and Gradgrind, who at least has some capacity to grow, follows Sissy to the circus for help. They find the hypocritical Tom ironically disguised in a mummer's costume. And the circle closes as the bloodless Bitzer crashes into them, still running, it seems, as though he had never stopped running since the night that he first chased Sissy Jupe. Now Gradgrind debates Bitzer for the safety of his son by using the language of compassion that he has learned from Sissy, and Bitzer counters with the arguments of cold logic that Gradgrind had once cited to Sissy in their discussion of statistics. But, while Bitzer defines "heart" and describes the philosophy of reasonable self-interest and mouths economic maxims, a dancing horse and a trained dog spirit Tom away. The circus' imagination foils Bitzer's utility.

Nature restores her balance at the end of *Hard Times*, and as we look back over the novel, we get a better understanding of how the imbalance occurred in the first place. Fact does not oppose nature. It is part of nature. Distortion arises when fact is seen as everything. The perversion of nature arises out of the imbalancing inflation of only one of its attributes while ignoring the other, fancy. In *Hard Times* all of nature is subject to and proved by time. Within the system of this novel, fact and fancy each has its own time scheme, and as the action moves ahead and the seasons change, fact and fancy, once separated, flow into each other. If, as the novel opens, the condition of fact controls, at its conclusion neither fact nor fancy does because they, too, have achieved balance. Dickens does not end with a "happily-ever-after" denouement. Characters must live out the consequences of their personal histories, and many of their futures will be painful. All of the perverted relationships of the novel have been in some way destroyed, affecting those involved in them. In the summing up Dickens tells us that only Sissy— her life unalloyed by artifice—will have a completely happy future. Mr. Gradgrind has learned that wonder complements fact, and the future holds promise for the growing Gradgrinds. Tom at last repents and dies loving Louisa. Louisa, though permanently scarred, looks forward to a life of some happiness. Finally, with the lesson of Louisa's life Dickens instructs the reader to temper his day-to-day reality with imagination so that, as, in time, his own fire grows cold, his heart will be light.

Certainly, a strong ideological line runs through the narrative of *Hard Times*. The individual incidents of the plot do have more lesson than richness. The characters, taken in their individual capacities, may well function more as symbols than as people. Previous *Hard Times* criticism has established these views with which, so far as they go, this paper does not take issue. But, if one is to understand the novel as a work of art, which most contemporary criticism argues that it is, one must capture a sense of the novel that transcends these fragmented interpretations and achieves a holistic one, that experiences the novel as a rich, unified, organic amalgam which is more than a collection of its parts. If the parts are simple, the whole is not. Simplistic materials, artfully set off against other simplistic materials and constellated throughout a carefully shaped whole, transform to rich complexity. In this monistic view *Hard Times* formally expresses its meaning as a single experience of narrative materials and narrative structures. The pattern of the novel is balance, and in the process of interior and exterior equilibrium, all of the materials balance all of the structures to create a final picture of order.

Randolph Splitter

GUILT AND THE TRAPPINGS
OF MELODRAMA
IN *LITTLE DORRIT*

DICKENS' *LITTLE DORRIT* has been seen as a seditious tract, a companion piece to Marx's *Das Kapital.*[1] *Little Dorrit* encompasses a whole society, but the theme of the social outcast and criminal returns us to the personal element which Edmund Wilson has shown to be at the heart of Dickens' work.[2] We are back in debtors' prison, which figures so darkly in *Pickwick Papers,* Dickens' first novel—in one of the interpolated tales and ultimately in the main story of innocent Mr. Pickwick himself. In fact, when Dickens was sent to work at the now-famous blacking factory, his own father was thrown into the Marshalsea Prison for failing to pay his debts. The strength of *Little Dorrit* is that an obsessive, traumatic memory has led Dickens to an entire social vision.

Mr. Dorrit, like all the other debtors, arrives in the Marshalsea thinking that he will soon be out again, that he is not really a debtor, not really in prison, that he is free to come and go as he pleases. He maintains this pretense of freedom for the rest of his long imprisonment, claiming that he stays out of choice, not compulsion. Indeed, he lives by numerous fictions. Life in the Marshalsea revolves around money, but he remains supremely unconscious of the fact. His daughter feeds and clothes him, working to provide for him, but in so doing she allows him to maintain the fiction that his children do not need to work for a living. Even the elaborate ceremony of the testimonials depends upon its being discreet, unstated, unacknowledged. As the Father of the Marshalsea, as the oldest resident of the place, he receives money from the other inmates, but he remains above it all, oblivious to the sordidness of the transaction, hardly soiling his hands with the money: the testimonials are wrapped up in a piece of paper, like something dirty, or appear as if by magic in little piles upon the table. Mr. Dorrit's punctiliousness, his sense of ceremony and propriety, seems like a defense against sordid reality, a way of denying the fact that he is an imprisoned debtor and that even now he needs money to survive; money itself is dirty. Indeed, the primitive, unconscious identification of money and excrement,[3] implicit in the dust heaps of *Our Mutual Friend*, underlies Dickens' whole view of Victorian society.

If Mr. Dorrit insists upon being a gentleman, "preserving the genteel fiction that they were all idle beggars together" (74), it is not just an empty pose. As an imprisoned debtor, an idle beggar, he is freed from the burden of earning a living; this is the hallmark of a gentleman, and this is what Little Dorrit tries not to compromise. Although he acts as the Father of the Marshalsea, her motherly care grants him a kind of childlike innocence which protects him from the dangers of the outside world. In fact, prison itself is a womblike haven: acknowledging their bankruptcy, accepting their punishment, the debtors have nothing more to fear (63). It is easy to enter the Marshalsea and (unlike the womb) not at all easy to get out, but the inmates, making a virtue of necessity, maintain a fantasy of reversal, pretend that their prison is a sanctuary, and deny that they wish to leave.

Plornish, the worker who cannot find work, and Bleeding Heart Yard itself, where working people cannot earn enough money to pay their rent, represent the working-class treadmill from which the debtors have escaped. The worker must literally earn his living, must pay for his existence with his labor, but since he can never make enough to get off the treadmill, he winds up living on "borrowed" time; his life is not his own. Life in the Marshalsea mirrors life outside, except that it is more ritualized, more primitive: instead of the cycle of wage slavery and capitalist profit, there is simple penny-pinching, palm-greasing, and a pretense of giving gifts. Norman O. Brown points out the close association between money and guilt, the identity of guilt and indebtedness,[4] as in the line from the Lord's Prayer which Dickens himself cites—"Forgives us our debts as we forgive our debtors" (47)—where sins are debts owed to God. According to Brown, the primitive custom of gift-giving is a magical sharing of guilt, and Dickens, throughout his work, celebrates the Christmas ritual of giving and sharing. The collegians of the Marshalsea enact a parody of this ritual, a token exchange of gifts, except that it is not actually an exchange. In the capitalist economy, the aim is not to give up money but to make it, not to share one's guilt but "to accumulate the tokens of atonement, the economic surplus." [5] Mr. Dorrit, as the Father of the Marshalsea, acquires his token offerings in a parody of capitalist accumulation.

Needless to say, the possession of money is highly ambivalent, a wish charged with guilt. This is the dilemma of the guilt-ridden Merdle, who (like Midas) cannot enjoy his own wealth, and of all those, like Arthur Clennam, infected by the mania for speculation, who identify with the father-figure Merdle and discover—upon his (and their) collapse—that they have been corrupted. In the society that Dickens shows us, the guilt of the moneymakers is projected onto their victims, onto those who don't have money—the poor, the debtors. In Victorian culture, bankruptcy is a moral failure and work, which is experienced by the workingman as a punishment, a life of expiation for the sin of being poor, is a moral duty. The astonishing fact that debtors are thrown into prison is a sign of the society's guilty, pathological obsession with money. The debtors in the Marshalsea, stamped as criminals, are society's scapegoats; and, significantly, Merdle himself turns out to be a crook.

But money is not sufficient to pay one's debts, one's burden of guilt. As her father prepares to leave the prison, Little Dorrit makes a telling observation: "It seems to me hard that he should have lost so many years and suffered so much, and at last pay all the debts as well. It seems to me hard that he should pay in life and money both." (422). In other words, time is money; Mr. Dorrit pays with his life. The bitter recognition is that his life is *not* one of idle pleasure, that he is *not* free to spend it as he wishes. Debtors' prison is simply the logical reduction of "wage slavery," and Little Dorrit's insight is akin to Marx's surplus-value theory of labor. The worker must constantly earn more money in order to survive, yet his labor (his life) is turned into someone else's profit; the debtor, who does no work, turns no one else's profit, and yet his time is enslaved in an absurd parody of the worker's lot, in which the surplus-value goes up in smoke.

The society of the Marshalsea is founded upon mutually accepted fictions, a collective fantasy of denial, but the principles which govern the larger society are no less "fictional." Money itself is an official fiction, whose value is only symbolic. Merdle's name (Fr. *merde*) confirms the identification of money and excrement, but Merdle finds no sensual gratification in his accumulated wealth. He is a modern capitalist, a financier who deals in paper fortunes but knows inside himself that the paper is only paper. He turns out to be a forger and a thief, but in this he only exposes the true role of the capitalist, proving that money is not a thing of value but a way of cheating people. If society confers a magical value upon money, then the modern economy may seem to resemble a system of "black magic."

As Dickens shows us, the logic of putting debtors in prison is irrational and neurotic. In fact, Lionel Trilling claims, in his discussion of the prison image in this novel, that "Dickens anticipates one of Freud's ideas, . . . nothing less bold and inclusive than the essential theory of the neurosis." [6] Trilling is speaking of the "economic" balance between guilt and gratification, between superego and id: "The organization of the internal life is in the form, often fantastically parodic, of a criminal process in which the mind is at once the criminal, the victim, the police,

the judge and the executioner." [7] The economics of gratification is an
economics of scarcity; only guilt shows a surplus, and it keeps growing
at a high rate of interest. It is not simply that the neurotic never overcomes his own guilt, but—and this is Dickens' theme—that guilt is a
relation among individuals, virtually *the* relation among individuals: between the criminal and his victim, the judge and the criminal, the rich
man and the poor man. The debtor is imprisoned because he cheapens
the value of money, even as unsuccessful suicides were once executed
because they seemed to cheapen the value of human life.

The Marshalsea prison is an image of the entire society; it is the
heart of it, its center of guilt, and also a refuge from it. The prison is
known, pathetically, as the College of the Marshalsea, the school of experience or, simply, of life's defeats. The debtors' prison, the secret
heart of the modern city, may be Dickens' Yale College and his Harvard, to borrow Melville's analogy, but the idea of grown men regress-
ing to their schooldays has ambiguous implications. There are women
and children in the Marshalsea—part of the morbid unreality of the
prison is that family life goes on pretty much as it does on the outside—
but only the men, who have failed in their role as breadwinners, have
to be there. The real life of the place, the life of ritual and fantasy, is
strictly male, and its special clublike argot, with names like "the
Snuggery," suggests a hopeless, pathetic attempt at warmth and intimacy.

When Little Dorrit is born inside the prison, Mr. Dorrit is merely a
helpless bystander who does not seem capable of fathering a child. The
fact that she is born in prison, the Child of the Marshalsea, makes Little
Dorrit the child of society; all the other inmates claim "a kind of pro-
prietorship" in her. It draws attention to her birth while it obscures her
origins, her parentage, as if she were an orphan or an illegitimate child.
But in this way Little Dorrit's prison-birth, like that of Perdita in *The
Winter's Tale,* serves to preserve her innocence, to deny that she has
anything to do with actual sexual intercourse. So she resembles the innocent Christ-child, born of woman but conceived without sin. Or, by a
simpler logic, the unconscious logic of reversal, she is innocent because
she is born in debtors' prison, the reservoir of society's guilt. The Marshalsea may be an unlikely nursery, but, like all Dickens' poor found-
lings, like Oliver Twist, Little Dorrit remains untarnished by her low
origins.

What we have found in the Marshalsea—the obsession with money
and class, the hypocrisy and guilt—leads us out again to the overt social
themes of the novel. Although *Little Dorrit* descends into the depths of
personal guilt, it is also a condition-of-England novel, an ironic, satirical
portrait of Victorian society. The endless activity of the Circumlocution
Office is not merely a study in bureaucratic inefficiency ("how not to do

it"), but, as in Kafka, a way of organizing the state.[8] The Barnacles, who staff the Office, who run the business of the state, are a parody of a family, and their language—"howling labyrinths of sentences" (408)—is a parody of official rhetoric, sheer circumlocution. They spout a rhetoric of evasion and denial but, according to Dickens, the whole of society, typified by English travelers on the Grand Tour ("a superior sort of Marshalsea" [511]), is constructed out of an unspoken agreement to maintain official lies. Thus Mrs. Gowan conducts a charade of spurious gentility on the fringes of "real" Society. The houses on Harley Street, where Merdle lives, have identical façades, but these only mask their inner defects. Merdle is accepted by Society, because of his money, but not by his chief butler, who holds to the orthodoxy of class divisions more obsessively than any aristocrat.

Merdle's train of formal dinners—with allegorical figures like Bar, Bishop, and Physician, with the chief butler as a kind of silent chorus—enact a little morality play on the worthlessness of money and the downfall of the great, with Merdle himself as the type, say, of magnificence, incarnated in the familiar Victorian type of the upstart millionaire, capitalist and confidence man, and anticipating Trollope's portrayal of Melmotte in *The Way We Live Now*. The high society of Dickens' London is just as elusive and intangible as Proust's Faubourg Saint-Germain—more so, because Dickens' perspective is inescapably middle-class—but all the parasites and impostors are agreed on the qualifications for membership and the need to maintain standards. Indeed, it is not just "high society" but the whole social structure of Victorian England that is founded on an illusion, namely, the magical virtue of money, the belief that those who have it deserve it.

Arthur Clennam, the mild-mannered, passive hero of *Little Dorrit*, suffers from a failure of will and purpose, a kind of paralysis comparable to his mother's physical condition, a sense of helplessness almost as severe as prison-bound Mr. Dorrit's. After a stern, repressive childhood and a long exile doing work that he hated, he renounces all social ambitions and quits the family business. Indeed, suspecting that his father has wronged someone, he fears to take his father's money. Arthur seems to take his father's guilt upon himself, but his almost obsessive suspicion implies that he is projecting his own guilt onto his father. Of course he has done nothing wrong, but he may have learned, growing up in the Clennam house, to blame himself for everything. In fact, it is not money so much as guilt—a need to pay off debts, to make restitution—which is passed on from father to son. Behind the tainted money lies a deeper, more basic childhood conflict: Arthur's fear of assuming his father's role betrays a guilty wish to do just that, and the wronged party, the victim at least of fortune, turns out to be his mother. If Arthur's gloomy depression seems like prolonged, exaggerated grief over his father's memory, it may feed—as did Hamlet's, who also suffers from a paralysis of the will—on his own sense of guilt.[9] The opposition of guilt and desire leaves him unable to act at all.

But Arthur's guilt-ridden impotence stems not so much from his weak, ineffectual father, whom he seems to take after, as from the oppressive and overbearing figure whom he takes to be his mother. The black-shrouded widow, entombed in a gloomy house and surrounded by images of death (33), beyond the reach of time (34), seems like death itself, not a helpless invalid but an omnipotent destroyer. Her hysterical paralysis—the symptom disappears, briefly, after she confesses her long-guarded secret—is, like Arthur's inner paralysis, a sign of guilt.[10] Arthur imagines that his parents are responsible for the misfortunes of the Dorrit family and that Mrs. Clennam's virtual imprisonment is a kind of recompense for Mr. Dorrit's (89). These two parental figures preside (as well as they can) over the course of the novel, and, significantly, in Arthur's scheme, the mother (Mrs. Clennam) seems to have punished the father (Mr. Dorrit) like an upstart child who has presumed to play an adult role, taking away his money and appropriating it for herself. Mr. Dorrit, the passive, childlike father who is punished for his economic failure, may be, for Arthur, a substitute for his own businessman father. Indeed, he may be, at least in this, a substitute for Dickens' own bankrupt, imprisoned father. Dickens' hero Arthur feels a guilty kinship with the father who is punished for no apparent fault of his own. In this scheme both father and son are like helpless children under the sway of a single all-powerful parent, a tyrannical mother. Beneath the pale shadow of father-son rivalry lies an even more primitive and more serious conflict between mother and child.[11]

Arthur's theory of retribution, his moral accounting of guilt and expiation, has a psychological point as well. Mrs. Clennam, who seems to punish the innocent, winds up punishing herself for that very act, taking the guilt upon herself. The suffering inflicted on others, the guilt projected onto convenient scapegoats, finally comes home to roost, as if to prove that bad mothers are punished in the end. By the same token, however, child Arthur internalizes the familial and social guilt he seeks to expose. Indeed, calling attention to his own personal conflicts, he renounces all sexual ambitions and confines his pursuit of women to passive daydreams. His fear of assuming an adult sexual role is so strong that he denies his real feelings and calls his more impulsive self, the self that falls in love with Pet Meagles, *nobody* (200). If the character in *Bleak House* who turns out to be Esther Summerson's father goes by the name of Nemo (Lat. nobody), it may be because sexual impulses tend to be anonymous, unauthorized, and independent of one's personal control. Dickens originally intended to call this novel, ironically, "Nobody's Fault," but Arthur's guilt is itself so pervasive that he denies even the most innocent of desires.

In fact, the inhibited, lackluster hero of *Little Dorrit* may tell us less about inner conflicts than a more peripheral character, Miss Wade, whose own "History of a Self-Tormentor" is a kind of Dostoievskian *tour de force*, a relentless exposure of psychological motives, a case history of paranoid jealousy. She is an orphan, an illegitimate child, brought up in a substitute family, like the uncomplaining, always-grateful Esther Summerson in *Bleak House*,[12] but unlike Esther, she resents her position in life, rejecting the pity and condescension of those who claim to be kind to her. She imagines a conspiracy of persecution against her and, mistrusting all attempts at friendship, tries to turn her friends into enemies, trying to make them hate her. "I have the misfortune of not being a fool" (662), she says, claiming the preternatural "insight" of paranoiacs [13] and turning even that against herself. She develops passionate attachments, but these too are sabotaged by her own jealous suspicions. She becomes a governess, like Esther Summerson, Jane Eyre, and numerous other Victorian heroines, and the ambiguity of that position—half parent, half servant—only aggravates her insecurity. Her illegitimacy, the feeling that she is "not like other people" (667), is the source of gnawing doubt and shame, and it is, finally, her mother whose love she cannot trust but desperately needs.

If Miss Wade conceives a jealous hatred for Pet Meagles, it is not only because she is a romantic rival but because, as her parents' pampered favorite, she is a sibling rival as well. And in the Meagles family Miss Wade discovers her own "double," the image of herself at a younger age, the object of pity rather than love, Tattycoram. This girl is an orphan, a foundling of unknown parentage, and she too occupies an ambiguous, equivocal place—part servant, part child—in the family. Tatty is not without gratitude, but she resents the unequal treatment given to her "mistress" Pet, who is "always petted and called Baby" (26) even though she is the older of the two. Tattycoram's self-punishing tantrums demonstrate even more clearly the kind of inner conflict that rages within Miss Wade. Like her bad angel, the ungrateful, mistrusting side of her own divided feelings, Miss Wade inflames Tattycoram's resentment and also, in effect, "seduces" her, becoming the mother she would like to have had to the child she once was.

As Tattycoram's case implies, Miss Wade may not be simply the victim of delusions and her grievances may not be without foundation. Cutting through the myth of disinterested love, she shows us not only that love may hide more selfish motives but also that anger, jealousy, and hatred, reflecting deeper needs, may be the masks of love. She impresses upon us not only the social consequences of illegitimacy, but also the uncertainty that any child feels about his mother's love and about his own mysterious origins. Is it too much to suggest that Miss Wade is, however obliquely, a stand-in for Arthur Clennam, who is also an illegitimate child? Seen through her eyes, Pet Meagles, the spoiled child, the object of parental love, represents what Arthur would like to be, while Tattycoram, the foundling, the stranger in her own home, represents what in fact he is. Though both are suspicious of other people's motives, Miss Wade's angry resentment is, for Arthur, only a nameless, undefined guilt; her self-torment is reduced, in him, to vague anxiety, depression, and paralysis. But her embittered history could be the disguised, displaced record of his unconscious thoughts.

Both Tattycoram and Miss Wade are, like Arthur, divided against themselves, but Dickens makes this inner division visible by showing us pairs of characters bound together by powerful, though ambivalent, identifications—Miss Wade and Tattycoram, Tatty and Pet. Flintwinch's twin brother appears, in Affery's waking dream, as his mirror double, and Pet Meagles has a dead twin sister: such interchangeable twins are a staple of mistaken-identity comic plots, but Dickens' use of this stock device only reminds us of deeper, psychological divisions. In post–Romantic, nineteenth-century fiction the idea of the double—or of the self divided into separate personalities—becomes not simply a convenient device but a central theme,[14] culminating (one might say) in Freud's image of a mind split by the conflicting demands of impulse and repression, desire and guilt. In characters like Mr. Dorrit, Mr. Merdle, and Mrs. Clennam, unexpected outbreaks point to the existence of private lives which are normally, but not permanently, repressed. In Arthur's case, the repression is so strong that his second, private self is hardly manifest; there is just one impotent, withdrawn, guilt-ridden man—and, perhaps, "nobody." Because he is, briefly, imprisoned for debt in the Marshalsea and because he questions, cautiously, the values upon which society is based, this passive figure takes his unlikely place in Dickens' gallery of criminals and social outcasts, but for him social injustice has personal, private origins. In short, Arthur is Dickens' hero not because he rebels but because he is almost, like Oliver Twist, David Copperfield, Esther Summerson, and Pip, an orphan.

The hero of *Little Dorrit* may seem bland and innocuous, but many of the minor characters are (typically) "characters," exaggerated comic caricatures or humors.[15] Like all caricatures, their personalities are limited—in fact, rigidly obsessed, like Mr. F.'s aunt, whose stiff, mechanical, doll-like appearance (157) tells us what she is like—but also well defined, sharply drawn, and highly conspicuous. The essential feature of humors is repetition, their inability to change, and Dickens' humors are often identified, simply, by a gesture or phrase compulsively repeated and symptomatic of their obsession. More broadly, the

Barnacles are characterized by their evasive rhetoric and even Mr. Dorrit has a formal, fastidious style of his own. A more obviously "humorous" style is Flora's barely punctuated, barely coherent verbal flood; for Flora, speech itself is a compulsive act. Dickens' characters tend to resemble stock comic types: the Barnacles are parasites on the social organism, Merdle resembles the character of the miser, Mr. Dorrit is the pedant of the Marshalsea, and Rigaud (moustache and all) is a stock villain, a descendant of the medieval Vice, but in its most extreme form (Mr. F.'s aunt or, less violently, Flora) the Dickensian humor is a robot-like machine entirely cut off from conscious, human control.

If the humor illustrates the principle of unconscious compulsion, the paralysis of Mrs. Clennam, whose wicked stepmother role makes her a stock fairy-tale type, shows us an even more rigid repression of these same dangerous and anarchic impulses. Indeed, if the superabundant life of Dickens' humors seems to come from Dickens himself, to reflect his own comic exuberance, it is because emotions which, if seriously acknowledged, might threaten him are projected onto them. To the extent that they are displaced, peripheral figures, cut off from the author's own ego, they allow him to give in to unconscious impulses, to let himself go. It is for this reason that Dickens' villains are often more lively, more compelling, and more "humorous" than his drab, colorless heroes. It is not only our detachment from these humors, our confidence that we are free from their obsessions, that, enabling us to laugh at them, makes them comic; it is also our secret participation in their ridiculous and irrational compulsions, a kind of mock regression which gives us a feeling of harmless, innocent pleasure.

The close relationship of Dickens and his readers, confirmed by the extraordinary impact of his highly theatrical readings, is well known. With a style full of arch circumlocutions and unsubtle ironies, Dickens sometimes sounds as pedantic as Mr. Dorrit, repeating himself until even the dullest reader will not have missed the point. But the comic showman who plays all the parts in the show, who impersonates his eccentric characters like an ventriloquist with his puppets, is a different, less inhibited kind of humor, an *auctor gloriosus* (braggart writer) who exaggerates everything, mixes fact with fiction, and seeks to impress us with his virtuosity, his sheer verbal exuberance. The opening of a Dickens novel is often a self-conscious *tour de force,* and the scorched, burnt-out overture to *Little Dorrit,* though it may not compare with the foggy opening of *Bleak House,* is a case in point. The universal habit of staring (1), exemplified by the white-hot eye of the sun, suggests a total invasion of privacy, a violation of all possible hiding-places. Dickens' rigid, mechanical, puppetlike humors sometimes seem like inanimate objects, but that kind of depersonalization is reversed here, where houses, walls, and streets are (like the sun) given the power of sight and turned into animate creatures. This confusion between animate and inanimate seems to imply a childlike view of things, one in which inner, private fears are projected onto the outside world, and the fear of exposure inherent in this obsession with staring seems like agoraphobia, fear of open spaces, of being exposed to people's stares, fear of the light instead of the child's fear of the dark. The conscious artificiality of the rhetoric tends to neutralize, to seal off the emotion (fear) raised by the "staring" fantasy, but if we take the fantasy seriously, we realize that we have entered a world where a child's "paranoid" fears merge with reality.

Indeed, the world of *Little Dorrit* sometimes takes on a hallucinatory, dreamlike quality, as in Affery's waking dreams (where *she* stares, transfixed, at forbidden sights) and in the mysterious noises that make her think the house is haunted. These sights and sounds point to the secret prehistory of the novel, the set of mysterious circumstances surrounding the hero's birth, but there is an increasing feeling of tension and suspense which demands that the hallucinations be explained, that the characters wake up from their dreams. The division of the novel into two books, "Poverty" and "Riches," pretends to satisfy this demand, but the reversal of Mr. Dorrit's fortunes turns out to be illusory. Life in the Marshalsea had been a self-contained dream in which Mr. Dorrit denied not only the facts of imprisonment and poverty but even the reality of his own suffering; after he escapes from this nightmare, he denies that it ever existed. His newfound wealth enables him simply to fulfill the role of gentleman that he had already acted out in prison and to deny even more vigorously that he has ever been anything else. He is released from prison but not from the imprisoning strategy of repression that governs his life.

When Arthur himself is imprisoned, crossing the line between creditors and debtors, sympathizers and victims, free citizens and "criminals," he is forced to assume the burden of his dead father's guilt and of that other dead father, Mr. Dorrit's. His depression is translated, inside the prison, into a physical illness, but in the economy of the novel his punishment is meant to satisfy outstanding debts, to expiate the secret guilt that he has been trying for so long to expose. Doyce finally appears, miraculously, to settle Arthur's actual debts and rescue him from prison; his good fortune is as unconditional and immediate as Mr. Dorrit's when *he* is freed from prison. If this melodramatic turn of events seems like mere wish fulfillment, it implies that Arthur is still in the role of a helpless child. Doyce is a "good" father and Merdle a "bad" one: the father gives and the father takes away, but in either case the child remains at the mercy of the father's—of fortune's—whims. Indeed, fortune is traditionally identified as a woman, and in this novel the fathers themselves must submit (like children) to the greater authority of a mother, most notably the terrible deathlike figure played by Mrs. Clennam. The realities of social power give way to fantasies of more primitive powers.[16]

So too Little Dorrit, who appears as the loving mother who will nurse him back to health, is the real source of Arthur's good fortune. When Mrs. Clennam finally reveals her guilty secret—above all, the fact that she is not Arthur's mother—to Little Dorrit, she is also revealing the source of the mysterious guilt that so obsesses Arthur, the guilt that ties the Clennams to the Dorrits. The codicil that Mrs. Clennam has suppressed makes Little Dorrit a substitute for Arthur's real mother, and Mrs. Clennam's guilt is, literally, a debt owed to Little Dorrit. If the codicil itself seems nothing more than an implausible, incredible plot-contrivance, still it suggests that the events surrounding the hero's birth are a kind of "family romance," a fantasy of replacing "bad" parents with "good" ones.[17] As in a fairy tale, the child-hero is brought up by a wicked stepmother (deadly instead of life-giving) who has replaced the original loving mother of the hero's dreams. The pure, virtuous mother is, ironically, a "fallen" woman, but she is presented as an innocent victim. Arthur, virtually an orphan like his mother, takes her guilt upon himself: in the last analysis, his guilt (like Miss Wade's) is hidden in the secret of his illegitimate birth. In fact, Arthur illustrates, if not literally, the impotence Freud ascribes to men who idealize their mothers: he avoids romantic attachments and "overestimates" the objects of his love, afraid of tarnishing their virtue, because they are unconscious replacements for his mother.[18]

But the orphan child-mother who suffers unjustly at the hands of a wicked stepmother seems suspiciously like a child's projected fantasy, the fantasy of a mother in his own image. Little Dorrit, who is childlike and motherly at the same time, is the embodiment of that fantasy. Dickens compares her to Cinderella (running title, xiv), a girl brought up by a wicked stepmother, and she herself tells a sentimental fairy tale about her secret Prince Charming (xxiv). She takes care of her father, but she is also a "little mother" to the big, overgrown "child" Maggy, who is in fact a grossly distorted version of Little Dorrit herself, fixed at age ten, forever a child. If Maggy is big and Little Dorrit little, if Little Dorrit is mistaken for Maggy's child, this reversal of their actual roles only underscores the ambiguity of Little Dorrit's own identity. As a child, she is the most innocent and virginal of mothers, whose kiss might redeem even a prostitute (175). Her ambiguous position, permanently childlike and yet old before her time, associates her with two other child-women, Esther Summerson, the "little old woman" of *Bleak House,* and the dolls' dressmaker Jenny Wren in *Our Mutual Friend.* As with Little Dorrit, Esther's shy, retiring, grandmotherly character masks and postpones romantic possibilities. Jenny treats her father as her child and sews dresses for dolls as if they too were her children; actually, she herself is a child who, instead of playing with her dolls, must earn her living by them. Her bent and crippled body, which prevents her from being a mother as well as from being a child like all the others, is a clearer and harsher version of Little Dorrit's "defect," her small size. Like Jenny Wren, Little Dorrit, forced to grow up too soon, might be neither child nor mother, and her "defect" seems to be a sign (almost like Hester Prynne's scarlet letter) that she is not like other women, less conventionally beautiful but also more virtuous.

Poverty too is a sign of Little Dorrit's innocence. When she has lost her money, when Arthur has passed through debtors' prison, they are restored to innocence and therefore free to love. Together they renounce the guilt-ridden, magical value society confers upon money. The guilty secret of the codicil is passed from the "bad" mother (Mrs. Clennam) to the "good" mother (Little Dorrit), even as Arthur himself is, seemingly, restored to the good mother who bore him, but the mothers keep the secret to themselves. Again, Arthur is like a child in the care of omniscient, godlike parents, without any knowledge of their mysterious ways. If the *Oliver Twist*-like, fairy-tale-discovery plot tends to turn the question of social guilt into a family secret, this secret— which mothers don't tell their children—is, finally, the secret of their mysterious origins. Motherhood itself becomes a kind of original crime in which the mother is either the "criminal" (Mrs. Clennam) or the innocent victim (the dead orphan girl). Arthur, anticipating Kafka's childlike heroes, never learns what the Clennams are guilty of, but Little Dorrit, who takes the guilty secret upon herself, "forgives" the debt owed, through her, to his mother. In this way she serves as a kind of virgin mother in a postdated immaculate conception, removing the stain of Arthur's illegitimate birth. As the difference in their ages implies, their marriage represents a child's conception of the ideal family, the union of parent and child.

But then this "happy ending" is just a wishful fantasy, a magical recovery of childhood innocence under the aegis of an impossibly idealized mother. As such, it solves nothing: the larger society remains unchanged, and the newly married couple are just a tiny island of repose in the maelstrom. If Arthur himself cannot undo his childish dependence on parental figures, his neurotic attachment to the past, then Dickens' happy ending seems like a literary confidence-trick which fools us into thinking that the issue of guilt has been settled. But as we have seen, the conflicts that paralyze Arthur are acted out by other characters; the real energy of the book is invested elsewhere. Even if Arthur remains in the dark, we don't. The mystery seems to be solved, and the feeling of tension and suspense is replaced by one of relief.

So, too, the melodramatic catastrophe of the plot—the explosion in the Clennam house—represents a release of energy, the outward emblem of all those climactic revelations. Arthur suffers a near-fatal illness, but a worse fate is displaced onto a scapegoat, Rigaud, who is broken into tiny pieces and buried alive. Arthur is released from prison, but the release from inner compulsions is displaced onto characters like Affery, who, bursting with secrets, breaks down and tells her dreams; Mr. Dorrit, who starts to betray his true feelings about the Marshalsea and whose death is itself a release; and Mrs. Clennam, who divulges the prehistory of the novel and (in a temporary remission of symptoms) walks away from her wheelchair. Even Merdle breaks free of social restraints by committing suicide. There are, in fact, a whole series of characters who break down, say what has been on their minds, do what they have always wanted to do, or come to some recognition of themselves. The paradigm of these self-recognitions is the release of the humor from his obsession. So, by the end of the novel, Flora becomes a little calmer, a little less manic, Pancks rebels against Casby the patriarch and becomes his own man, and Tattycoram leaves her bad angel Miss Wade and returns to the Meagles fold. But Tatty's repentance is simply a reflection of her guilt, not a release from it. Her acceptance of blame is a surrender to arbitrary parental authority, a plea for love and security (like Arthur's fairy-tale marriage) at any cost. The escape from anxiety is more a wish than a reality, but one can carry out that wish by accepting guilt (like the Marshalsea debtors) as well as by fighting against it.

The humors who become less restless, less anxious, less driven by irrational needs, show us the compulsive, irrational, "humorous" quality of even the more central characters. But the author of *Little Dorrit* is himself a kind of obsessive, compulsive humor who treasures up the secrets of his plot, revealing nothing more than teasing clues, until they explode in a final, melodramatic burst of revelations at the end. In this book, where every pleasure is suspect, tinged with guilt, Dickens himself, who seems to enjoy what he is doing, postpones full gratification and indulges instead in the mixed pleasure of waiting, holding onto his cards as long as possible. Prolonging tension and anxiety for the sake of future pleasure seems slightly masochistic, but there is also a certain sadistic overtone to the way Dickens manipulates his readers. In fact, Dickens' whole mechanism of suspense—withholding secret information, keeping the outcome in doubt until, like Affery, he bursts—becomes (if one may speak clinically) a kind of anal-sadistic strategy. If he manipulates his readers the way the capitalist Merdle manipulates gullible investors, he does so by ascribing a magical, symbolic value not to money but to those long-treasured secrets that seem, in the end, much more empty and meaningless than we had ever expected.

As Chesterton put it seventy years ago: "It is characteristic of

Dickens that his atmospheres are more important than his stories. . . . The secrecy is sensational; the secret is tame. . . . It seems almost as if these grisly figures . . . were keeping something back from the author as well as from the reader." [19] The "silly document advantageous to the silly Dorrits," as Chesterton calls it, is somewhat of a letdown after Arthur's wild suspicions. Mrs. Clennam is *not* responsible for putting Mr. Dorrit into prison, and we never even find out who is; that information is lost in the Circumlocution Office forever. The inheritance which finally comes to Mr. Dorrit is completely unexplained, completely fortuitous, but that other inheritance, contained in that silly document appended to old Mr. Clennam's will, serves to explain fortuitousness, to explain the whims of fortune. Its point is that everything is related, that everyone in the society is linked by money, that the present is bound to the past by money, and that there is an inequality, an imbalance, an instability, in these economic relations, like entropy in physics, which is identical with guilt. The problem is that the relations are so complex and far-reaching that they appear fortuitous; they hang by the thread that links the Clennams to the Dorrits.

Unexpected inheritances, huge financial collapses, and long-suppressed codicils may be facts of Victorian life, but they seem like acts of God, parental rewards and punishments from beyond the grave. Guilt is historical, handed down from parents to children along with vain attempts at restitution; family conflicts are never resolved, simply passed on. This is the meaning of the codicil, in which is condensed the history of the Clennam family, in which a strong father and a weak one, a bad mother and a good one, preside over the birth and subsequent fate of a very uncertain hero. There is no gratification, only repression, from which one never escapes: Arthur's mother will never receive restitution; Mr. Dorrit will never be the man he was before he entered prison; Mrs. Clennam will never walk, or speak, again; and Arthur himself will never learn the secret of his origins. In this sense the balance between guilt and gratification, between superego and id, is unequal. The pleasure that has been repressed, postponed till some future day of judgment, is never recovered; time cannot be undone. The debtors' prison becomes an image of the mind itself, where one pays one's debts at the cost of one's life.

Dickens' view of society, in *Little Dorrit*, is a child's vision of parental authority or, worse, of no authority at all, of children abandoned to a world run on mysterious, magical principles and sustained by guilt. Guilt is the universal disease which one tries to escape by contaminating someone else, and it comes from that original abandonment, from a child's fear that his parents don't love him after all. In Dickens' own case, his brief exile in the blacking factory must have fused, in his mind, that childish fear of abandonment and the Victorian middle-class fear of falling into poverty. If the shame of his father's bankruptcy reinforced and compounded his own fear, his father's imprisonment, punishing the parent who abandoned him, must have given him a secret, disturbing satisfaction. Still, finally, his father's failure could only have redoubled his sense of abandonment, shattering his faith in parental authority and omnipotence.[20]

Dickens shows us how childish fears may give rise to a magnified, nightmarish, but not unfounded, vision of adult reality. He also takes refuge in childish wish-fulfillment, exchanging Miss Wade's paranoid hostility for Little Dorrit's sentimental piety. Indeed, we may wonder if, in a larger sense, his anarchic and unprincipled comedy doesn't undercut his serious social criticism. Just as in *Oliver Twist*, the fairy-tale-discovery plot offers no real solution to the social problems that have almost engulfed the hero. And yet the elaborate, climactic ending of *Little Dorrit* represents at least a return of the repressed. We are denied the epiphany that Dickens seems to promise us, but the verbal exuberance, the comedy of humors, the sentimentality, the happy ending, and the whole mechanism of suspense—everything that can be subscribed under the name of melodrama—all this is a substitute for it. The trappings of melodrama are the signs of a compulsive, guilt-ridden attempt at liberation, an attempt to undo repression.

On the one hand, the fortuitousness of the plot reflects the terrible Kafkaesque nightmare of modern society. In Northrop Frye's words: "For all its domestic and sentimental Voctorian setting, there is a revolutionary and subversive, almost a nihilistic, quality in Dickens's melodrama that is post-Romantic, has inherited the experience of the French Revolution, and looks forward to the world of Freud, Marx, and the existential thriller." [21] But that fortuitousness has a design of its own, a design whose origins lie in the unconscious past. The whole Dickensian artifice goes to show the significance of that hidden, unconscious world: that way—making the past present, the unconscious conscious—liberation lies, the kind of liberation that the "fortuitous," fantastic quality of fiction makes possible. It is true that the hero is not really freed from guilt, that the anxiety manifested in the novel is not dispelled; what Dickens gives us is an imitation of liberation, an elaborate sleight of hand. The point of the artifice—of which the artificer, the *auctor gloriosus*, is trying to convince himself—is that the nightmare of modern society is only a nightmare, a dream, a fiction, after all.

Peter Christmas

LITTLE DORRIT:
THE END OF GOOD AND EVIL

THE LITERARY and religious conventions which Dickens followed all his career prescribed an opposition between villainy and virtue whose extreme poles, whatever complexities might turn up in between, remained fixed and simple. However, the great power of *Little Dorrit* consists chiefly in the peculiar and deliberate nature of its transformation of this convention, effected at the same time as a literal conformity to it. That an expected form is often at odds with one attempting to modify it has often been demonstrated to be a source of new vitality. But Dickens is not ordinarily credited with this kind of sophistication, so that his resistance here to literary convention has passed unnoticed and unpraised. For this novel's very foundation is built upon the substitution of one set of contraries for another: Good and Evil confront each other in the most satisfactorily exemplary fashion in *Little Dorrit* in the persons of Amy Dorrit and Rigaud, the "Child of the Marshalsea" versus the cosmopolitan gentleman, yet the struggle which Dickens' art toiled simultaneously to express was that between Reality and Gentility.

In the purity of their natures both Amy and Rigaud still have every appearance necessary for captains in a quasi-theological battle, but since the conventional stuffing has been replaced by Reality and Gentility, now raised almost to the pitch of metaphysical principles, they become much more useful, when taken in combination, as a critical method by which to examine society. Not that *Little Dorrit* is unique among Dickens' works in displaying a tendency to turn from the personal to the social, from the particular and idiosyncratic to the general and systematic. But the tendency is crystallized here in its most intense and self-conscious form. So much of the author's effort has gone into expanding the terms of his new opposition till the result is a full-length exposure and description of a concealed aspect of social relations. He starts from a moral dichotomy but strives thenceforward to achieve a unity of effect whose meaning subsumes the moral into the political.

I shall take Gentility first, Reality next, and then suggest what general conclusions Dickens was enabled to draw by the use of his new vocabulary.

— *I* —

In *Little Dorrit* a group of families is intended to represent society as a whole. Each family represents a class. Starting from the top and going downward they are the Barnacles, the Merdles, the Gowans, the Meagleses, the Clennams, the Dorrits, and the Plornishes. In the respectively abstract and bloodless portrayal of the Barnacles and Merdles, Dickens speaks out of his own lower middle-class origins: the rulers are a remote constant and the barrier between the idle laborer and the respectably poor is the most impenetrable of any that divide the classes. The author's interest is confined to the four families in the middle; his interest in the Gowans, Meagleses, Clennams, and Dorrits derives from the relationship that each family forms with Gentility—for Rigaud establishes a connection with all four—and from the vicious knot of human relationships that each family ties. The particular way each knot is tied reveals the author's assessment of the class in question.

Both Gowans genteelly impose on their fellow countrymen, who in their turn recognize the imposition and either submit to it as the order of things or willingly collaborate. The mother is a public pensioner, one of the "gypsies of Hampton Court"; the son is a dilettante and salaried by his deferential father-in-law. When Gowan married the Meagles fortune, the corrupt social contract is sealed by Mrs. Merdle, the interpreter of Society's oracles, giving her consent to the match as blood acquiring property, and by his mother's pretense that her own reluctant consent has been extorted by the scheming ambition of the Meagles family—a pretense to which they silently bow.

The Meagleses, though the victim of the family above them, do not earn our unmixed pity. Meagles himself is John Bull, as is evident in the novel's opening pages when he is abroad: he is gruff, hearty, and well intentioned. The narrowness and philistinism would no doubt be conceded by a Meagles himself with cheerful pride. More to the point here are the sentimentality and overprotective coziness with which he has brought up his surviving daughter Pet, with the result that, thus spoilt, she is blind to the genuine merit of Arthur Clennam and vulnerable to the spurious charm of Henry Gowan. Father and daughter together tie this knot, and the moral obtuseness arising from the sentimentality then reaches out to include Tattycoram, the adopted ward of the family. Meagles and Pet both treat her as a servant rather than as a replacement for the other dead daughter, so that she is made equally vulnerable to the sinister Miss Wade. Tattycoram is denied even straightforward resentment since she is well aware that she has nonetheless enjoyed genuine kindness for which she must owe a debt of gratitude. As with the Gowans, the tangle is insolubly complicated yet at the same time harmoniously self-supporting. Considering that Meagles is a member of that thrifty, industrious, and prosperous middle-class which had hitherto been Dickens' bulwark, it is startling that the purpose here is to connect him, directly though subterraneously, with the book's most painfully complex character. Cheeryble self-complacency is indeed but the other side of the coin to the self-hatred of Miss Wade, just as the Merdles and the Plornishes inhabit a single system in whose successful functioning they both cooperate, albeit the former are the winners and the latter the losers. The John Bull in Meagles, however, extorts a residual attachment on Dickens' part, and Tattycoram is made to return cap in hand at the end to listen to a lecture from her employer-father. Amy Dorrit is the text, though, not Pet, whose true nature, sentimental like his own, he never has to face up to. In return for the author's leniency toward him, Meagles has only to pay his unhappy daughter's husband a stipend indefinitely and be patronized in return.

The Clennams, the third of these middle-class families, have wrapped themselves in a knot cruder than the two preceding ones because it carries the main burden of the intrigue. The burden, even in the experienced hands of a master of the convention, has become so heavy that the obscure mass of details becomes a way of transcending the convention by exposing its irrelevance. Mrs. Clennam, sitting paralyzed in a wheelchair above the offices of her dilapidated colonial trading company, muttering of vengeance, guilt, and atonement, with her rascally crony Flintwinch and his brutalized wife Affery hovering around her, together form a clear tableau of evil. One waits, knowing the way of such plots, only to discover which one of the other characters they have wronged and from what quarter nemesis is likely to arrive. Just as Meagles, the character with the most ingratiating exterior, is linked to Miss Wade, so the least ingratiating, Mrs. Clennam, is similarly linked to Amy Dorrit. Mrs. Clennam is genteel in Dickens' special sense by the fact of her holding up to public scrutiny a conscious façade of untruth, if only that of her prosperous respectability—it is a façade which literally collapses at the end.

Finally, with the Dorrits we touch home ground for the author. These are the people who, like himself, speculate the most anxiously as to what it is that constitutes a gentleman and who feel the greatest foreboding that they will be found wanting. William Dorrit, a soured version of Micawber, is viciously bound to his willing victims, who are his immediate family and the prison population in general. While he

profits from his children's work and extorts tribute money from those
whom he can browbeat or move to pity, everyone combines to maintain
a veil of well-bred euphemism concealing the Reality. In return for
their complicity Tip, Fanny, and the "collegians" are rewarded by a
reflection of Dorrit's genteel pretensions, so that the Reality of being in
prison is evaporated in a haze of mendacity. As with Tattycoram's
being divided between justifiable resentment and justifiable gratitude,
the knot here is given a final twist when one considers that Dorrit's
euphemistic system is a corruption of a courageous psychological tactic,
adopted in part to maintain self-respect through long years of humiliation. The case is complicated even further by Dorrit's hints to Amy that
she should equivocate with the turnkey's proposal of marriage and by
his response to the news of his release, when he acknowledges for the
first time that he had known his children work for a living. It would
seem that there is a line within even the realm of self-deception between self-deception in good faith and vulgar lying. Dorrit feeds off
the Reality of his solvent brother Frederick who, like Amy, connives at
his pretenses out of compassion, and is sucked dry as a result.

Rigaud, the archetypal gentleman, holds a handful of threads,
each of which binds one of these four principal families to him. When
the English middle-class characters have reached a point where Gentility has sufficiently perverted their souls, this diabolical figure appears
obligingly at hand.

He plays Lucifer to Amy when he lights her down the staircase of
the Great Saint Bernard, though she is proof against his further advan-
ces. Her one weakness is her love for Clennam, but since this does not
burgeon into jealousy of Pet, Rigaud remains powerless. However, the
thread that leads from the beaming Meagles through Pet and Tattycoram to Miss Wade provides a perfect set of conditions for Rigaud's
nature to expand, and it is no surprise to find him hovering around
Miss Wade as courier and paid spy. With the Clennams, Rigaud is indispensable as midwife to the intrigue. But the fourth family, the
Gowans, gives him his most interesting opportunity. Despite Dickens'
dislike of Gowan, the turbid affection that the author is later to feel for
Eugene Wrayburn is already in evidence. Rigaud turns up as the intimate family friend of the newly married couple, in spite of Pet's
marked aversion to him. It is Gowan's breezy cynicism that opens the
door.

> It appeared, before the breakfast was over, that everyone
> whom this Gowan knew was either more or less of an ass, or
> more or less of a knave; but was, notwithstanding, the most
> lovable, the most engaging, the simplest, truest, kindest,
> dearest, best fellow that ever lived. The process by which this

unvarying result was attained, whatever the premises, might have been stated by Mr. Henry Gowan thus: "I claim to be always book-keeping, with a peculiar nicety, in every man's case, and posting up a careful little account of Good and Evil with him. I do this so conscientiously, that I am happy to tell you I find the most worthless of men to be the dearest old fellow too: and am in a condition to make the gratifying report, that there is much less difference than you are inclined to suppose between an honest man and a scoundrel." The effect of this cheering discovery happened to be, that while he seemed to be scrupulously finding good in most men, he did in reality lower it where it was, and set it up where it was not; but that was its only disagreeable or dangerous feature. (204–5)

Dickens might have forgiven Gowan for being a sponger and a dilettante, but that the free and easy charm might lack a critical sense is beginning to trouble the author. Gowan ought to know better and do better. He is of the class that might, according to Dickens, have provided a defense against the cold winds blowing across England from the Continent. The revolution of 1848 and the autocracy that followed it could not fail to disturb an English onlooker, for there was cause for alarm across the whole range of political prejudices, from Left to Right. Gowan's class still had its usefulness in *Bleak House*. But instead of defense, Gowan is a fifth column in *Little Dorrit*'s England. Compare the vein of the speech above with Rigaud's self-justifying outburst; at first sight there is little resemblance between the bland shrug of the one and the violent scorn of the other: " 'I sell anything that commands a price. How do your lawyers live, your politicians, your intriguers, your men of the Exchange? How do you live? How do you come here? Have you sold no friend? Lady of mine! I rather think yes! . . . Society sells itself and sells me: and I sell Society.' " (749)

It is Dickens' point that, just as Meagles' kindliness had its flabby underside of sentimentality, so Gowan's tolerance is akin to the Rigaud point of view. These two cases are like William Dorrit's effort to keep up a brave front to adversity: the corruption of the best is the worst. In one sense it is, after all, true that "there is much less difference than you are inclined to suppose between an honest man and a scoundrel." Be that as it may, Rigaud and Gowan become practically indistinguishable, and only Pet, with her virtue gained largely by acquaintance with Amy, holds her husband back from a complete embrace with his cosmopolitan Devil: " 'Painters, writers, patriots, all the rest who have stands in the market. Give almost any man I know, ten pounds, and he will impose upon you to a corresponding extent; a thousand pounds— to a corresponding extent; ten thousand pounds—to a corresponding extent. So great the success, so great the imposition. But what a capital

world it is!' cried Gowan with warm enthusiasm. 'What a jolly, excellent, lovable world it is!' " (310)

Furthermore, Gowan is connected to the Barnacles. When young
Ferdinand Barnacle talks about Merdle's collapse, the similarity to
Gowan is evident; the affinity with Rigaud's amoral scoffing now ex-
tends into the heart of England's ruling class.

> "A consummate rascal, of course," said Ferdinand, "but re-
> markably clever! One cannot help admiring the fellow. Must
> have been such a master of humbug. Knew people so well—got
> over them so completely—did so much with them!"
> In his easy way, he was really moved to genuine admira-
> tion. . . .
> "Pardon me, but I think you really have no idea how the
> human bees will swarm to the beating of any old tin kettle; in
> that fact lies the complete manual of governing them." (738)

In this respect, middle-class common sense shares an affinity with
ruling-class arrogance. Dickens has Clennam speculate whether there
was not in even Meagles, because of his contempt for Doyce's intelligence, "any microscopic portion of the mustard-seed that had
sprung up into the great tree of the Circumlocution Office" (194). The
sturdy yeoman and the dashing young squire are alike, then, in moral
stupidity, and it is appropriate that the former uncomplainingly puts
up the cash for the latter. In this the small system of personal and family relationships coincides with the larger social system.

The intention here is twofold. The leveling force of stupidity, uniting every class in a common disparagement of ideas, theory, and even
intellect itself, meets the specious amiability and pretense of harmless-
ness, of basic decency and English niceness with which these attitudes
are defended. Ferdinand Barnacle catches the tone perfectly:

> "Look at it from the right point of view, and there you have
> us—official and effectual. It's like a limited game of cricket. A
> field of outsiders are always going to bowl at the Public Service,
> and we block the balls.". . .
> "Believe me, Mr. Clennam," said the sprightly young Bar-
> nacle in his pleasantest manner, "our place is not a wicked
> Giant to be charged at full tilt; but, only a windmill showing
> you, as it grinds immense quantities of chaff, which way the
> country wind blows." (736–38)

Rigaud is a hollowly allegorical character because the symbolic content that went into his conception has been diffused among the realistic
characters whose Gentility has brought them under his influence. As

we have him he is, perhaps, the residue of two half-fulfilled intentions.

First, the opening encounter with him in Marseilles, together with Meagles' remarks about "allonging and marchonging," suggest that he was once meant to owe something to the French tradition of revolutionary change through violence. And perhaps Edmund Wilson was right to draw a parallel with Louis Napoleon,[1] who had come to power just four years before, with the aid of a great deal of Bonapartist propaganda. The spectacle of this raffish confidence man, after years of disreputable travel in foreign countries, managing to impose an imperial dictatorship on the ruins of the idealism of 1848, must have appeared an event whose symbolism was hard to resist, however hard to define. If Wilson's identification is true, Dickens seems to have felt tempted to bring his assessment of the French emperor into some kind of significant relationship with middle-class people living in England. It is an important part of Dickens' view of Gentility in *Little Dorrit* that it is a method of compelling others to accept one at one's own false evaluation. The paltry Napoleon II, with a great name and many resounding slogans, may be seen as genteel in this sense, but the novel as it stands does not warrant making more of this than a conjecture.

It may be, secondly, that Rigaud is not unconnected with the original title, *Nobody's Fault.* This was meant, apparently, as irony at the expense of those who refuse responsibility for their misdeeds by passing them off as the will of Providence.[2] Rigaud may be what remains of this ironic view of Providence; as such he is an expression of a blurred conception at the novel's center. For if Dickens wanted to show people caught in a huge web of social interrelatedness in which *Nobody's Fault* would lose its irony, he was also anxious to avoid the accompanying pitfall of lapsing into a Gowan-like refusal to judge. On the one hand, therefore, the menacing rent-collector Pancks is fully exculpated and some pity is found even for Merdle, but on the other, the Barnacles, Bar, Bishop, and the Stiltstalkings, when once they have been drained of all life, are condemned without reservation. Rigaud is an attempt to solve this problem. He is made diabolically potent yet must remain always subordinate to characters whose evil he can only promote, not initiate. Thus he is not the first mover of evil but the accomplice of an evil that other people have found for themselves and for which they must take responsibility.

But then this second intention with regard to Rigaud becomes redundant after Dickens has abandoned Evil for the corrupt knottedness of social relations which in this novel forms the diseased tissue where Gentility breeds. That is to say, it may be unreasonable to put blame on an individual Merdle for behavior which his whole society endorses, but correction, like charity, can at least begin at home: Gentility is a blight that starts with the individual heart and yet can stand for a nation's ills, whereas Evil, understood as a magical mystery of the Dostoevskian type, disarms any attempt to grasp the bridge between the social part and the social whole. The traditional charge against Dickens is true: he could indeed not portray a gentleman properly, but it is because he was trying to do so much more with his gentlemen than mere portraiture.

— 2 —

Against the vast tangled net of Gentility, locking together the middle classes of England in a bond of misery and threatening to draw England's rulers into the toils of Continental mismanagement, *Little Dorrit* pits Reality, which is represented almost exclusively by Amy. Dickens evidently felt the match might appear uneven. Physician, for instance, is unexpectedly forgiven the dubious company he keeps with Bar and Bishop because it must be made clear that Amy stands for an idea other than mere Goodness: "Where he [Physician] was, something real was. And half a grain of reality, like the smallest portion of some other scarce natural productions, will flavour an enormous quantity of diluent" (702).

Amy's strength is no more specifically Christian love than it is abstract Goodness; [3] the point is, she knows better than anyone else what is real and what is not: "Sitting opposite her father in the travelling-carriage, and recalling the old Marshalsea room, her present existence was a dream. All that she saw was new and wonderful, but it was not real; it seemed to her as if those visions of mountains and picturesque countries might melt away at any moment, and the carriage, turning some abrupt corner, bring up with a jolt at the old Marshalsea gate. . . . It was from this position that all she saw appeared unreal; the more surprising the scenes, the more they resembled the unreality of her own inner life as she went through its vacant places all day long." (463)

A far more formidable foe than Rigaud is Amy's own father, seconded by her governess. The former teaches her to forget the Reality she has known in the past (" 'I say, sweep it off the face of the earth and begin afresh. Is that much? I ask, is *that* much?' "), and the latter teaches her to avoid knowing it in the future (" 'be ignorant of everything that is not perfectly proper, placid, and pleasant' "). Together they are the forces of Gentility assaulting Amy's fortress of saving Reality.

Amy is distinguished from Pet and Flora by her having more Reality than these other two women who had preceded her in Clennam's affections. That she can estimate the true value of Flora's pathetic memories and of Pet's loveless marriage is far more to the point than that she is not conventionally nubile. Indeed, Amy's inadequacy as a wife is not as important as some readers have maintained.

It is true that Clennam persists in addressing her as his child, even in his final declaration of mature love in the Marshalsea (II, xxix), and our own age is apt to disapprove of love not properly sexual. But the child in Amy is ambiguous; for all others, apart from Clennam, she is Little Mother. It is not that she is a child, but that perhaps by being a mother, she is in touch with childhood and everything that Dickens and his contemporaries associated with childhood. In fact, child and mother are here transposable terms, for what is in question is the healing force of love. In *Little Dorrit* this is not a Victorian truism. On the contrary, Dickens is carefully making an almost technical point about how a mind can be repaired. The future appears feasible only when the past has been filled in. It is not that Amy is not enough of a woman to be a wife, but that she is made to be more than a wife—a sister, daughter, and above all, mother as well. That is to say, Dickens stakes all on one relationship which must redeem all the others if they are missing. Thus the insipidity of romantic married love according to his usual convention is immeasurably enriched, but enriched in the only terms which that convention would permit, namely the nonsexual. "At no Mother's knee but hers [Nature's] had he ever dwelt in his youth on hopeful promises, on playful fancies, on the harvests of tenderness and humility that lie hidden in the early-fostered seeds of the imagination; on the oaks of retreat from blighting winds, that have the germs of their strong roots in nursery acorns. But, in the tones of the voice that read to him [Amy's], there were memories of an old feeling of such things, and echoes of every merciful and loving whisper that had ever stolen to him in his life" (815).

Clennam, without a mother, a home, or any affection till early middle age, is not so much unhappy as empty. His sole memory of love is the pathetic Flora. He is not like Pip, who becomes wiser because of being unhappy and finding out what a cheat success is. The Clennam we see at the beginning starts with what Pip spends a novel to get; what he lacks is a Joe Gargery to have tended his childhood. This is what Amy must do first, wedding or no wedding. Clennam and Magwitch are similar in that they must be loved on trust before they can turn into a husband or a father, respectively.

If not in connection with Amy, the author's involvement in Clennam makes itself sufficiently felt when he gazes at the river and is tempted to "compound for its insensibility to happiness with its insensibility to pain" (I, xvi). For *Little Dorrit* is explicit that insensibility to pain is a deadly lure. This is one of the most powerful and frightening ideas of the book. It is the deliberately placed alternative to the optimism of the saving particle in every soul. Yielding to numbness is a far worse fate for the insulted and the injured than yielding to the goad of wealth and worldliness. Amy and Clennam as they stand together on the last page must keep intact their vulnerability to pain as well as resist its shocks. The first of the following passages concerns Clennam, and the second Dorrit—that is to say, with and without the saving particle:

> For a burning restlessness set in, an agonized impatience of the prison, and a conviction that he was going to break his heart and die there, which caused him indescribable suffering. His dread and hatred of the place became so intense that he felt it a labour to draw his breath in it. The sensation of being stifled sometimes so overpowered him, that he would stand at the window holding his throat and gasping. At the same time a longing for other air, and a yearning to be beyond the blind blank wall, made him feel as if he must go mad with the ardour of the desire. . . . Two nights and a day exhausted it. It came back by fits, but those grew fainter and returned at lengthening intervals. A desolate calm succeeded; and the middle of the week found him settled down in the despondency of low, slow fever. (754).

> The time had been when the Father himself had wept, in the shades of that yard, as his own poor wife had wept. But it was many years ago; and now he was like a passenger aboard ship in a long voyage, who has recovered from sea-sickness, and is impatient of that weakness in the fresher passengers taken aboard at the last port. He was inclined to remonstrate, and to express his opinion that people who couldn't get on without crying, had no business there. (223)

However, the almost universal dissatisfaction with Amy felt by the novel's readers is not without grounds. If she is a fitting consort for Clennam, she is nevertheless lacking in herself. The deficiency is hard to formulate, especially when one has claimed so much for her in other respects. In brief, the mere presence of Miss Wade in the novel is the cause of the trouble. She jars on the conventions to which Amy so securely belongs. The great passage (II, xxi), "The History of a Self-Tormentor," must stand alone in its own chapter, since it cannot be assimilated by the rest of the book. Dickens' usual method in seeking to achieve psychological complexity is to exhibit a comparatively simple character in numerous relations with other strongly individualized but equally simple characters in a variety of telling incident. Delving so deeply in a single character, particularly a minor one, must obtrude as an isolated piece of virtuosity. Yet, isolated or not, Miss Wade does express a perspective on human motives and needs which throws Amy into rather meager relief. It is as if Miss Wade stands for all the things Dickens knew about people, but which he was loath to confront directly, for artistic and moral reasons, so bound did he feel to the exigencies of lively caricature and resolved endings. Her self-torment does not proceed from gothic anguish or inherited curse, the love affair with Gowan cannot be held to be the cause, nor does Tattycoram's companionship have any appreciable effect on her. Dorrit, Tip, and Fanny might be said to be beyond the power of healing love, but Miss Wade simply belongs in a world outside such a conception. Yet, however seldom she appears, she shares more of the author's intelligence than any other character in the whole large cast. Her speech to Tattycoram when Meagles comes to take her back is both a true and a false account of the facts of the case, but only Miss Wade, together with Dickens, sees that side of Meagles at all.

> "You can be, again, a foil to his pretty daughter, a slave to her pleasant wilfulness, and a toy in the house showing the goodness of the family. You can have your droll name, again, playfully pointing you out and setting you apart, as it is right that you should be pointed out and set apart. (Your birth, you know; you must not forget your birth.) You can again be shown to this gentleman's daughter, Harriet, and kept before her, as a living reminder of her own superiority and her gracious condescension." . . .
> Poor Mr. Meagles's inexpressible consternation in hearing his motives and actions so perverted, had prevented him from interposing any word until now. (328)

Perhaps it was the artist in Gowan that made Miss Wade say, "He was the first person I had ever seen in my life who had understood me" (669). But Dickens dared not go any further into either the love affair or into what it might mean to be an artist. Miss Wade's being present at all in *Little Dorrit* is displacement enough. Amy offers moral reality but Miss Wade verges on literal realism.

— *3* —

Although Dickens lavished so much art on depicting the opposition between Gentility and Reality, my having labored behind in his footsteps to sketch his intentions should not blind one to another of his intentions, equally important but contrary in its effect. For Dickens was determined in *Little Dorrit* to avoid a structure which depended on a straightforwardly dualistic tug-of-war. He may set up a system of con-

traries and wish one to grasp their separate identity, but he is equally
intent on describing their synthesis. After all, *Little Dorrit* is straddled by
Hard Times (1854) and *A Tale of Two Cities* (1859)—the one, with its
formula of "kindness and patience and cheery ways," an appeal for political quietism, and the other a costume drama which gives one the undeniable impression of an author letting off bottled-up steam. *Little
Dorrit* mediates between these two brief and mediocre productions; it
consciously seeks and achieves a unique balance of a kind that is of central importance to Dickens' whole work. Usually he worked by a zigzag
method of redressing balances, character by character or book by book.
Harmony of a single effect he never appeared to desire so much as in
Little Dorrit. The indignation over a corrupt society that one finds in
Hard Times and *A Tale of Two Cities* is still there in *Little Dorrit*. Nevertheless, indignation does not belong at its center. Clennam seeks justice
but has not an atom of indignation.

   Little Dorrit's attempt to harmonize the emotions that provoked
Hard Times and *A Tale of Two Cities* is reflected in the almost diagram-
matic set of oppositions: "Poverty" in Book I versus "Riches" in Book
II, or the opening chapter, "Sun and Shadow." The emotions concerned are love and justice. Although Dickens spent most of his writing
life demonstrating the need for both and exhibiting the pathos or de-
structiveness caused by their absence, he did so in passages that were
organically separate from each other. In *Little Dorrit* he combines their
relations in ways unfamiliar to him, whose purpose is to show that
righteous anger and Christian humility are a complicated mixture and
may even be mutually antagonistic. That is why this novel is Dickens'
most courageous intellectual feat, for in it he supplies his own most
subtle reservation about the strident calls to the public conscience that
were such a feature of his earlier work,[4] and also invents the most satisfactory version of love that his romantic convention could bear. The
sexual anomalies of bourgeois marriage on the one hand, and philanthropy and reform on the other, can scarcely be said to reach a definitive clarification in *Little Dorrit*. But they are at least made more
serious by being brought into a qualifying proximity with one another.
The novel's final paragraph, where Clennam and Amy are joined and
about to descend once more into the thick of life, is impressive in itself
and impressive as a conscious example of the proximity in question:
that is to say, Clennam, with his vague longing for justice and his quite
unfocused need to make restitution, marries Amy, who has spent her
life in good works, unrequitedly loving her father, brother, and sister.
Justice and love are fused. But it is only a way of survival that is being
offered, not a solution to the world. Merdle, the Barnacles, Casby, and
the others remain at large.

   Despite the novel's bifurcated structure, then—rich and poor, light and dark, hot and cold, confined and free—the main idea is not so much a seesaw as a seamless interrelatedness.

> Grapes, split and crushed under foot, lay about everywhere. The child carried in a sling by the laden peasant woman toiling home, was quieted with picked-up grapes; the idiot sunning his big goître under the leaves of the wooden châlet by the way to the waterfall, sat munching grapes; the breath of the cows and goats was redolent of leaves and stalks of grapes; the company in every little cabaret were eating, drinking, talking grapes. A pity that no ripe touch of this generous abundance could be given to the thin, hard, stony wine, which after all was made from the grapes! . . .
> As the heat of the glowing day, when they had stopped to drink at the streams of melted ice and snow, was changed to the searching cold of the frosty rarefied night air at a great height, so the fresh beauty of the lower journey had yielded to barrenness and desolation. (431–32)

That a thing can have antithetical attributes and yet still retain its unity is the point here. Thus it is not a question of balancing out one stretch of narrative against another: for instance, showing the Dorrits first with money and then without money. Rather, both these accounts of experience should be thought of as unified by a single set of conditions that subsume them throughout, regardless of the point at which the intrigue has at any time reached. This is the relevance of the multiple images of confinement, evident to every reader. They are a way of expressing this unity of the conditional in life, under whatever variety of guise. Thus bifurcation tends always toward a harmony of eventual effect.

The opening chapter of the first book, "Sun and Shadow," is a magnificent piece of Dickensian bravura offering a vision of humanity caught in the toils of a necessity that is partly Rigaud's debased sansculottism, partly Vanity Fair and partly original sin: "Hindoos, Russians, Chinese, Spaniards, Portuguese, Englishmen, Frenchmen, Genoese, Neapolitans, Venetians, Greeks, Turks, descendants from all the builders of Babel, come to trade at Marseilles, sought the shade alike." Religion alone gives shelter from the glare: "The churches were the freest from it. To come out of the twilight of pillars and arches— dreamily dotted with winking lamps, dreamily peopled with ugly old shadows piously dozing, spitting, and begging—was to plunge into a fiery river, and swim for life to the nearest strip of shade."

This is a bold and strong effect in simple outline, it would seem. Yet the outline soon wavers. Rigaud, introduced in the same chapter as the passages above, is described as being "chilled" in his Marseilles prison cell. Is it the virtue of prison shade which, like church shade, produces this shiver in the villain? But shortly after, much is made of another prison shade which has a different meaning: "Little Dorrit parted from them at the door, and hastened back to the Marshalsea. It fell dark there sooner than elsewhere, and going into it that evening was like going into a deep trench. The shadow of the wall was on every object. . . . 'Why not upon me too!' thought Little Dorrit, with the door yet in her hand" (245).

Then, suddenly, in the first chapter of the second book, "Fellow Travelers," the counterpart to "Sun and Shadow," all these terms are reversed. Now it is the heat of the monastery which protects from a cold that kills rather than soothes: "While all this noise and hurry were rife among the living travellers, there, too, silently assembled in a grated house half-a-dozen paces removed, with the same cloud enfolding them and the same snow flakes drifting in upon them, were the dead travellers found upon the mountain." Religion is still the constant on which this second equally savage dichotomy turns: "Seen from these solitudes, and from the Pass of the Great Saint Bernard, which was one of them, the ascending Night came up the mountain like a rising water. When it at last rose to the walls of the convent of the Great Saint Bernard, it was as if that weather-beaten structure were another Ark, and floated on the shadowy waves."

But what of religion after the cruel and stupefying clamor of church bells in London as Clennam arrives on a Sunday evening? This passage (I, iii) could be explained away as religion of the perverted Calvinist type that we are about to discover in Clennam's mother. That might be valid enough, though odd considering that Dickens is clearly not particular about sectarian distinctions in a work where the Roman church can be allowed to stand for Christianity itself—and this to a reading public whose prejudices he knew and for a large part shared. But these reverses happen too often; everywhere an implied meaning is matched by its opposite.

Imprisonment is destructive of the best in people, as can be seen everywhere, yet it is specifically said of Clennam, in the chapter entitled "The Pupil of the Marshalsea" (II, xxvii), that if he had not been condemned to prison the last indispensable factor in his maturing love for Amy would have been lacking. Confinement of what is harmful is a protection for those at large, as is the case with the quarantine restrictions in Marseilles, or with Rigaud who, Dickens insists—in a long harangue against "philosophical philanthropy" (I, xi)—in this instance stands for that element in human nature that is irremediably resistant to human care. (It is significant that even Amy can only shudder impotently at him and remain herself inviolable.) However much prison may protect the world against Rigaud, the same chapter points out that

Rigaud was himself protected by guards and prison walls against the vengeance of outraged justice. Dorrit, too, is protected, and he exults in what he calls his freedom within the Marshalsea, but chiefly the shield is against Reality. When Reality finally bursts in on him in the great scene of Mrs. Merdle's farewell dinner (II, xix), and he babbles pathetically of the old prison in the midst of all the splendor, he is merely destroyed. Even his selfishness toward Amy returns intact for his last moments of life. On the other hand, Reality bursts in upon Mrs. Clennam with just as much destructive force, but it also brings a brief spell of saving clarity and genuine reparation. The monk of the Great Saint Bernard tries to explain to Dorrit that an effort of will can transform incarceration into a beneficent retreat (II, i). But the explanation is to one whose ferocious paroxysm of anger and frustration at being locked up on the eve of release (I, xxxv), throws light on another and very sinister variety of will power, considering the long years of Dorrit's apparently cheerful serenity beforehand. Once more the difference is between two aspects of a single thing. Then again, the places of confinement can on the one hand be pestholes of misery or viciousness, such as the Circumlocution Office or Mrs. Clennam's house, or, on the other hand, they can be real communities such as Bleeding Heart Yard, whose fellowship consoles its occupants for their undeniable bondage. Finally, one might be tempted at least to venture the observation that confinement, whether understood as stone walls or as the psychology of a Miss Wade, was man-made—invidious barriers against freedom and nature and so on. But to do so would be to underestimate the scale of Dickens' conception: "Black, all night, since the gate had clashed upon Little Dorrit, its iron stripes were turned by the early-glowing sun into stripes of gold. Far aslant across the city, over its jumbled roofs, and through the open tracery of its church towers, struck the long bright rays, bars of the prison of this lower world" (763).

If life itself is to be thought of as the realm of limitation, one is diverted finally from any effort to change it and is thrown back on Amy Dorrit for a solution. Not that Clennam's effort on behalf of justice is very energetic or thoroughgoing; apart from his personal and family atonement, he merely accompanies Meagles in a visit to the Barnacle stronghold and ends up as partner to the gentle Doyce. Thus muted, justice can be accommodated to love, and we are surely to take the "sunshine and shade" of the great final paragraph as a deliberate modification of the harsh alternatives of the book's beginning. It is an example of the seemingly effortless conversion of a debilitating convention—the happy ending—to higher ends. The happiness of the married protagonists is to be carefully distinguished from mere optimism. Dickens breathed new life into a dead form precisely by taking out the optimism. There is of course a price to be paid for such an accommodation: it is the loss of that energy and that warm jollity of human fellowship which mean so much to Dickens elsewhere. We get instead the drab spirits but heart-breaking pathos of "Little Dorrit's Party" (I, xiv). Instead of the black and white glare of "Sun and Shadow," there is the triumph of ordinariness and the mean achieved by reconciliation, though we may feel Amy's share is greater than Clennam's. This is because the novel as a whole knows that Rigaud and Gowan are right: society is indeed bought and sold, and Clennam must necessarily not press his righteous claims too hard, or Amy could never have pacified him: "They went quietly down into the roaring streets, inseparable and blessed; and as they passed along in sunshine and shade, the noisy and the eager, and the arrogant and the froward and the vain, fretted and chafed, and made their usual uproar."

— *4* —

The synthesis of opposing conflicts in *Little Dorrit* mattered to Dickens because it was the artistic metaphor which enabled him to move from the portrayal of society as England to society as a system without national boundaries. *Bleak House* (1852–53) had been, like *Little Dorrit,* an attempt to express how a society was bound up together, class by class. But the earlier book had implied the comparatively genial idea of the family of England, where the slum diseases of Tom-All-Alone's might not only impose a unifying blight on even the highest in the land, by infecting them with the afflictions of the poor, but also provide a satisfyingly compact target for a reformer's zeal. The upper class of *Bleak House* is not excluded from our sympathy and the whole book is an appeal to those who have power for more responsible behavior.

One might read *Little Dorrit* as a deliberate reaction against having made such an appeal. The emphasis is no longer even on unjust institutions. It is not simply that the effectiveness of reform seems now much reduced, but that the target for reform has expanded to such a degree as to have been changed in kind. To correspond to this widened scope, the scene of action is no longer confined to England. With the two most important chapters, one set in Marseilles, the other in the Swiss Alps, each standing at the head of the novel's two books, England now figures as merely the foreground of a larger picture which is intended, in its account of underlying system, to be all-embracing.

Intimations of this large matter appear in small but ubiquitous ways. To begin with, Dickens is uneasy about where his people get their money. Even Clennam's savings and Amy's legacy are not sufficiently above suspicion but that they must be lost before the lovers are allowed to find each other. The author's discomfort is most evident in his inclination to avoid the subject. If every source of money is tainted, the novel would be peopled only by villains and would leave no room for those, like Meagles, who are intended to inhabit a crucial middle ground in the moral sense. Nevertheless, that the world is indeed peopled by those who participate in a general villainy is also very much Dickens' point.

In *Little Dorrit* money is everywhere felt but remains always invisible. This is a theme, of course, that *Great Expectations* will take up in earnest. And after being handled there so reticently, with the connection between a convict's Australian sheep-farming and English pretensions being left, after all, to our inference, it surfaces like a spouting whale with the mountains of excrement in *Our Mutual Friend*. Where people get their money from is a concern that keeps scratching at Dickens' mind in a way that separates him from other English novelists and lifts his stature so far above him. Earlier in his career anxieties could be allayed if a character was kind and worked for the money, but now even this is no longer enough: Meagles is no longer morally secure in his income, as Clennam, his financial double, well knows. The problem is crystallized in law, because law is the theoretical justification for the way in which the money is distributed. If law holds its peace at a distribution Dickens knew to be wrong, then he was able, for all his unintellectual cast of mind, to achieve a distinction between legality and justice which still impresses one with its extraordinary intellectual courage. Consequently, lawyers trouble Dickens. Angus Wilson says of *Great Expectations:* " 'But the strangest, most enigmatic figure in the book, perhaps in all Dickens' work, is Jaggers. Who is he, this Prospero, this manipulator, agent and source of Pip's and Estella's fortunes? Is he good and benevolent as he sometimes seems? Or cynical and malign as he appears at other times? It is almost impossible to pin him down. Yet around him undoubtedly hangs the guilt—social and personal—that is the pervading theme of the book, and for all his hand-washing he is never free of it.' " [5]

Why does Jaggers in particular have so much guilt hanging round him? It is perhaps because he is not merely subject to the law in the way everyone else is, he is triumphant in the law, his wits and fluency guarantee its power over people's lives and bring him money and fame. One might even say that it was he who, in his capacity as a lawyer, made Magwitch what he was and then transported him as a felon to Australia. Small wonder he washes his hands so assiduously; it is to prevent himself from drawing the conclusions which Dickens himself draws from such a passage as the following:

> "Now, I ask you, you blundering booby," said my guardian [Jaggers] very sternly, "once more and for the last time, what the man you have brought here is prepared to swear?"

Mike looked hard at my guardian, as if he were trying to learn a lesson from his face, and slowly replied, "Ayther to character, or to having been in his company and never left him all the night in question."

"Now, be careful. In what station of life is this man?"

Mike looked at his cap, and looked at the floor, and looked at the ceiling, and looked at the clerk, and even looked at me, before beginning to reply in a nervous manner, "We've dressed him up like—" when my guardian blustered out:

"What? You WILL, will you?"

("Spooney!" added the clerk again, with another stir.)

After some helpless casting about, Mike brightened and began again:

"He is dressed like a 'spectable pieman. A sort of a pastry-cook."

"Is he here?" asked my guardian. (159)

The mixed feelings and thoughts that Dickens has about Jaggers he has already had about the resourceful detective Bucket of *Bleak House*. (Is he good or bad?—He serves the law and nothing else. Does that worry him? Should it worry us?) In *Little Dorrit* the corresponding figure is Pancks the rent collector. He grinds the poor of Bleeding Heart Yard, with a suitable philosophy to salve his conscience—" 'But I like business. . . . What's a man made for?' "—yet not only does he finally recognize his own instrumentality in a larger and legal scheme of things, but also turns out to be the cause, again working through none but legal channels, of the Dorrit family's release from prison. However, as a mixture of kindheartedness beneath a formidable exterior—an exterior which alone enables him to survive—Pancks reminds one more of Wemmick than of the more complex Jaggers. *Little Dorrit* contains the Jaggers doubt in nothing less substantial and effective a form than the Marshalsea prison itself, of course. Stone walls mark out the legal way in which money has been distributed.

Probably Dickens intended something similar with regard to justice vis-à-vis law when he introduced smuggling into the novel: an infraction of the law that could be relied upon for sympathy from many an honest Englishman. The good-hearted Cavalletto has come to be Rigaud's cellmate on account of a smuggling conviction; the Marshalsea is described as having a special smugglers' enclosure, distinct from the debtors' quarters; the Great Saint Bernard is mentioned as a refuge for smugglers. However, Dickens does not develop the idea, perhaps feeling that the law-abiding criminals elsewhere in the book represented it better. Smuggling in *Little Dorrit* must remain an aborted embryo of a theme Dickens was determined to come to terms with, and even Jaggers does not perhaps finish it off properly for him.

The invisibility of money in *Little Dorrit* makes it a furtive specter round every corner of the novel. We see the people but never the money, nor the sources of money, nor any work that might make money. Thus the impression which accumulates is that some people behave atrociously and others suffer because something has been dislocated in their merely personal relations. To bring in money as a real presence would have been to rationalize the dislocation, and Dickens chose not to do so. That money is no longer real in the novel—real in a moral and even tangible sense—is evident in the irony of such a passage as the following:

> "It seems to me hard," said Little Dorrit, "that he [her father] should have lost so many years and suffered so much, and at last pay all the debts as well. It seems to me hard that he should pay in life and money both." . . .
> The prison, which could spoil so many things, had tainted Little Dorrit's mind no more than this. Engendered as the confusion was, in compassion for the poor prisoner, her father, it was the first speck Clennam had ever seen, it was the last speck Clennam ever saw, of the prison atmosphere upon her. (422).

Thus the theme of Reality seals up this ultimate meaning of *Little Dorrit*. The inquiry as to what is real ranges from the clouds billowing around the Great Saint Bernard, giving it an air of insubstantiality, to poor Flora's fantasies of lovelorn romance; from Merdle's stock to Clennam's callow hopes of marriage with Pet. But it is Amy who finally dominates the inquiry. With her it is not that the disagreeable is in itself a force for spirituality: the grimy and wretched walls of the Marshalsea are preferable to Venice—"the crowning unreality"—with its transparent walls and illusion of limitlessness, because the inhabitants of a debtors' prison know where money comes from. In this connection *Great Expectations* is again the inevitable comparison. While Pip, the newly-made gentleman, was waiting to meet Estella on her trip to London, he paid a visit to Newgate prison and is overwhelmed with a vague shame. The rich girl who had laughed at him for being common now sneers loftily at the convicts as " 'Wretches!' " (xxxiii). It takes the whole novel for Pip to learn to love a convict and accept that part of his childhood on the marshes which belonged to the prison ships: "I thought of the beautiful young Estella, proud and refined, coming toward me, and I thought with absolute abhorrence of the contrast between the jail and her. . . . I beat the prison dust off my feet as I sauntered to and fro, and I shook it out of my dress, and I exhaled its air from my lungs" (xxxii).

Clennam, too, has to learn this final lesson in Reality, as the "Pupil of the Marshalsea," after he had momentarily flouted it in his disastrous flutter on the Stock Exchange. This is where *Little Dorrit*'s expanded sense of reality converges with the theme of money's invisibility. For money, properly understood, is not a symbol of exchange value with a life of its own; it is, rather, the fruit of work. A miraculous legacy does not make money any more visible to William Dorrit; it merely gives its apparition the haphazard quality that belongs to a casino. Merdle on the Stock Exchange is in one sense holding nothing but paper in his hands and is thus at the center of his society's unreality; but when he falls, the work which inheres in that paper goes with him. Clennam the investor becomes Clennam the imprisoned debtor in order to learn that Marx's labor theory of value is not a literal description so much as a moral protest. When Dickens dwells on the idea of secrecy the substance behind his fascination is a simpleminded wonder at how toil could be transformed into pieces of paper. Secrecy is the word that must carry the weight of the mysteriousness of this transformation, the bafflement of one who contemplates it, and the extraordinary vitality of unreal paper that can be lost and found like William Dorrit's freedom.

> As he went along, upon a dreary night, the dim streets by which he went, seemed all depositories of oppressive secrets. The deserted counting-houses, with their secrets of books and papers locked up in chests and safes; the banking-houses, with their secrets of strong rooms and wells, the keys of which were in a very few secret pockets and a very few secret breasts; the secrets of all the dispersed grinders in the vast mill, among whom there were doubtless plunderers, forgers, and trust-betrayers of many sorts, whom the light of any day that dawned might reveal; he could have fancied that these things, in hiding, imparted a heaviness to the air. The shadow thickening and thickening as he approached its source, he thought of the secrets of the lonely church-vaults, where the people who had hoarded and secreted in iron coffers were in their turn similarly hoarded, not yet at rest from doing harm; and then of the secrets of the river, as it rolled its turbid tide between two frowning wildernesses of secrets, extending, thick and dense, for many miles, and warding off the free air and the free country swept by winds and wings of birds. (542)

Deborah A. Thomas

DICKENS' MRS. LIRRIPER
AND THE EVOLUTION
OF A FEMININE STEREOTYPE

THE FEEBLENESS of Dickens' feminine characters is notorious. In the world of his fictions, as in many other worlds, women are uneasy subjects, and few critics have been able to follow the seemingly endless parade of little angels and larger female evils without an uncomfortable feeling that in this area at least the Inimitable might have done better. George Gissing remarked, as early as 1898, "Today the women must be very few who by deliberate choice open a volume of his works," [1] and the ensuing three-quarters of a century have not endeared Dickens to the feminist cause. Kate Millett, for example, remarks: "It is one of the more disheartening flaws in the master's work that nearly all the 'serious' women in Dickens' fiction, with the exception of Nancy and a handful of her criminal sisters, are insipid goodies." [2] Less polemical readers likewise find Dickens' women difficult to embrace: Edwin Pugh described Little Nell, Agnes Wickfield, and their seraphic sisters as "femininanities," [3] while V. S. Pritchett noted that his "women are also fools, in his comedy, pettish in love, tiresome in childbirth, perpetually snuffling, continuously breeding." [4] With fictional fools and angels thus populating the field, one might be forgiven for fearing to tread therein. However, the extent to which Dickens actually relied upon these stereotypes as his art developed is an important subject, and in the midst of such visceral overgeneralization, some of his significant accomplishments in depicting female personality have been overlooked.

To a large extent the distinction between colorless heroines and colorful comic figures is justified, at least in the early fictions, although characters such as Nancy in *Oliver Twist,* the Marchioness in *The Old Curiosity Shop,* and Edith in *Dombey and Son* are notable exceptions. Critics have often explained Dickens' use of such stereotypes, both serious and comic, in terms of his Victorian cultural assumptions as well as his personal disappointments. On the one hand, Philip Collins remarks that Dickens' "limited ideal of womanhood" reflects "the limitations of a middle-class, middle-brow Englishman, of the mid-nineteenth century." [5] On the other hand, Angus Wilson contends that Dickens' frustrated adolescent romance with Maria Beadnell (whose parents spurned him as financially ineligible), following upon his feeling of rejection by his mother (whom he never forgave for wishing him to continue in the blacking warehouse), permanently distorted the depiction of women in his fiction.[6] Ian Watt has likewise argued recently that the oral perspective of the rejected child in Dickens' novels appears in his "segregation of women characters into asexual angels or frustrating witches." [7] Within this biographical context it is often suggested that Dickens' misguided mother is partially caricatured in the obsessively talkative, incurably romantic Mrs. Nickleby, while the unfortunate Maria Beadnell is diversely reflected in the immaturely angelic Dora Spenlow and the maturely ludicrous Flora Finching. The increased complexity of Estella in *Great Expectations,* Bella Wilfer in *Our Mutual Friend,* and Rosa Bud and Helena Landless in *Edwin Drood* is similarly attributed to Dickens' experience with Ellen Ternan late in his career: he may have learned that young women are more complicated than he earlier assumed.[8] Nevertheless, while exploring this admittedly valuable social and personal background, critics have generally overlooked one of Dickens' most remarkable adult female characters, Mrs. Lirriper, who appears not in his novels but in two of his short works created for the Christmas season. This oversight is unfortunate, for his contributions to *Mrs. Lirriper's Lodgings* and *Mrs. Lirriper's Legacy,* the extra Christmas numbers of *All the Year Round* for 1863 and 1864, strikingly illustrate at least one of the comic feminine stereotypes with which he worked and the way in which he transformed it.

As Mrs. Lirriper reveals in her opening words of the first of these stories, she belongs to Dickens' long line of phenomenal conversationalists:

> Whoever would begin to be worried with letting Lodgings that wasn't a lone woman with a living to get is a thing inconceivable to me my dear, excuse the familiarity but it comes natural to me in my own little room when wishing to open my mind to those that I can trust and I should be truly thankful if they were all mankind but such is not so, for have but a Furnished bill in the window and your watch on the mantelpiece and farewell to it if you turn your back for but a second however gentlemanly the manners, nor is being of your own sex any safeguard as I have reason in the form of sugar-tongs to know, for that lady (and a fine woman she was) got me to run for a glass of water on the plea of going to be confined, which certainly turned out true but it was in the Station-House. (*Lodgings,* 1)[9]

The environment depicted by this verbal torrent is matter of fact. Mrs. Lirriper is a London lodging-house keeper, a widowed "lone woman with a living to get," and the remainder of the beginning of *Mrs. Lirriper's Lodgings* proliferates with details about her friends and temporary enemies, her hired girls, her business tribulations, her longtime lodger and close associate Major Jemmy Jackman, her adopted grandson Jemmy, and her own meanderingly talkative self. Contemporary readers were delighted with her: the *Saturday Review*, for example, pronounced her a creation "which Mr Dickens has scarcely, if ever, surpassed," [10] and John Forster later declared that Mrs. Lirriper "took her place at once among people known to everybody; and all the world talked of Major Jemmy Jackman, and his friend the poor elderly lodging-house keeper of the Strand, with her miserable cares and rivalries and worries, as if they had both been as long in London and as well known as Norfolk Street itself. A dozen volumes could not have told more than those dozen pages did. The *Legacy* followed the *Lodgings* in 1864, and there was no falling off in the fun and laughter." [11] In terms of the often-echoed distinction between serious heroines and nonserious, comic figures such as that implied in Millett's comment that "nearly all the 'serious' women in Dickens' fiction . . . are insipid goodies," Mrs. Lirriper occupies a unique position. She is a thoroughly "serious" character in the sense of being the major figure in the works bearing her name and of being a "poor, elderly" woman occupied with "cares and rivalries and worries," yet she is also intrinsically a source of "fun and laughter." Moreover, she is not a haphazard manifestation or mutation, but the clear result of an evolutionary process in Dickens' art.

Stages in this process can be seen in some of Dickens' earlier comically talkative women. In one of the few critical discussions of Mrs. Lirriper, Harry Stone has observed that her seemingly random, but inwardly organized, remarks reveal a definite advance in Dickens' "rendering of individualized interior consciousness" [12] previously represented by the meandering associations of Mrs. Nickleby and Flora Finching. In this respect Mrs. Lirriper is simply the most sophisticated member of Dickens' gallery of garrulous women. She is, however, linked to Mrs. Nickleby and Flora not only in terms of her distinctive style of speech but also in terms of a well-established comic tradition, for the stock comic character of the eccentrically talkative, no-longer-youthful woman, usually unmarried, usually with romantic inclinations, whose features recur in varying degrees in all three characters is by no means the exclusive property of Dickens. Versions of this type range from Chaucer's Wife of Bath to Sheridan's Mrs. Malaprop, and, as Jane Stedman has pointed out, the unlovely, middle-aged "dame" figure, evident near the end of the nineteenth century in the dramas of W. S. Gilbert, was a popular stereotype on the mid-Victorian stage. [13] In view of this tradition, Mrs. Lirriper reveals significant changes not only in Dickens' representations of the operation of the human mind but also in his attitude toward conventionally ridiculous feminine characteristics. One of his earliest fictional works illuminates his initial approach.

A tale in *Sketches by Boz* entitled "The Boarding-House," first published in the *Monthly Magazine* in May and August of 1834, illustrates the often overweight outlines of the figure whose traces reappear in Mrs. Nickleby, Flora, and Mrs. Lirriper. In this early tale, three middle-aged women predominate: two widowed boarders looking for husbands, as well as Mrs. Tibbs, who runs the lodging house and customarily outtalks and effaces her unfortunate mate. Of these women the most relevant for this discussion is the boarder introduced as Mrs. Bloss, a "carnivorous" hypochondriac who eats "one mutton-chop in bed at half-past eight, and another at ten, every morning" (293).[14] She is usually just described in this tale, but when she speaks she has a tendency to confuse words in a manner resembling that of Mrs. Malaprop (or a more immediate cousin might be Theodore Hook's Mrs. Ramsbottom, mentioned by Dickens in a letter of 1837,[15] who likewise has this conversational abnormality). Her arrival at the boardinghouse quickly demonstrates her vocal peculiarities as she expresses a desire for "a state of retirement and obtrusion" in a remarkable voice which sounds "as if she had been playing a set of Pan's pipes for a fortnight without leaving off" (292). Mrs. Bloss turns out to be a former cook who gave the deceased Mr. Bloss "very little peace in his time" (292) and whose second marriage, to a Mr. Gobler, a fellow lodger who suffers from impaired digestion, is one in which her own tastes predominate, "wafted through life by the grateful prayers of all the purveyors of animal food within three miles round" (310). At this stage in his career, Dickens' hand is shaky: Mrs. Bloss turned Gobler is a shadowy, imperfectly delineated person; the male characters are generally as crudely drawn as the female ones; and the focus of Dickens' humor is not always clear.[16] Nevertheless the stereotype which Mrs. Gobler represents is apparent: an eccentrically talkative, domineering, husband-hunting widow, bent on finding a second spouse presumably to master as she did her first. The response which she seems intended to arouse is understandable in terms of Bergson's definition of comedy: "The comic is that side of a person which reveals his likeness to a thing, that aspect of human events which, through its peculiar inelasticity, conveys the impression of pure mechanism, of automatism, of movement without life. Consequently it expresses an individual or collective imperfection which calls for an immediate corrective. This corrective is laughter, a social gesture that singles out and represses a special kind of absent-mindedness in men and in events."[17] At the outset of Dickens' career this "exceedingly vulgar, ignorant, and selfish" (294) woman is only a

mechanically functioning figure whose antisocial behavior must be re-
formed by laughter; she is a satiric, unsympathetically treated example
of what an ideal woman should never be.

Mrs. Nickleby seems at first only a more pronounced and polished
duplication of this stereotype. The first distinguishing trait, an unusual
style of speaking, is her hallmark. As her remarks to her daughter on
the subject of the weather indicate, her most conspicuous characteristic
is an extended version of Mrs. Gobler's occasional verbal idiosyncrasy,
which now becomes a reflection of the "curious association" of Mrs.
Nickleby's thoughts:

> "Kate, my dear," said Mrs. Nickleby; "I don't know how it is,
> but a fine warm summer day like this, with the birds singing in
> every direction, always puts me in mind of roast pig, with sage
> and onion sauce, and made gravy."
> "That's a curious association of ideas, is it not, mama?"
> "Upon my word, my dear, I don't know," replied Mrs. Nick-
> leby. "Roast pig; let me see. On the day five weeks after you
> were christened, we had a roast—no, that couldn't have been a
> pig, either, because I recollect there were a pair of them to
> carve, and your poor papa and I could never have thought of
> sitting down to two pigs—they must have been partridges.
> Roast pig! I hardly think we could have had one, now I come to
> remember, for your papa could never bear the sight of them in
> the shops, and used to say that they always put him in mind of
> very little babies, only the pigs had much fairer complexions;
> and he had a horror of little babies, too, because he couldn't
> very well afford any increase in his family, and had a natural
> dislike to the subject. It's very odd now, what can have put that
> in my head!" (529)

At such moments, Gissing's assessment is almost irresistible: "Mr. Nickleby died in the prime of life; what else could be the fate of a man
doomed to listen to this talk morning, noon, and night?" [18] Her second
traditionally comic trait, domination of her deceased husband, is less
significant than her present garrulousness, but it is important in terms
of the plot of *Nicholas Nickleby*, for the only occasion on which she over-
ruled the unfortunate Mr. Nickleby proved utterly disastrous. As the
first chapter, which "Introduces all the Rest," explains, she persuaded
him to become involved in the unsuccessful speculation which ruined
him financially and so discouraged him that he died; this untimely
demise, in turn, threw his survivors on the untender mercies of his
brother Ralph. The important feature of Mrs. Nickleby's error in terms
of her own personality is the fact that, at her cynical brother-in-law's
suggestion, she easily persuades herself that she is "the amiable and

suffering victim of her late husband's imprudence" (28) rather than the cause of his misery. Moreover, this willingness to yield to delusion is linked to her manifestation of the third conventional characteristic. Unlike the onetime Mrs. Bloss, Mrs. Nickleby is not seriously interested in finding a second husband, but, just as she weaves fantasies of wealth and romance on the slightest provocation, she cherishes the flattering illusion that the mad gentleman in small-clothes who throws vegetables over the garden wall at her is an eligible and serious suitor for her hand.

In these respects Mrs. Nickleby is simply a more successful version of Mrs. Gobler, yet she does not fit precisely into the mold of her predecessor. Her speech pattern is not just a mechanical fixation but a reflection of her surroundings, and her bizarre verbal associations provide an insight into the actual movement of her thoughts. Even the narrator cannot deny her a kind of sympathy. Her self-excusing conviction that she has been victimized by her late husband is explained as part of "the irritability of sudden poverty" (119), and her fantasies about her vegetarian courtship are attributed to human vanity: "Although there was no evil and little real selfishness in Mrs. Nickleby's heart, she had a weak head and a vain one" (484). When she speaks, as in her musings about birds and pigs, the confident exuberance with which she demonstrates her weakness and vanity is infectious. Throughout the novel her absurdly connected ideas and impossible dreams float buoyantly above her inauspicious surroundings, and in the end, despite all probability, her optimistic faith that she and her children will succeed to spectacular good fortune proves triumphant. Ultimately Dickens' humor seems best explained not so much in Bergson's terms as in those of Freud, "the ego's victorious assertion of its own invulnerability": "It refuses to be hurt by the arrows of reality or to be compelled to suffer. . . . Humour is not resigned; it is rebellious. It signifies the triumph not only of the ego, but also of the pleasure principle, which is strong enough to assert itself . . . in the face of . . . adverse real circumstances." [19] As Margaret Ganz has emphasized, this transcendent quality lies at the heart of Dickens' most characteristically comic work: "That capacity of Dickens the humorist to effect a reconciliation between the tragic and comic elements of our life . . . is one of his most significant achievements. For it makes possible through laughter the pleasurable transcendence of the threats and perplexities in man's existence." [20] We laugh *at* Mrs. Gobler, but we are lured to laugh *with* Mrs. Nickleby, and our laughter is, to a large extent, tolerant. Dickens may have conceived the latter character against the background of a familiar comic stereotype, in a spirit of maternal animosity, but he embodied this original conception through his own increasingly distinctive comic vision.

Other figures in Dickens' work, such as Mrs. Todgers in *Martin Chuzzlewit,* display some of the features of this stereotype, but the nearest relative of Mrs. Nickleby in terms of verbal style and romantic dreams is Flora Finching in *Little Dorrit.* At the same time, movement from one of Dickens' early, primarily lighthearted novels to one of his darkest brings a dramatic shift in perspective. The world inhabited by Flora is far more grim than that of *Nickleby,* yet the treatment accorded to the later character's versions of the three conventionally ridiculous feminine frailties in question is paradoxically even more sympathetic than that given almost a decade earlier to the follies of Mrs. Nickleby. Once again, Flora—the lily turned peony, the boyhood sweetheart grown fat and florid—is eccentrically talkative. Once again, as her interweaving of romantic recollections with breakfast preparations indicates, her words tumble over one another in a bizarrely connected stream:

> "Romance, however," Flora went on, busily arranging Mr. F's Aunt's toast, "as I openly said to Mr. F when he proposed to me and you will be surprised to hear that he proposed seven times once in a hackney-coach once in a boat once in a pew once on a donkey at Tunbridge Wells and the rest on his knees, Romance was fled with the early days of Arthur Clennam, our parents tore us asunder we became marble and stern reality usurped the throne, Mr. F said very much to his credit that he was perfectly aware of it and even preferred that state of things accordingly the word was spoken the fiat went forth and such is life you see my dear and yet we do not break but bend, pray make a good breakfast while I go in with the tray." (283)

However, Flora's fusion of remembered proposals with current meals, leaving the reader as well as Little Dorrit "to ponder over the meaning of her scattered words" (283), flows much more smoothly than Mrs. Nickleby's laborious and slow-moving association of summer days, roast pigs, and babies; as Stone has noted, Flora's fusion is more indicative of the genuine leaps of human thought.[21] Likewise, the second traditionally comic trait, domestic domination, is softened and presented in Flora simply as self-indulgence. She remembers Mr. F as a "most indulgent husband, only necessary to mention Asparagus and it appeared or to hint at any little delicate thing to drink and it came like magic in a pint bottle it was not ecstasy but it was comfort" (285). In addition, the role she assumes, that of a dependent eighteen-year-old girl under her father's roof, is essentially self-indulgent, for, as the novel makes clear, this dependency is artificial. It is part of her "mermaid condition" (286)—her insistence upon combining past and present—in which, in this novel filled with prisoners, she has immured herself. Finally, for Flora even more clearly than for Mrs. Nickleby, the conventionally ludicrous pursuit of a husband is only the pursuit of an illusion. She quickly discerns at their first reunion that she has disappointed Clennam's expectations, but throughout most of the remainder of the novel, she happily nourishes the fantasy that their former relationship still exists and joyfully bids farewell to "the ashes of departed joys" (820) only when his impending marriage to Little Dorrit makes the fantasy impossible.

In any case, Flora's "fluttered" (826) enjoyment of Clennam's wedding does not mark the end of this kind of comic character for Dickens' fiction. With Mrs. Lirriper, six years after the conclusion of *Little Dorrit,* Dickens returned to a figure much like her predecessors yet significantly different, and the differences underscore his increasing sensitivity toward at least one kind of feminine personality. Like that of the tale in *Sketches by Boz,* the setting is again a boardinghouse, but the dissimilarity between the wooden lodger Mrs. Gobler and this mentally active lodging-house keeper is a striking illustration of the degree to which Dickens' style has developed in the intervening years. The speed with which Mrs. Lirriper fuses the existence of her professional worries with examples of these worries in the opening paragraph of *Mrs. Lirriper's Lodgings* ("have but a Furnished bill in the window and your watch on the mantelpiece and farewell to it if you turn your back for but a second however gentlemanly the manners") smoothly outdistances the slow-moving musings of Mrs. Nickleby. In addition, Mrs. Lirriper's associations are more consistently rooted in her everyday experience than those of Mrs. Nickleby and Flora Finching where Dickens occasionally seemed to interject farfetched details, such as Mrs. Nickleby's fear of giving birth to a second Shakespeare or the late Mr. F's seven proposals, for their own surprising sakes.

In marked contrast to the generally omniscient style of *Nickleby* and *Little Dorrit,* the opening chapters of both *Mrs. Lirriper's Lodgings* and *Mrs. Lirriper's Legacy* are first-person monologues in which she alone explains her existence. As Stone has pointed out, in these chapters Dickens is experimenting with interior monologue in order to produce "a representation of consciousness which was at once private and complex and at the same time convincing and illuminating," and the introduction of the *Legacy* goes even further than the *Lodgings* to verge in places on stream-of-consciousness narration: [22]

> Being here before your eyes my dear in my own easy-chair in my own quiet room in my own Lodging House Number Eighty-one Norfolk-street Strand London situated midway between the City and St. James's—if anything is where it used to be with these hotels calling themselves Limited but called Un-

limited by Major Jackman rising up everywhere and rising up
into flagstaffs where they can't go any higher, but my mind of
those monsters is give me a landlord's or landlady's wholesome
face when I come off a journey and not a brass plate with an
electrified number clicking out of it which it's not in nature can
be glad to see me and to which I don't want to be hoisted like
molasses at the Docks and left there telegraphing for help with
the most ingenious instruments but quite in vain—being here
my dear I have no call to mention that I am still in the Lodgings as a business hoping to die in the same and if agreeable to
the clergy partly read over at Saint Clement's Danes and concluded in Hatfield churchyard when lying once again by my
poor Lirriper ashes to ashes and dust to dust. (*Legacy,* 1)

The impact of the free-flowing beginnings of these Christmas numbers
is subsequently muted as accounts of the lodgings and the legacy un-
fold. Punctuation becomes more conventional, Mrs. Lirriper's style
grows less allusive, and the episodes she relates are unashamedly sentimental. The concluding chapter of the *Lodgings* is presented in the
words not of Mrs. Lirriper but of her friend Major Jemmy Jackman,
though she does narrate the final chapter of the *Legacy,* an improve-
ment which enclosed the latter Christmas number in one enveloping
point of view. Nevertheless, despite this eventual retreat from what
briefly suggests the uninhibited associative style of Molly Bloom,
Dickens has clearly moved beyond the satiric treatment of feminine
speech with which he began in *Sketches by Boz.* Here, to an even greater
degree than with Mrs. Nickleby and Flora Finching, Dickens seems to
be using the customary verbal eccentricity associated with this kind of
comic character to demonstrate the movement of human thought. As
in dramatic monologues such as Browning's "Fra Lippo Lippi," the
result encourages sympathy to such an extent that Mrs. Lirriper's foi-
bles—her small jealousies, her uneducated mistakes, her rambling style
of speaking—almost go unnoticed.

Simultaneously, the evidence of domestic domination apparent in
the earlier characters emerges in Mrs. Lirriper simply as domestic and
worldly competence. As her emphasis on "my own easy-chair in my
own quiet room in my own Lodging House" makes clear, she is completely in charge of her own establishment. She is obviously a successful
businesswoman who pays her late husband's debts, acquires enough
money to support herself and her less capable dependents, and, in the
process, learns about human nature ("wishing to open my mind to
those that I can trust and I should be truly thankful if they were all
mankind but such is not so"). Nevertheless, while marriage, widow-
hood, and thirty-eight years in the lodging business have made her

abundantly aware of human weakness, they have failed to make her cynical. She does open her mind not only to the reader but also to her friend and financially irregular lodger, Major Jemmy Jackman. In a sense, her friendship with the Major, eventually joined by their informal grandson and godson Jemmy, is a sexless, mirror image of the traditional male-dominated marital arrangement. Mrs. Lirriper relies upon the Major's advice, but any emotional dependence is countered by her undisputed financial superiority. As she tactfully explains in the *Lodgings,* he entered her boardinghouse after quarreling with her rival Miss Wozenham, who detained his luggage, over an unspecified but apparently rent-related issue: "Such was the beginning of the Major's occupying the parlours and from that hour to this the same and a most obliging Lodger and punctual in all respects except one irregular which I need not particularly specify, but made up for by his being a protection and at all times ready to fill in the papers of the Assessed Taxes and Juries and that" (4). In both Christmas numbers, this generally unmentioned but undenied economic factor remains at the background of their relationship. Moreover, as the Major's repeated obsequious allusions to "my esteemed friend" and "my respected friend" in his monologue at the close of the *Lodgings* indicate, he is conscious of and content with his subordinate position in the household.

Mrs. Lirriper's personality is essentially maternal. Like an expanded and inverted version of the harried Mrs. Todgers in *Martin Chuzzlewit,* who buries a kind heart beneath a preoccupation with the mundane demands of operating a lodging house, Mrs. Lirriper openly mothers the Major as she mothers Jemmy and jokes about their similarly juvenile excitement as they prepare to investigate her French legacy. Behind the joking, however, is the actuality of her attitude toward the small society collected around herself. In both the *Lodgings* and the *Legacy* she tirelessly cares for the physical and emotional needs of what often appears to be a large extended family including not only Jemmy and the Major but also her lodgers, her hired girls, her competitor Miss Wozenham, Jemmy's unwed mother who dies in the house after having been deserted by a seducer, and even Jemmy's father, whom she finds repentent on his deathbed in France. Furthermore, her maternal instincts are closely linked to her manifestation of the third conventionally comic trait evident in her prototypes: the pursuit of a husband and youthful romance. Her mind not only moves more rapidly from past to present than those of any of her predecessors, but she is also better able to separate the two. Her age is indeterminate although apparently greater than that of Flora, Mrs. Nickleby, or the mechanical Mrs. Gobler, yet even her flashbacks to earlier days are level-headed.

"I am an old woman now and my good looks are gone but that's me my dear over the plate-warmer and considered like in the times when you used to pay two guineas on ivory and took your chance pretty much how you came out, which made you very careful how you left it about afterwards because people were turned so red and uncomfortable by mostly guessing it was somebody else quite different, and there was once a certain person that had put his money in a hop business that came in one morning to pay his rent and his respects being the second floor that would have taken it down from its hook and put it in his breast pocket—you understand my dear—for the L, he says, of the original—only there was no mellowness in *his* voice and I wouldn't let him, but his opinion of it you may gather from his saying to it 'Speak to me Emma!' which was far from a rational observation no doubt but still a tribute to its being a likeness, and I think myself it *was* like me when I was young and wore that sort of stays." (*Lodgings,* 2)

Emma Lirriper knows that her youth is gone and that no one can ever take the place of her mellow-voiced dead husband. Like her predecessors, however, she still cherishes the dreams of youth, in this case the dreams of her adopted grandson Jemmy. The Christmas number for 1863 ends with Jemmy's childish vision of an ageless, deathless, eternally affluent world in which everyone lives happily ever after, while the Christmas number for 1864, showing a world in which things fail to go quite so well, reveals Jemmy's boyish belief in "trust and pity, love and constancy" (48), and both concluding illusions are sustained against the background of Mrs. Lirriper's compassionate knowledge that experience often has disproven them.

With this knowledge, she emerges as neither a mechanical object of laughter nor a serious heroine but a complex figure who is aware of the difficulties of the world, yet humorous despite them. She is too old and too funny to be an angel, too practical and too kindly to be a joke, and too prominent in the position given her by Dickens to be dismissed as an aberration. Undeniably, clichés still abound in her characterization. Her dedication to domestic order is unoriginal; a few of her verbal problems, such as her difficulty with French in the *Legacy,* are labored; and the deathbed scenes which she describes in both fictions can seem excessive to modern taste. Her personality appears less distinct and her mind less flexible in the latter portions of her monologues than her freeflowing associations wane, and her effortless rearing of Jemmy in both numbers is the kind of experience of which mothers may dream but seldom know. Nonetheless, whatever the artistic limitations of his achievement, Dickens' conception of Mrs. Lirriper remains significant.

In many ways she embodies the deepest impulses of his art. According to Northrop Frye, a major goal of Dickens' comedy is to break through the obstructions inhibiting congenial humanity and to reconstitute society on a more familial basis:

> In most of the best Victorian novels, apart from Dickens, the society described is organized by its institutions: the church, the government, the professions, the rural squirearchy, business, and the trade unions. It is a highly structured society, and the characters function from within those structures. But in Dickens we get a much more freewheeling and anarchistic social outlook. For him the structures of society, as structures, belong almost entirely to the absurd, obsessed, sinister aspect of it, the aspect that is overcome or evaded by the comic action. The comic action itself moves toward the regrouping of society around the only social unit that Dickens really regards as genuine, the family.[23]

In Frye's terms, Mrs. Lirriper's character is that of an amiable humor, although the features which identify her personality are more indicative not only of her congeniality but of her inner nature than those of Flora and Mrs. Nickleby. She knows clearly that the world beyond her control is not as she would make it, yet within the society that she creates for the occasion of this Christmas number, she is dedicated to the proposition "that what is must never take precedence over what ought to be."[24] The best description of the overall tone of these chapters which open and close the two numbers is perhaps that offered by Forster, talking specifically about Dickens' depiction of the character of Doctor Marigold in the Christmas number of the following year but focusing on features that are equally apparent in his treatment of Mrs. Lirriper: "the wonderful neighbourhood in this life of ours, of serious and humorous things; the laughter close to the pathos, but never touching it with ridicule."[25] Both Mrs. Lirriper and Doctor Marigold are parental figures and the attitude they adopt in terms of the world threatening themselves and the children they take under their protection is much like that described by Freud: "the humorist acquires his superiority by assuming the role of the grown-up . . . while he reduces the other people to the position of children."[26] Flora's concern for Mr. F's impossible Aunt is a step in this protective direction, but Dickens' complete vision of the familial ideal is reserved for the eyes of Mrs. Lirriper. The laughter here is intentionally "close to the pathos," much as pathos may seem infelicitous to modern palates. Like Mrs. Lirriper herself, we remain acutely aware of the fragility of this vision at the very moment when she imposes it through the power of her words.

The conclusion to which these words lead a reader is that, like his comedy, Dickens' characterization of women is not so simple as is sometimes believed. The possible reasons for Mrs. Lirriper's presence at this point in Dickens' career are manifold. In September 1863, a few months before the appearance of *Mrs. Lirriper's Lodgings,* Dickens' own never-quite-forgiven mother died. His complex response to this event combined with whatever satisfaction he may have found or yearned to find with Ellen Lawless Ternan is undoubtedly reflected to some degree in the personality of Mrs. Lirriper (whose initials, E. L., likewise distinguish the names of his late heroines: Estella, Bella Wilfer, and Helena Landless, often associated with Ellen). The full explanation of this character, however, rests not in Dickens' life but in the way in which he transmuted life through the force of his imagination. In this instance we can observe him, like all compulsively creative artists, reworking his own earlier compositions, delving within his own published but never quite finished products, and deepening his own previous conceptions.[27] The result is a competent, compassionate, at times mentally flexible, very nearly sympathetically portrayed woman who evolves from what was, earlier on, simply a ridiculous example of feminine error. Admittedly, by twentieth-century standards based on microwave ovens and modern child-care centers, the concept of feminine potential remains limited: woman's role, at best, appears to be maternal, and her sphere, at largest, is shown to be an extension of the domestic scene. The important point, however, is not that Mrs. Lirriper reflects a view of woman's nature that now seems dated but that Dickens' art is never stagnant, that his view of feminine personality gradually deepened as this art developed, and that here, as elsewhere in his writing, we can see him transforming convention with the humorous vitality of his distinctive imagination.

William M. Burgan

THE REFINEMENT OF CONTRAST: MANUSCRIPT REVISION IN *EDWIN DROOD*

ASSESSMENTS OF Dickens' last, unfinished novel have varied widely, but most readers agree on at least one point—the superlative quality of its prose. As Edmund Wilson remarks, "In this new novel . . . Dickens has found a new intensity. The descriptions of Cloisterham are among the best written in all his fiction: they have a nervous concentration and economy (nervous in the old-fashioned sense) that produce a rather different effect from anything one remembers in the work of his previous phases. We are far from the prodigal improvisation of the poetical early Dickens: here every descriptive phrase is loaded with implication." [1] My aim in this paper is to consider this peculiar excellence in the light of changes that Dickens made in the manuscript of the novel, which is now housed with other items in the Forster collection at the Victoria and Albert Museum. [2]

Restraint is perhaps the first quality to strike the reader who comes to the descriptions in *Drood* with a sense of Dickens' style derived from either his rambling early works or the social fables of his later years. There is in *Drood* a quietness, a dependence on the evocative force of literal language, a discretion even in the use of figurative language that suggest a peculiar reserve on the part of a writer whose descriptive flair is customarily a matter of exuberant display. In turning to the manuscripts for insight into the changed goals of Dickens' style in his last work, one may feel some surprise in discovering how naturally he adapted himself to the requirements of this unwonted stylistic austerity, how little the restraint of *Drood* appears to have derived from excision. As in the revising of works very different in their linguistic texture, Dickens proves to be primarily engaged in augmenting rather than curbing his initial ideas. His frequent refinement of images characteristically takes the form of additions that enrich them, often through analyzing them into distinct, symmetrically poised components. Hence the

[167

importance of those contrasts which Margaret Cardwell, editor of the Clarendon edition of the novel, cites as one principal focus of revision in *Drood*.[3]

In the manuscript excerpts quoted in this paper, I have omitted to record only two categories of revision: first, immediate repetitions of a deleted phrase, which add nothing new; and second, altered punctuation. Changes of punctuation were so numerous in the processing of the manuscript for publication that the effort to register all of them is distracting and—when one is presenting relatively few cases—potentially misleading.[4] In general, I have stylized Dickens' revisions as follows. Material from the base line of the manuscript is printed in Roman. Italics indicate material added in manuscript or in the proofs of the monthly numbers.[5] Deleted words appear inside angle brackets, with question marks used to signify doubtful readings. When I have been quite unable to read a deleted passage, I have placed square brackets around an italicized estimate of the number of canceled words. But since I have tried to keep speculation to a minimum, readers with a particular interest in one or another of these hard cases should not assume that their own examination of the manuscript would prove equally fruitless.

A simple example will help to clarify this method of transcription. In the statement that Neville and Helena Landless passed below Crisparkle, "along the margin of the river, in which the town fires and lights already shone, making the landscape bleaker," the emended clause would be transcribed as follows: "in which the town fires and lights already shone, making the landscape ⟨bleak and ?dismal? *by [one word] by strong contrast*⟩ *bleaker*." [6] Regrettably, such transcriptions are hard to follow. The point of giving them this form is to furnish as much evidence as possible about the process of thought that led to the final version. In the present instance, for example, Dickens initially notes the effect of light in intensifying the prevailing gloom. Moving to block the inference that the reflections are major sources of bleakness in themselves (or that he is writing carelessly), he then replaces the second adjective with the explanatory phrase about contrast. But such explicitness apparently strikes him as heavy-handed, so he reverts to "making the landscape bleak." Last of all, in working on the proofs of the monthly number, he realizes that the comparative, "bleaker," will eliminate ambiguity without cost to elegance.

I should like now to examine some revisions that work a deeper change in the Cloisterham settings. The manuscripts show Dickens using contrast for a variety of purposes, several of which may converge in a single revision. It may therefore be useful to list here the aims and techniques with which this paper is chiefly concerned. These are: 1) the augmenting of symbolism; 2) the enhancement of stylistic tension through paradox and unconventional figurative language; 3) the control of tone; 4) the elaboration of simple images through analysis into discrete components, or through reinforcement by other, parallel images; 5) the isolation of contrasting aspects in closely similar phenomena.

Significant contrasts in *Drood* sometimes turn on the choice of a single adjective. For example, when the diabolical Jasper returns to his duties as choirmaster at the Cathedral, after the opium trance that opens the novel, Dickens notes that "the choir are getting on their *sullied* white robes, in a hurry" (I, 2; i, 3). As the reader soon learns, this hurry reflects the indiscipline of the Cathedral as a functioning institution, and "sullied" reinforces that impression.[7] At the same time, however, the soiled robes refer symbolically to Jasper's deeply false position, and so initiate a counterpoint between institutional sloth and individual depravity that attends the portrayal of his public self throughout the novel. The irony of this connection becomes explicit in one of the few excisions that seem regrettable (it was clearly made in the interests of bringing the length of the monthly number down to the specified limit),[8] a short passage deleted from the end of the eloquent account of Jasper's music as a destructive sea.

⟨Among the ⟨white robes⟩ *dirty linen* that ⟨were⟩ *was* already being ⟨plucked⟩ unbuttoned behind with all the expedition compatible with ⟨?languid? [*one word*]⟩ *a feint of following Mr. Tope* ⟨*in procession round the corner*⟩ *and his mace in* [*one word*] *procession round the corner* was the robe of Mr. Jasper. He threw it to a boy ⟨and [*six words*]⟩ ⟨*who sadly* [*three words*] *wanted "getting up" by some laundress*⟩ *and he and Mr. Grewgious walked out* of the Cathedral, talking as they went.⟩ (⟨III⟩, 8; ix, 74, n. 1)

In his last description of the Cathedral, Dickens works a curiously poignant change on this contrast between Jasper and the choir, as he describes the gradual filling of the Cathedral for early service (the whole of this interior is a travesty of the immediately preceding vision of the empty church, transformed by a summer morning into an emblem of "the Resurrection and the Life"):

Come a very ⟨small⟩ *small and straggling* congregation *indeed:* chiefly from Minor Canon Corner and the Precincts. Come Mr. Crisparkle, fresh and bright, and his ministering brethren, [*two words*] not quite so fresh and bright. Come the choir in a hurry (always in a hurry, and struggling into their *night*-gowns at the last moment *like children shirking bed*), and comes John Jasper ⟨at their head⟩ *leading their line.* (VI, 20; xxiii, 215)

The same paragraph at the close of the first chapter that contains the image of sullied white robes also illustrates a principal source of the ominous atmosphere of the Cloisterham settings, the sense of latent as opposed to overt menace. As the service begins, "the intoned words, 'WHEN THE WICKED MAN—' rise among groins of arches and beams of ⟨roof⟩ [*one word*] *roof* awakening ⟨massive⟩ *muttered* thunder⟨s⟩" (I, 2; i, 4). In substituting "muttered" for "massive," Dickens replaces an obvious effect with a subtly divided one, setting an emotional key from which he' deviates seldom and with correspondingly striking impact. Only at rare, climactic moments does his imagery partake of a violence matching Jasper's intent, as in the storm on the night of the murder. More often, a linguistic and pictorial subtlety verging on oxymoron conveys such uneasiness as that which marks the first description of the Cathedral Close:

> ⟨The day is waning⟩ Not only is the day waning, but the year ⟨?too?⟩. The *low* sun is ⟨fiery [*one word*] flaming⟩ *fiery* and yet cold behind the ⟨monastery⟩ [*one word*] *monastery* ruin, and the Virginia creeper on the Cathedral wall has [*one word*] showered half its deep-red leaves down on the pavement. ⟨It has⟩ *There has been* rain⟨ed⟩ this afternoon, and a wintry shudder ⟨comes and goes [*three words*]⟩ *goes* [*three words*] *among* the little pools on the cracked uneven flagstones and through the *giant* elm trees as they ⟨[*one word*]⟩ shed tears weep⟩ *shed* [*one word*] *a gust of tears.* Their fallen leaves lie strewn *thickly* ⟨?round?⟩ about⟨,⟩. ⟨and⟩ *Some* [*one word*] *of these leaves, in* a timid *rush,* ⟨flight of them try to take⟩ *seek* sanctuary within the low arched ⟨door⟩ Cathedral door. (I, 3; ii, 4)

"Fiery and yet cold" and "a timid rush" pair antithetical qualities as unexpectedly as "muttered thunder," [9] while "a gust of tears" reflects the frequent tendency of style in *Drood* to assimilate figurative language into the texture of literal representation. In this case, such assimilation results from the curious expedient of placing an actual element of the scene—the gust that shakes the trees—in a metaphorical relationship to the metaphor of weeping. And all these details—sun, scattered raindrops and dead leaves—embody a salient feature of the Cloisterham descriptions, a blend of natural beauty with elegiac sadness and nameless apprehension.

The same complex feeling attends a second glimpse of the close, following on a reference to Jasper's evident disorientation at the service (the effect of his stay in London) as reported by Mr. Tope to Canon Crisparkle and the Dean:

> They all three look towards an old stone gatehouse crossing the Close, with an arched thoroughfare *passing* beneath it.

Through its latticed window, a fire shines out upon the *fast* darkening scene, involving in shadow the pendent masses of ivy and creeper covering ⟨its front⟩ the building's front. *As* ⟨T⟩ the deep [*one word*] *Cathedral* bell ⟨?struck?⟩ strikes the hour, a ripple of wind goes through these *at their distance,* ⟨as if it were⟩ *like* a ripple of the solemn sound that hums ⟨in⟩ *through tomb and* tower, ⟨and turret, and ?defa?⟩ *broken* niche and [*one word*] defaced statue, *in the pile* close at hand. (I, 4; ii, 5)

In this first view of Jasper's gatehouse, Dickens begins to establish its place in the symbolic patterning of light and darkness that serves as one of the main structural principles of the novel. Closely studied manipulation of light characterizes all of Dickens' mature fiction, but in *Drood* he devotes more care than ever before to suggesting the swift passage of time in the daily cycle from sunrise to sunset, and the sinister character of the fire emblematic of "the Wicked Man." So the first, premonitory image of the gatehouse shows Jasper's window shining in the darkness with which Dickens will increasingly identify him; and the emended "fast-darkening" deftly heightens the impression of oncoming night.

It is typical of the play of contrast in such descriptions that the shift from "tower and turret" to "tomb and tower" should introduce an antithesis of high and low at the same time that it enhances sonority and emotional suggestion. Dickens' revisions in all his works reveal intense concern for vividly realized spatial relationships. Even his cleanest manuscript pages often bear deletions and insertions in behalf of this particular aspect of sensory awareness, and the present instance points to the unusual emphasis which the special features of the Rochester setting encouraged him to lay on the vertical axis of his pictorial scheme. In *Drood,* there is a frequent sweeping of the narrator's eye from river to hilltop, crypt to tower. Similarly, on the horizontal axis, the ripple of wind and hum of the bell unify a scene clearly delimited by the gatehouse and the Cathedral, which Dickens places in antithetical relationship to each other by inserting "at their distance" to qualify the masses of ivy on the gatehouse, and "in the pile" to fix the location of the niches and statues near the three characters whose point of view determines the perspective of the whole vignette. More often than not, touches of this kind occur—as here—in the context of prose so rich in poetic overtones that the translation of spatial awareness into syntactical symmetry passes unnoticed. But it is upon such care in disposing firm contours that more fluid agents of atmosphere, like the wind and the sound of the bell, depend for their full effect.

The phrase, "broken niche and defaced statue," illustrates a further aspect of that binary cast of mind for which the word "contrast" often seems too restrictive. Niche and statue are elements of a single image bifurcated in the interests of sharper visualization and affective redundancy, so that the idea of "ruin" becomes at once more concrete and more emotionally emphatic. One sees the same principle at work in a later scene—an ominous view of the ruins and the river at twilight, including a detail originally recorded simply as "the restlessness of the sea gulls," then analyzed into more concrete elements, "the restless-⟨ness⟩ *dipping and flapping* of the ⟨sea⟩ *noisy* gulls" (III, 4; x, 80). The change calls attention to the fact that redundancies of this type are never mere repetitions.. The pleasing assonance of "dipping and flapping" accompanies an exact discrimination of the two elements of motion comprising the birds' flight.

The pursuit of subtle sensory discriminations is nowhere more telling than in the revisions of Jasper's "night with Durdles," a moonlight exploration of the Cathedral crypt and tower, the importance of which appears clearly in Dickens' plan for the monthly number: "Lay the ground for the manner of the Murder, to come out at last. . . . Night picture of the Cathedral." [10] As Jasper and Durdles descend into the crypt, the narrator remarks: "The lantern is not ⟨?needed?⟩ wanted, for the moonlight strikes in at the groined windows, ⟨[*one word*]⟩ *bare* of glass⟨.⟩, *the broken* ⟨[*one word*] *framing*⟩ *frames for which cast*⟨s⟩ *patterns on the ground.* ⟨?and with?⟩ The heavy pillars which support the roof ⟨?throw?⟩ *engender* masses of black shade ⟨upon the ground⟩, but between them there are lanes of light" (III, 23; xii, 106). In its initial form, this passage portrays a single visual contrast: the pillars block the light coming through the windows, and so cast shadows on the ground. Dickens then doubles the image. By inserting the detail of the broken frames, he refines his basic pictorial dualism of light and dark into a juxtaposition of hard-edged, linear silhouettes against broad, alternating masses of light and shade, and the darkness "engendered" by the pillars becomes a form of energy coeval with light.

Jasper's preference for darkness is a given of the whole episode. To pass the time before setting out, he "withdraws . . . to his piano. There, *with no light but that of the fire,* he sits chanting *choir-music* in a low and beautiful voice, for ⟨some time ?some? three two⟩ *two or three* hours; in short, until it has been for some time dark, and the moon is about to rise" (III, 21; xii, 103). And the lamplight in his room during his absence has an ominous color: *"One might fancy that* ⟨T⟩the tide of life ⟨[*four words*]⟩ *was* stemmed by Mr. Jasper's own Gate House. ⟨Its⟩ *The* murmur *of the tide* is heard beyond; but no wave passes the archway, over which his lamp burns ⟨behind⟩ red behind his curtain, as if the building were a [*one word*] Lighthouse" (III, 23; xii, 105–6).

Durdles' lantern, which is not "wanted" in the moonlit crypt, proves useful as the two men climb the tower staircase: "Durdles has lighted his lantern, by drawing from the ⟨[*one word*] cold wall *a speck*⟩

cold hard wall a spark of that mysterious fire which lurks in everything, and, guided by this speck, they clamber up among the cobwebs and the dust" (III, 25; xii, 107–8). The contrast between inert matter and mysterious fire strikes Dickens first, perhaps because of its metaphorical affinity with Jasper's mesmerism. He then sharpens his descriptive focus by characterizing the fire as "a speck." But finally, employing his favorite device of redundancy-through-close-discrimination, he substitutes the more literal and evocative "spark," and moves "speck" to a context in which its use to identify a larger and brighter light enables him to suggest the scale of the dark tower. The same craftsmanlike concern for accuracy and nuance marks the climax of this "night picture":

> Their way lies ⟨among⟩ *through* strange places. Twice or thrice they emerge into level *low*-arched galleries, whence they can look down into the moonlit nave; and where Durdles, waving his lantern, shows the dim angels' heads upon the corbels of the roof, seeming to watch their progress. Anon, they turn into narrower and steeper ⟨stairs⟩ staircases, [*one word*] and the night air begins to blow upon them, and the [*one word*] chirp of some startled jackdaw or frightened rook precedes the ⟨violent⟩ *heavy* beating of wings ⟨and⟩ *in a confined space, and the* beating down of dust *and straws* upon ⟨them. At lengths⟩ their heads. At last, leaving their light behind a stair—for it blows fresh up here—[*one word*] *they* look down on Cloisterham, fair to see in the moonlight: its ⟨ruins down below⟩ *ruined* habitations and sanctuaries of the dead, ⟨down below;⟩ *at the tower's base:* its *moss-softened* red-tiled roofs and red-brick houses of the living, clustered beyond: its river winding ⟨?down?⟩ down [*two words*] from the mist on the horizon, as though that were its source, and [*two words*] already ⟨*lashing and*⟩ heaving ⟨and ?foaming?⟩ with ⟨the⟩ *a restless* knowledge of its approach towards the sea. (III, 25; xii, 108)

The development of the image of the birds shows especially well how sensory discrimination and contrast can at once heighten the impact of particular narrative moments and bind these firmly into a logically articulated structure. Dickens first writes, "the violent beating of wings and beating down of dust upon them." Howard Duffield has suggested that Jasper, as a "Thug" devoted to the Hindu goddess of destruction, would have regarded the rooks' cry, heard within sight of the river, as an omen favorable to the murder.[11] Duffield's conjecture is both persuasive and hard to establish firmly. What cannot be doubted is Dickens' aim to give the rooks a sinister suggestiveness throughout the story. It therefore comes as no surprise that he should at first have characterized the beating of their wings as "violent." But we have al-

ready noticed that for the most part Dickens dwells upon the potentiality rather than the actuality of violence in the settings of *Drood,* and the
recasting of this image involves a simultaneous restraint and intensifying of emotional force. While "heavy" is intrinsically a less threatening
word than "violent," the added notation of the close quarters in which
climbers and birds confront each other brings into the narrative a sen-
sation quite absent from the earlier version—the visceral revulsion that
most people feel on having to share "a confined space" with frightened
birds. While no longer so plainly prophetic of the murder, the incident
becomes a more gripping objective correlative for the impulse behind
this quest.

The effect of the spatial phrase on our response to the birds is so
vivid that we may overlook the preparation it affords, through contrast,
for the release from confinement that immediately follows. Revulsion
yields to relief and sudden pleasure in the vista of town, river, and
countryside. On several occasions, Dickens associates such tranquil pan-
oramas with violent crime, and it is interesting to compare the present
instance with the aerial view of London and its environs on a moonlit
summer night which immediately precedes Mr. Tulkinghorn's murder
in Chapter xlviii of *Bleak House.* In keeping with the usual stance of the
omniscient narrator in that novel, the description unfolds in clearly
defined units, marked by repetitions and close variants of the phrase,
"a still night," while the Thames, whose course from inland country
through the city to the sea unites the scene pictorially, furnishes a
means of setting the dark menace of London against the peace of the
natural world. In the view from the tower, the rhetorical frame is much
less explicit; there is little repetition (the relative infrequency of this
device in its more pronounced forms sets *Drood* apart from all the other
omniscient narratives of Dickens' later years) and the placing of the
town in the natural landscape is remarkable for integration of the two
rather than for contrast between them. This point is especially worth
stressing in the present examination of revisions that constantly direct
our attention to the symmetrical logic underlying Dickens' most deli-
cately nuanced prose. For the impression of subtlety in *Drood* is not an
illusion: if anything, the reverse is true, and there is some danger of
forgetting, as we note one instance of conscious balancing after another, the rhythmic variety that filters out the heavy accent of descriptive oratory. The actual impression is one of dreamlike continuity and
stillness. Yet the means employed to secure it retain the dual character
of all the other descriptions and resolve themselves under analysis into
a system of contrasts within contrasts.

Describing the view of Cloisterham from the tower, Dickens first
writes of "its ruins down below." Checking himself in the course of
writing the sentence, he chooses instead the familiar, dual pattern: "its

ruined habitations and sanctuaries of the dead down below," afterward replacing the last phrase with the more precise spatial orientation, "at the tower's base." For the moment, at least, the Cathedral belongs wholly to the dead, while the houses of the living are touched with the innocence of sleep.[12] The inserted adjective, "moss-softened," epitomizes the poetic control with which Dickens builds his settings in *Drood*. The note of color and softness, the sheer sound of the word, convey the Cloisterham values of "good age" and natural life, the peace Jasper seeks to destroy. Such prose defeats all efforts to separate sensory concreteness from thematic implication. Just as the ghostly atmosphere of the crypt depends for its effect on the precision with which Dickens plays off sharp silhouette against shadowy mass, so the sense of threatened peace in the sleeping town depends on the discrimination of colors that are barely discernible in moonlight—the dark green of the moss, the cool red of roof-tiles and bricks.

At the conclusion of the view from the tower, the same preference for imagery of unrest over that of turmoil that informs the change from "violent" to "heavy" leads Dickens to delete the participle, "lashing," from the phrase "lashing and heaving," and to characterize the river's foreknowledge of its destiny by the inserted adjective "restless." But when, rarely, violence does erupt in the Cloisterham setting, he shows a corresponding eagerness to heighten its impact, and he does so in part by clarifying the spatial logic of his imagery. In the storm on the night of Drood's disappearance,

> the darkness is augmented and confused, by flying dust *from the earth,* [*two words*] dry twigs from the trees, *and* ⟨*fragments from the rooks' nests up in the tower*⟩ great ragged fragments from the rooks' nests up in the tower. ⟨The trees themselves[*two words*] and creak⟩ *The trees themselves so toss and creak,* as this tangible part of the darkness madly whirls about, that they seem in peril of being torn out of the earth. (IV, 16; xiv, 130)

What begins as a brief listing of windblown debris turns into a firm, three-part progression from earth to sky, with the symbolism of rook and tower assuming its appropriate place at the climax of the series. As in "Tempest," the most heavily revised chapter in *David Copperfield*, Dickens here takes pains to give a lucid structure to the representation of chaos.

We have noticed by now a number of different sources of the peculiar quality of the settings in *Drood*. Through almost all, there runs a complex dialectic between two sorts of grouping, the balance of opposites and of closely similar phenomena. Sometimes the opposites are aspects of a single thing or event, as in "muttered thunder" and the sun that is "fiery and yet cold," sometimes they are phases of a sequence, as when the confinement of the tower suddenly opens on a panorama of Cathedral, town, and river, bounded only by the horizon. Such contrasts of course intensify perception of the elements contrasted. But the peculiar vividness of the Cloisterham setting owes much to the discrimination of phenomena that resemble each other as closely as the two kinds of shadow in the crypt or the three kinds of "tangible darkness" whirled about in the storm. In short, Dickens makes us see the world of this novel by asking us to imagine sights that solicit attention as urgently as a spark in a pitch-black stairwell, and also by asking us to register differences of light and texture so subtle that we normally either take them in without noticing or must strain our eyes to see them. As Edwin Drood and Rosa stroll by the river on the evening of their last meeting, the sadness and ominousness of the occasion find embodiment in a singularly precise rendering of the visual obscurity of twilight: "The ⟨water moaned and⟩ *moaning water* cast its ⟨dripping⟩ seaweed ⟨?*sadly dripping*? at their feet and⟩ *duskily at their feet when* they turned to leave its margin; and the rooks hovered ⟨above *around*⟩ *above* them ⟨[*one word*] restless splas⟩ with ⟨[*one word*] cries⟩ hoarse cries, ⟨[*one word*] as a ?confusion? of⟩ *darker* splashes in the darkening air" (IV, 7; xiii, 119). After Drood's disappearance, as the search parties carry their work into the night, the river is "[*one word*] *specked* with lanterns, and lurid with fires" (IV, 20; xv, 136). And Rosa, fleeing from Jasper, looks out from her train window over London, where "⟨there⟩ *down below* ⟨*there*⟩ lay the gritty streets with their yet un-needed lamps ⟨lighted⟩ *aglow*, on a hot *light* summer night" (V, 20; xx, 176).

The most memorable exercise of sensory acuteness in *Drood* is Crisparkle's effort to locate the source of his feeling that there is something amiss at Cloisterham Weir, something which he ultimately identifies as Drood's gold watch, caught in the timbers at one corner of the falls. This discovery tends to confirm the suspicion that Drood's disappearance points to murder rather than to a mere impulsive departure from Cloisterham. Since Dickens stresses the oddity of the intuition that something in the place requires investigation, and since Crisparkle arrives on the scene without conscious intention, after a meeting with Jasper, it seems likely that Jasper has mesmerized him, employing posthypnotic suggestion to lead to the discovery of a planted clue. This hypothesis would account for the extraordinary pains Dickens takes with the manuscript draft of the whole episode. It may also account for the fact that it was this portion of the narrative that he chose to expand when he found that he had fallen short of the requisite length of his monthly number by some twenty lines.[13] To help make good this deficiency, he inserted three substantial passages that do not appear in the manuscript at all. To the information that Crisparkle often walked to the Weir, yet was so preoccupied that he only became conscious of his whereabouts when he heard the sound of falling water, Dickens adds this glimpse of puzzled self-scrutiny—

> *"How did I come here!" was his first thought, as he stopped.*
> *"Why did I come here!" was his second.*
> *Then, he stood intently listening to the water. A familiar passage in his reading, about airy tongues that syllable men's names, rose so unbidden to his ear, that he put it from him with his hand, as if it were tangible.* (xvi, 142)

There follows a paragraph from the manuscript in which the narrator comments that no search had been made for the body at this point in the river, since it was two miles upstream from the place where Drood and Landless had gone to watch the storm. The scene is superficially unremarkable: "The water came over the Weir, with its usual sound on a cold starlight night, and little could be seen of it; yet Mr. Crisparkle had a strange idea that something unusual hung about the place." Here Dickens makes his second substantial insertion: *"He reasoned with himself: What was it? Where was it? Put it to the proof. Which sense did it address? No sense reported anything unusual there. He listened again, and his sense of hearing again checked the water coming over the Weir, with its usual sound on a cold starlight night"* (xvi, 142). Resolving to pursue his search in the morning, Crisparkle goes home for a night during which the Weir runs through his sleep. When he returns the next day, something catches his eye. The third insertion occurs at this point, comprising all but the last sentence of the following paragraph:

> *He turned his back upon the Weir, and looked far away at the sky, and at the earth, and then looked again at that one spot. It caught his sight again immediately, and he concentrated his vision upon it. He could not lose it now, though it was but such a speck in the landscape. It fascinated his sight. His hands began plucking off his coat.* For it struck him that at that spot—a corner of the Weir—something glistened, which did not move and come over with the glistening water-drops, but remained stationary. (xvi, 143)

The speck is, of course, Drood's gold watch.

Although the need to "lay the ground" for later disclosures and the need to pad an insufficient text may explain the genesis of this highly circumstantial account, they give little idea of its significance. For this is the scene in which Crisparkle acts out the meaning of his name, serving as the medium of that acuteness which realizes light and annihilates obscurity and deception. It does not matter that he is quite possibly being deceived, manipulated, at this moment in the story.

What matters is the clarity of his seeing, hearing, and feeling. And his patient interrogation of his senses has a special relevance to the uniqueness of descriptive style in *Drood*. Dickens always writes with singular alertness to sensory experience. But in no other novel does he concentrate so intently on fine discriminations, straining "those hawk's eyes of his" (to use his own epithet for Crisparkle) to capture subtle shades of difference-in-similarity, and so involving his readers in strenuous efforts of vicarious perception.

The reward for such efforts is a sense of fine-grained distinctness rather different in the quality of its appeal from the startling solidity and aggressively physical presence of the material world in the other novels. Leaving aside the kinesthetic effects that have led various directors and literary critics to stress Dickens' anticipation of the movies—effects abundantly present in the scenes we have examined—the prose of *Drood* is also reminiscent of certain Renaissance paintings and of that school of modern still photography which aims at recording natural beauty with more than natural resolution of detail, so that edges and textures barely noticed in everyday perception have an air of heightened and yet literal actuality. Such analogies are at best merely suggestive and bear on the value of the *Drood* settings in relation to the norm of Dickens' descriptive art rather than on some absolute, intrinsic exactness and copiousness of representation. The common factor in the analogy is a *sense* of clarity and detail: like all writers, Dickens must achieve his ends with an economy of specification that is severe by comparison with the visual record of a snapshot, let alone the landscapes of Giovanni Bellini or Ansel Adams. But he resembles these artists in conceiving of light as his basic "metaphor of value," and in articulating that metaphor through the refinement of contrast.[14]

I have reserved for final consideration a passage which illustrates especially well the interaction of the various stylistic traits that give *Drood* its peculiar subtlety and force. Because the effort to follow Dickens' revisions is sure to impair the rhythm of this eloquent set piece, I shall first quote it as it appears in the printed text. The occasion is the visit of Rosa's guardian, Mr. Grewgious, to the Cathedral where Jasper is leading the choir in the evening service.

> So, [Mr. Grewgious] descended the stair again, and, crossing the Close, paused at the great western folding-door of the Cathedral, which stood open on the fine and bright, though short-lived, afternoon, for the airing of the place.
>
> "Dear me," said Mr. Grewgious, peering in, "it's like looking down the throat of Old Time."
>
> Old Time heaved a mouldy sigh from tomb and arch and vault; and gloomy shadows began to deepen in corners; and

damps began to rise from green patches of stone; and jewels, cast upon the pavement of the nave from stained glass by the declining sun, began to perish. Within the grill-gate of the chancel, up the steps surmounted loomingly by the fast darkening organ, white robes could be dimly seen, and one feeble voice, rising and falling in a cracked monotonous mutter, could at intervals be faintly heard. In the free outer air, the river, the green pastures, and the brown arable lands, the teeming hills and dales, were reddened by the sunset: while the distant little windows in windmills and farm homesteads, shone, patches of bright beaten gold. In the Cathedral, all became grey, murky, and sepulchral, and the cracked monotonous mutter went on like a dying voice, until the organ and the choir burst forth, and drowned it in a sea of music. Then, the sea fell, and the dying voice made another feeble effort, and then the sea rose high, and beat its life out, and lashed the roof, and surged among the arches, and pierced the heights of the great tower; and then the sea was dry, and all was still.

Mr. Grewgious had by that time walked to the chancel-steps, where he met the living waters coming out. (ix, 73–74)

In process of revision, the passage looks like this:

⟨He⟩ *So, he* descended the stair again, and, crossing the Close, [*one word*] *paused* at the great *Western* ⟨door⟩ folding-door of the Cathedral, which stood open on the fine *and* bright, *though short-lived,* afternoon, for the airing of the place.

"Dear me," said Mr. Grewgious, peering in, "it's like looking down the throat of Old Time."

Old Time heaved a mouldy sigh from tomb and arch and vault; and gloomy shadows began to deepen in corners; and damps *began* to rise from green patches [*one word*] of stone; and jewels, ⟨reflected on⟩ *cast upon* the pavement of the nave from stained glass by the declining sun, began to ⟨fade⟩ *perish.* ⟨Afar off through⟩ *Within*⟨;⟩ the grill-gate of the chancel, up the steps ⟨?surmounted?⟩ *surmounted* [*one word*] *loomingly* by the ⟨organ⟩ *fast* darkening organ, white robes could be ⟨ seen [*six words*]⟩ *dimly seen, and one feeble voice,* rising and falling ⟨?as if? [*three words*]⟩ in a cracked monotonous [*one word*] mutter⟨ing⟩ could [*two words*] at intervals be faintly heard. ⟨Without *Outside*⟩ *In the free outer air,* the river, the green pastures *and* the *brown* arable lands, the *teeming* hills and dales, *were reddened by the sunset: while the distant little windows in windmills* and farm ⟨buildings⟩ *homesteads,* ⟨were touched a [*three words*]⟩ shone, ⟨?bright burnished?⟩ *patches* ⟨?of bright burnished gold?⟩ *of bright* [*one word*] *beaten gold.* ⟨Inside, all was *Inside,*⟩ *In the Cathedral, all became* grey, ⟨dusky⟩ *murky,* and sepulchral, and the

cracked monotonous mutter went on like a dying voice, until the
[*one word*] *organ and the* choir burst forth, and drowned it in a
sea of music. Then, the sea fell, ⟨as once it did when rebuked⟩
and the dying voice made another ⟨feeble struggle [*three words*]⟩
feeble effort ⟨for it⟩, and then the sea rose *high,* and beat its life
out, and ⟨rose to⟩ *lashed* the roof, and ⟨rolled⟩ *surged* among
the arches, [*two words*] *and pierced the* [*three words*] *heights of the
great tower;* and then ⟨all was still and silent; lo⟩ the sea was dry,
and all was still ⟨and silent⟩.
    Mr. Grewgious had by that time walked to the chancel-steps,
where he met the living waters coming out. (⟨III⟩, 8; iv, 73–74)

    Two of the manuscript insertions, "though short-lived," and "fast
darkening," intensify the sense of the swift onset of night, while the
stress on mortality becomes more explicit as "fade," in the initial account of the "jewels cast upon the pavement of the nave by the declining sun," is replaced by "perish." The latter verb is the more striking
because, whereas "fade" represents a modulation from metaphor back
to literal reality, "perish" mixes the metaphor of the jewels with an antithetical image of what is organic and mortal. The reflected light, the
literal reality, can be likened either to jewels or to perishing life; but to
place the two metaphors in direct relationship to each other is to create
a more extreme case of the same linguistic tension that distinguishes
"muttered thunder," and a doubling-back of figurative language upon
itself similar to "shed a gust of tears."
    Of particular interest in the present study is the insight this pas-
sage affords into the way Dickens uses contrast in organizing a paragraph. He at first locates the scene within the chancel as "Afar off," assuming the point of view of Mr. Grewgious as he enters the nave
through the western door, and strains to make out the white robes of
the choir, which he can only see "through the grill-gate." The idea of a
strongly marked contrast with the natural world beyond the Cathedral
then occurring to Dickens, he begins the sentence about the out-of-
doors, "Without," and substitutes "Within" for "Afar off." But as he
proceeds to move back into the Cathedral at the climax of the scene,
with the annihilation of the priest's voice by organ and choir, he
prefers to open the formal, rhetorically pointed contrast with the image
of natural beauty, in order to be able to close it with the second view of
the Cathedral interior. So he substitutes "Outside," for "Without," and
opens the final sentence with "Inside." Last of all, echoing an image introduced earlier in the phrase, "for the airing of the place," he substitutes "In the free outer air" for "Outside," and "In the Cathedral" for
"Inside."
    The sentence containing the sudden glimpse of the countryside il-
lustrates quite clearly the way in which Dickens analyzes a general im-

Page and chapter references in the text are to *The New Oxford Illustrated Dickens* (London: Oxford University Press, 1948–58), unless otherwise noted.

ALBERT D. HUTTER: *Reconstructive Autobiography*

1 John Forster, *The Life of Charles Dickens*, 2 vols. (London: J. M. Dent, 1966); Edmund Wilson, "The Two Scrooges," in *The Wound and the Bow*, rev. ed. (1952; reprinted., London: Methuen, 1961), pp. 1–93; Jack Lindsay, *Charles Dickens* (London: Andrew Dakers, 1950); Steven Marcus, "Who is Fagin?" in *Dickens: From Pickwick to Dombey* (New York: Simon & Schuster, 1968), pp. 358–78. It should be noted that Marcus' primary aim is a fresh reading of *Oliver Twist*, not a biographical reappraisal of Dickens. A number of modern critics integrate their own understanding of Charles' reaction to Warren's with their reading of specific texts; see, for example, George H. Ford, "David Copperfield," in *The Dickens Critics* (New York: Cornell University Press, 1961), pp. 349–65; Robert L. Patten, "Autobiography into Autobiography: The Evolution of *David Copperfield*," a forthcoming essay in a volume on *Victorian Autobiography;* Warrington Winters, "Dickens' *Hard Times:* The Lost Childhood," in *Dickens Studies Annual,* 2 (1972), 217–36; Harry Stone, "The

Genesis of a Novel: *Great Expectations*," in *Charles Dickens 1812–1870,* ed. E. W. F. Tomlin (New York: Simon & Schuster, 1969), pp. 110–31; and "The Love Pattern in Dickens' Novels," in *Dickens the Craftsman: Strategies of Presentation,* ed. Robert B. Partlow, Jr. (Carbondale: Southern Illinois University Press, 1970), pp. 1–20. Leonard Manheim's analysis of father-son conflict in Dickens' life and fiction involves a specific reappraisal of Wilson's analysis, which reached "only a part of the truth" ("The Law as 'Father,' " *American Imago* 12 [Spring 1955], 17–23); see also "The Personal History of David Copperfield," *American Imago* 9, no. 1 (April 1952), 21–43, and, most recently, "A Tale of Two Characters: A Study in Multiple Projection," in *Dickens Studies Annual,* 1 (1970), 225–37.
2 *Charles Dickens* (1906; reprinted ed., New York: Schocken, 1965), p. 37.
3 W. Robertson Nicoll, *Dickens's Own Story* (London: Chapman & Hall, 1923), p. 13; Margaret Lane, "Dickens

on the Hearth," in *Dickens 1970,* ed. Michael Slater (New York: Stein & Day, 1970), pp. 153–71; Thomas Wright, *The Life of Charles Dickens* (New York: Scribner's, 1936), p. 43.

[4] *Charles Dickens* (1898; reprinted ed., London and Glasgow: Blackie & Son, 1929), p. 14.

[5] See, for example, Edgar Johnson, *Charles Dickens: His Tragedy and Triumph,* 2 vols. (New York: Simon & Schuster, 1952); K. J. Fielding, *Charles Dickens: A Critical Introduction,* 2d ed. (Boston: Houghton Mifflin, 1964); and Angus Wilson, "Dickens on Children and Childhood," in *Dickens* 1970, ed. Michael Slater (New York: Stein & Day, 1970), pp. 195–227; and *The World of Charles Dickens* (London: Martin Secker and Warburg, 1970), pp. 49–61. Julian Symons (*Charles Dickens* [New York: Roy Publishers, 1951], pp. 7–29) is psychological with a vengeance: he uses Kraepelin's *Manic-Depressive Insanity and Paranoia* to classify Dickens as manic-depressive, but fortunately " 'still in the domain of the normal,' " and bases much of his analysis on the "evidence" of Warren's.

[6] Lindsay's methodological limitations are compounded by his distortions of fact: he makes Elizabeth Dickens far more active than she was even in Charles's account. Lindsay, for example, had Elizabeth pay for Charles's first lodgings whereas Charles believed that it was his father who took the lodgings for him (Lindsay, p. 54; Forster, I, 24).

[7] Johnson, I, 45. In a more recent article on the life of Dickens ("Dickens: The Dark Pilgrimage," in *Charles Dickens 1812–1870,* ed. E. W. F. Tomlin [New York: Simon & Schuster, 1969], pp. 42–63), Johnson writes similarly of Charles's experience at Warren's:

> The experience was crucial for Dickens's entire future course. It is hardly fanciful to say that in the blacking warehouse that unhappy child died, and into his frail body entered the spirit of a man of relentless determination. Deep within him, he resolved that he should never again be so victimized. He would toil, he would fall prey to none of his father's financial imprudence, he would let nothing stand between him and ambition. He would batter his way out of all the gaols that confine the human spirit. (P. 45)

Angus Wilson follows Edmund Wilson in describing "these traumatic months at Warren's" and their importance for the novelist's ability to portray the criminal and the oppressed. Angus Wilson, however, is more critical of Dickens' tone: "The phrases pour out of the autobiographical narrative so that the speaker seems like the most strange of Dickensian characters, a grown human being utterly enclosed in a vivid stylization of his childhood self, cut off from all his own everyday rational, decent 'manliness' by a lament for his own lost innocence—in short, one of the isolated, verbalizing monsters of his own novels. And so in a sense he is—a little mad about what happened to him as a child, unjust, snobbish, and uncaring for others" (*The World of Charles Dickens,* p. 58).

[8] Ian Watt, "Oral Dickens," in *Dickens Studies Annual,* 3 (1974), 174.

[9] *Great Expectations* (London: Oxford University Press, 1953), p. 50. For a full description of the relationship between love and feeding in *Great Expectations,* see Barbara Hardy, "Food and Ceremony in *Great Expectations," Essays in Criticism* 13, no. 4 (October 1963), 351–63.

[10] Dickens' remark is from a letter describing the sudden death of his brother Alfred ("he . . . has left a widow and five children—you may suppose to whom"). He then goes on

to talk about Elizabeth Dickens: "My mother, who was also left to me when my father died (I never had anything left to me but relations), is in the strangest state of mind from senile decay; and the impossibility of getting her to understand what is the matter, combined with her desire to be got up in sables like a female Hamlet, illumines the dreary scene with a ghastly absurdity that is the chief relief I can find in it. Well! Life is a fight and must be fought out. Not new, but true, and I don't complain of it" (*The Letters of Charles Dickens,* ed. Walter Dexter [Bloomsbury: Nonesuch, 1938], III, 172; to Mrs. Dickinson, 19 August 1860). Here again is the bitterness toward his mother, but with their positions reversed: Charles can now afford to be ironic.

11 See *The Dickens World*, 2d ed. (1942; reprinted., London: Oxford University Press, 1965), pp. 202–3. Such an explicit statement is particularly interesting in a nonpsychoanalytic critic.

12 "Pots" had a clear anal meaning in the nineteenth century, and the term was also slang for a woman, usually a lower-class woman or prostitute. See Eric Partridge, *A Dictionary of Slang and Unconventional English* (London: Routledge and Kegan Paul, 1967). The second meaning allows us to speculate on the relationship between this "soiling" experience and the almost certain (and sudden) sexual education young Charles would have received on entering a new working environment around the beginning of puberty. But any serious reconstruction of Charles' introduction to sexual knowledge is impossible without the more detailed and explicit information which Dickens was unlikely to have made available to anyone, especially Forster.

13 Erik H. Erikson, "The Problem of Ego Identity," *Journal of the American Psychoanalytic Association* 4, no. 1 (1956), 74.

14 *The Letters of Charles Dickens,*

eds. Madeline House, Graham Storey, and Kathleen Tillotson (Oxford: Clarendon, 1965), I, 119; (?) 22 January 1836.

15 See also Dickens' letter to Forster, August 1844 (*Letters,* ed. Dexter, I, 618) and to Evans, 4 July 1849 (*Letters,* ed. Dexter, II, 159). And see Charles Kligerman, "The Dream of Charles Dickens," *Journal of the American Psychoanalytic Association* 18 (October 1970), 783–99.

16 1 November 1838; *Letters,* ed. House, I, 448.

17 See Paul C. Squires, "The Case for Dickens as Viewed by Biology and Psychology," *Journal of Abnormal and Social Psychology* 30 (1936), 468–73. Squires, in turn, relies on the earlier speculation of a 1934 article by H. B. Fantham in *Character and Personality.*

18 *Charles Dickens and His Family: A Sympathetic Study* (Cambridge: W. Heffer & Sons, 1956), p. 138.

19 See Franz Alexander, *Psychosomatic Medicine* (New York: W. W. Norton, 1950), pp. 85–215.

20 Peter Blos, *On Adolescence* (New York: Free Press, 1962), pp. 10–11.

21 There is some confusion over the exact date of the autobiographical fragment: Forster suggests 1847 in one place, several months before Dickens conceived the idea of *David Copperfield* in another (which would put it late in 1848 or early 1849), and several years before writing *Copperfield* in yet another reference. Edgar Johnson, noting these discrepancies, suggests somewhere between September 1845 and May 1846 (Johnson, I, 63 n.).

22 His son's emerging adolescent aggression may have also been an important part of this stimulus. See below.

23 D. W. Winnicott, *Playing and Reality* (New York: Basic Books, 1971), pp. 144–45.

24 *Collected Letters of Samuel Taylor Coleridge,* ed. Earl Leslie Griggs (Oxford: Clarendon, 1956), I, 389; to Thomas Poole, 19 February 1798. In

citing this passage Norman Fruman comments: "It seems curious for the letter to break off so abruptly, without even his usual affectionate compliments and regards. And it is with this pointed sentence. 'Our appetites were *damped* never satisfied—and we had no vegetables,' that the famous series of autobiographical letters comes so unexpectedly to an end, almost as if there was nothing more to be said" (Norman Fruman, *Coleridge, the Damaged Archangel* [New York: George Braziller, 1971], p. 24). Fruman's reading of this period, as of the whole of Coleridge's life, stresses the poet's strongly pathological character. Other biographers, like Walter Jackson Bate (*Coleridge* [New York: Macmillan, 1968]), portray Coleridge's childhood in the mildest of terms and focus instead on his success at Christ's, his closeness to school friends and relations and acquaintances in London. However, Bate tends to oversimplify motivation and to ignore modern psychological understanding. He claims that in Coleridge, for example, especially in dealing with others, "there was comparatively little of self. Above all there was nothing personally aggressive or competitive" (pp. 6–7). Lawrence Hanson (*The Life of S. T. Coleridge: The Early Years* [London: George Allen & Unwin, 1938], p. 17) strives for a more balanced approach.

> Coleridge, at a later date and in his best conventional manner, bewails the fate of his "weeping childhood, torn By early sorrow from my native seat." But it is difficult to believe that this "depressed, moping, friendless, poor orphan, half starved" represents more than a phase through which most of the boys had to pass. The conditions at the school must indeed have seemed grim to a newcomer: the brutality of some monitors, the fear-

someness of the punishments, the inadequacy of the food, were alone sufficient to chill the stoutest heart. But they were not the whole of school life, they did not even form the major part of it. . . . He possessed, even at that age, a highly developed capacity for bemoaning the loss of that which he had never enjoyed; and if he mistook a love of nature for a longing for home and shed some tears, it is not surprising.

What *is* surprising, however, is the suffering of the adult Coleridge, and Fruman argues persuasively for seeing the separation and loss of childhood in the adult's nightmares, anxieties, and dependencies.

25 *The Notebooks of Samuel Taylor Coleridge*, ed. Kathleen Coburn (London: Routledge and Kegan Paul, 1957), I, 1681 [references are to entry rather than page number]. For a full account of the deeply disturbing imagery of Coleridge's dreams and fantasies, see Fruman, pp. 365–412. Fruman notes that while some images may be attributable, as in any dream, to immediate life events, we need to see the child's conflicts in the adult's dreams; nor is it sufficient to explain these images as simply the results of an opium vision. See also Alethea Hayter, *Opium and the Romantic Imagination* (Berkeley: University of California Press, 1968).

26 Coleridge's record of his dreams, visions, and waking fantasies provides a rich source for substantiating this pattern of oral into anal and connecting it with the child's image of a frightening and dangerous mother, like the "frightful pale woman" who wants to kiss him and whose very breath "had the property of giving a shameful Disease" (*Notebooks*, 1250). Fruman, making a somewhat different argument, connects the dream

in which this woman appears with Coleridge's fantasy of the moon, where people are "exactly like the people of this world in every thing else except indeed that they eat with their Backsides, & stool at their mouths . . . their Breath not very sweet—but they do not kiss much & custom reconciles one to every thing" (Fruman, pp. 376–77). The pale woman of the dream gives way to another dream woman "of gigantic Height" who is changed "into a stool." Presumably Coleridge consciously intends "stool" to mean an article of furniture, but it is even more suggestive as a link between the dream and the anal fantasies, showing the child's perspective of a "gigantic" mother, his fear of the mother and of attachment itself (the kiss, the disease), and finally his fear and despair indicated by the transformation of food to excrement, apples to horse dung.

[27] *Notes Upon a Case of Obsessional Neurosis* (1909), *The Standard Edition of the Complete Psychological Works of Sigmund Freud,* trans. and ed. James Strachey et al. (London: Hogarth Press, 1953–64), X, 205.

WILLIAM J. PALMER: *Dickens and the Eighteenth Century*

[1] Albert Camus, *Lyrical and Critical Essays,* ed. Philip Thody, trans. Ellen Conroy Kennedy (New York: Alfred A. Knopf, 1968), p. 199.

[2] Cf. T. A. Jackson, *Charles Dickens: The Progress of a Radical* (London: Lawrence and Wishart, 1937); Jack Lindsay, *Charles Dickens: A Biographical and Critical Study* (New York: Philosophical Library, 1950).

[3] Joseph Gold, *Charles Dickens: Radical Moralist* (Minneapolis: University of Minnesota Press, 1972).

[4] Cf. J. Hillis Miller, *Charles Dickens: The World of His Novels* (Cambridge: Harvard University Press, 1958); William J. Palmer, "The Movement of History in *Our Mutual Friend,*" *PMLA* 89 (May 1974).

[5] Cf. Edmund Wilson, *The Wound and the Bow* (Cambridge: Harvard University Press, 1941), p. 40; Lionel Stevenson, "Dickens' Dark Novels 1851–1857," *Sewanee Review* 51 (1943), 398.

[6] Edgar Johnson, *Charles Dickens: His Tragedy and Triumph* (Boston: Little, Brown and Co., 1951).

[7] I have elsewhere discussed the positive images of light/imagination/love in "*Hard Times:* A Dickens Fable of Personal Salvation," *The Dalhousie Review* 52 (1972) and in "the Movement of History in *Our Mutual Friend,*" *PMLA* 89 (May 1974).

[8] Taylor Stoehr, *The Dreamer's Stance* (Ithaca, New York: Cornell University Press, 1965), pp. 98 ff. Robert A. Donovan one year later makes an even stronger assertion of the rightness of the "dark" novel descriptor in *The Shaping Vision: Imagination in the English Novel from Defoe to Dickens* (Ithaca, N.Y.: Cornell University Press, 1966), p. 208.

[9] For a discussion of Jarndyce and Jarndyce as an image of the world of *Bleak House* see *Charles Dickens: The World of His Novels,* p. 196, and for the cure of the absurdity of that world see pp. 206, 217.

[10] Lionel Stevenson, "Dickens's Dark Novels 1851–1857," p. 398.

[11] Miller, "The Geneva School," *The Virginia Quarterly Review* 63 (1967), 465.

[12] *Pickwick Papers,* 71.

[13] Humphry House, *The Dickens World* (London: Oxford University Press, 1941), p. 40.

[14] Louis Cazamian, *Le Roman Social en Angleterre* (Paris: H. Didier, 1934), I, 237.

[15] *Ibid.,* p. 240.

[16] From Shaftesbury's preface to his edition of Whichcote's *Select Sermons* (1698), as quoted by Basil Willey, *The Eighteenth-Century Background* (London: Chatto and Windus, 1946), p. 59.

17 Anthony Ashley Cooper, Third Earl of Shaftesbury, *Characteristics of Men, Manners, Opinions, Times* (London, 1711), I, 115–16.

18 Godwin's *Enquiry Concerning Political Justice*, ed. F. E. L. Priestley (Toronto: University of Toronto Press, 1946), p. 436.

19 Cf. Philip Collins, "Dickens's Reading," *The Dickensian* 60 (1964), 143, and Edgar Johnson, *Charles Dickens: His Tragedy and Triumph*, II, 1130.

20 Quoted by George H. Ford in *Dickens and His Readers* (Princeton, N.J.: Princeton University Press, 1955), p. 151.

21 The most famous statement of Dickens' acquaintance with eighteenth-century literature is the oft-quoted passage in Chapter iv of *David Copperfield*. Reiterations of and additions to this list can be found in Philip Collins, "Dickens's Reading," p. 138; and in Edgar Johnson, *Charles Dickens: His Tragedy and Triumph*, I, 270, and II, 1131. Earle Davis, *The Flint and the Flame* (Columbia: University of Missouri Press, 1963), p. 12, also adds a name which is important for this study, that of William Godwin.

22 Laurence Sterne, "Philanthropy Recommended," *Sterne*, ed. Douglas Grant, (London: Rupert Hart-Davis, 1950), p. 653.

23 Fielding's *Joseph Andrews* (New York: Holt, Rinehart and Winston, 1948), p. 6.

24 Sterne's *Tristram Shandy* (New York: Odyssey Press, 1940), p. 224.

25 Steven Marcus, *Dickens: From Pickwick to Dombey* (New York: Basic Books, 1965), pp. 29–30.

26 Other similarities between Jenkinson and Jingle are their idiosyncratic speech tags (Jenkinson's cosmogony speech, Jingle's fragmented sentences) and their facility at assuming false identities (Jenkinson's elaborate theatrical makeup, Jingle's use of aliases). They are both facile at confusing meaning both linguistically and metaphorically.

27 Joyce Cary, *The Horse's Mouth* (New York: Harper and Row, 1958), p. 4.

28 Smollett's *Roderick Random* (New York: New American Library, 1964), p. 95.

29 Godwin's *Caleb Williams* (New York: Holt, Rinehart and Winston, 1960), pp. 370–71.

ROBERT M. MCCARRON: Folly and Wisdom

1 Jack Lindsay, *Charles Dickens: A Biographical and Critical Study* (London: Dakers, 1950); J. Hillis Miller, *Charles Dickens: The World of his Novels* (Cambridge: Harvard University Press, 1958); J. C. Reid, *The Hidden World of Charles Dickens* (Auckland: University of Auckland Press, 1962); Jerome Meckier, "Dickens and King Lear: A Myth for Victorian England," *South Atlantic Quarterly* 71 (1972), 75–90. See also Leonard Manheim, "Dickens' Fools and Madmen," *Dickens Studies Annual*, 2(1972), 69–97, for a detailed psychoanalytic study of many of Dickens' fool-figures; this article, however, although an excellent clinical analysis of the fool, does not explore the complex dramatic, moral, or thematic functions with which Dickens endows this classic literary character.

2 William Willeford, *The Fool and His Scepter: A Study in Clowns and Jesters and Their Audience* (Evanston, Ill.: Northwestern University Press, 1969), p. 115.

3 *The English Dramatic Critics*, ed. James Agate (New York: Hill & Wang, 1958), pp. 124–25. This review, often erroneously attributed to Dickens himself, has been reattributed to Forster by William J. Carlton, "Dickens or Forster? Some *King Lear* Criticisms Re-examined," *The Dickensian* 61 (1965), 133–40. Dickens, however, undoubtedly knew the

review and, as Carlton notes, regarded the fool in the same laudatory fashion.

4   Robert F. Fleissner, "Haymarket Theatre," *Dickens and Shakespeare* (New York: Haskell House, 1965), p. 291.

5   Desiderius Erasmus, *The Praise of Folly*, trans. John Wilson (1668), ed. Hendrik Willem van Loon (1942; reprint ed., New York: Black, 1970), p. 244.

6   John Palmer, *Political and Comic Characters of Shakespeare* (1945; reprint ed., London: Macmillan, 1964), p. 384.

7   Gabriel Pearson, "The Old Curiosity Shop," *Dickens and the Twentieth Century*, ed. John Gross and Gabriel Pearson (London: Routledge and Kegan Paul, 1962), p. 88.

8   Garrett Stewart, *Dickens and the Trials of the Imagination* (Cambridge: Harvard University Press, 1974), p. 89.

9   Ibid., p. 105.

10   Enid Welsford, *The Fool: His Social and Literary History* (1935; reprint ed., Gloucester, Mass.: P. Smith, 1966), p. 326.

11   Robert Goldsmith, *Wise Fools in Shakespeare* (East Lansing: Michigan State University Press, 1955), p. 51.

12   Stewart, p. 111.

13   Steven Marcus, *Dickens: From* *Pickwick to Dombey* (New York: Simon and Schuster, 1965), p. 168.

14   Willeford, p. 235.

15   *Dickens and the Twentieth Century*, p. 104.

16   Welsford, p. 76.

17   For a further discussion of possible Shakespearean themes in *Barnaby Rudge*, see M. Rosario Ryan, "Dickens and Shakespeare: Probable Sources of *Barnaby Rudge*," *English* 19 (1970), 43–48.

18   James K. Gottshall, "Devils Abroad": The Unity and Significance of *Barnaby Rudge*," *Nineteenth Century Fiction* 16 (1961), 137.

19   Lindsay, pp. 100–101.

20   Although neither Hugh nor Dennis is as explicitly derived from the fool-tradition as Barnaby, a subtle relationship does exist. Hugh's wild naturalness, social isolation, rebelliousness, and insight are often attributes of the traditional fool. Dennis' stick, "the knob of which was carved into a rough likeness of his own vile face" (283), is an even more obvious connection to the fool-tradition.

21   Lindsay, p. 237.

22   Miller, p. 122.

23   Michael Steig, "*Martin Chuzzlewit*: Pinch and Pecksniff," *Studies in the Novel* 1 (1969), 181.

24   Ibid., p. 184.

25   Ibid., p. 185.

DAVID D. MARCUS: *Symbolism and Mental Process in* Dombey and Son

1   John Holloway, "Dickens and the Symbol," *Dickens 1970*, ed. Michael Slater (London: Chapman and Hall, 1970), p. 63.

2   J. Hillis Miller, *Charles Dickens: The World of his Novels* (Cambridge: Harvard University Press, 1958), p. 149.

3   William Axton, *Circle of Fire: Dickens' Vision and Style and the Popular Victorian Theatre* (Lexington: University of Kentucky Press, 1966), p. 257.

4   A number of critics have commented on the relationship of the internal and external worlds in Dickens' novels. See Dorothy Van Ghent, "The Dickens World: A View from Todgers's," *Sewanee Review* 58 (1950), 419–38. My work particularly builds on the insights of Miller into the tendency of individual characters to remake the world as a mirror of themselves, but by viewing this tendency as a principle that functions dramatically, I differ from Miller's conclusion that the central problem of the novel

"is how to break through the barriers separating one from the world and from other people" (p. 146). As I shall argue, the mind actively seeks such isolation as a condition of its existence.

5 Steven Marcus, *Dickens: From Pickwick to Dombey* (London: Chatto and Windus, 1965), p. 297.

6 See also John Lucas, *The Melancholy Man: A Study of Dickens' Novels* (London: Methuen & Co., 1970), p. 162.

7 This same verbal formula, with only very slight variations, is repeated twice more in this chapter, pp. 584 and 587.

8 Miller, p. 145.

9 Ibid., p. 149.

10 See Axton, pp. 235–61. Axton notes that both this passage and Carker's fevered journey are subjective accounts located within the character's mind, but his interest lies in Dickens' prose rhythms and use of melodrama, not mental process.

11 Marcus, p. 306.

12 Humphry House, *The Dickens World* (London: Oxford University Press, 1941), pp. 137–42.

13 Marcus, p. 309.

14 Ibid., p. 342.

15 Miller, p. 146.

ROBERT E. LOUGY: *Remembrances of Death Past and Future*

1 Several studies of *David Copperfield* have addressed themselves to this dissonance: James Kincaid's "The Structure of *David Copperfield*," *Dickens Studies*, 2 (1966), 74–95; Kincaid's chapter on *Copperfield* in *Dickens and the Rhetoric of Laughter* (Oxford: Clarendon Press, 1971), chap. vii; and J. Hillis Miller's "Three Problems in Fictional Form: First-Person Narration in *David Copperfield* and *Huckleberry Finn*," *Experience in the Novel*, ed. Roy Harvey Pearce (New York: Columbia University Press, 1968), 21–48.

2 Roland Barthes, *Writing Degree Zero and Elements of Semiology*, trans. Annette Lavers and Colin Smith (New York: Beacon Press, 1970), p. 39.

3 In his *Charles Dickens: Radical Moralist* (Minneapolis: University of Minnesota Press, 1972), Joseph Gold has spoken of *David Copperfield* as a novel about art: "To make metaphor is to make sense. To make art is to give meaning to the past and purpose to the present. *David Copperfield* is an exemplary tale of how art is made, why it is necessary and what purpose it serves" (p. 177).

4 Cf. Ernest G. Schachtel's observation in his "On Memory and Child-

hood Amnesia": "Memory as a function of the living personality can be understood only as a capacity for the organization and reconstruction of past experiences and impressions in the service of present needs, fears, and interests." This essay appeared in *A Study of Interpersonal Relations*, ed. Patrick Mullahy (New York: Hermitage, 1949), p. 8.

5 Martin Heidegger, *Being and Time*, trans. John Macquarrie and Edward Robinson (New York: Harper and Row, 1962). All subsequent references to this work will be from this edition, cited as *BT*.

6 For example, Leonard Manheim's "The Personal History of *David Copperfield*," *American Imago* 9 (1953), 23–43; and William H. Marshall's "The Image of Steerforth and the Structure of *David Copperfield*," *Tennessee Studies in Literature* 5 (1960), 57–66.

7 The most extensive discussion of this disparity and of its importance for the novel as genre is found in Georg Lukács' *The Theory of the Novel* (Cambridge: M.I.T. Press, 1971), 70–94, et passim.

8 Cf. David's own similar comment

about the relationship between fantasy and reality: "When my thoughts go back now, to that slow agony of my youth, I wonder how much of the histories I invented for such people hangs like a mist of fancy over well-remembered facts!" (169).
9 Samuel Taylor Coleridge, *Biographia Literaria,* from *The Portable Coleridge,* ed. I. A. Richards (New York: Viking, 1961), p. 475.
10 Cf. Janet H. Brown's comments in "The Narrator's Role in *David Copperfield,*" *Dickens Studies Annual,* 2 (1972), 197–207: "And Emily was long since dead to *him* [David]: when she fell in with Steerforth, she, like Steerforth, was as good as dead" (p. 201).
11 I have in mind here Edgar Johnson's account of the final years of Dickens' life and of how he, in spite of the advice of friends and physicians, engaged in a schedule of writing and public readings that he must have

known would kill him. See Johnson's *Charles Dickens: His Tragedy and Triumph* (Boston: Little, Brown and Company, 1952), 1102–4.
12 Lukács, pp. 85–93.
13 For an extensive discussion of this process of mystification, see Paul De Man's "The Rhetoric of Temporality," *Interpretation: Theory and Practice* (Baltimore: Johns Hopkins University Press, 1969), pp. 173–210.
14 See G. Armour Craig's "The Unpoetic Compromise: On the Relations between Private Vision and Social Order in Nineteenth-Century Fiction," *Society and Self in the Novel,* ed. Mark Schorer (New York: Columbia University Press, 1956).
15 Steven Marcus, *The Other Victorians* (New York: Basic Books, 1966), pp. 105–11.
16 Geoffrey H. Hartman, *Wordsworth's Poetry: 1787–1814* (New Haven: Yale University Press, 1964).

FRANK EDMUND SMITH: *Perverted Balance*

1 *The Great Tradition* (New York: New York University Press, 1963; orig. publ. 1948), pp. 227–28.
2 *Charles Dickens: The World of His Novels* (Cambridge: Harvard University Press, 1958), p. 226.
3 *The Maturity of Dickens* (Cambridge: Harvard University Press, 1959), p. 175.
4 *The Flint and the Flame: The Artistry of Charles Dickens* (Columbia: University of Missouri Press, 1963), pp. 216–17.
5 "Dickens' *Hard Times:* The Romance as Radical Literature," *Dickens Studies Annual,* 2 (1972), 237–54.
6 "Fettered Fancy in *Hard Times,*" *PMLA* 84 (1969), 520.
7 "The Bleak Houses of *Bleak House,*" *Nineteenth-Century Fiction* 25 (1970), 266.
8 "*Hard Times:* The Style of a Sermon," *Texas Studies in Literature and Language* 11 (1970), 1375–96.
9 "Miscultivated Field and Cor-

rupted Garden: Imagery in *Hard Times,*" *Nineteenth-Century Fiction* 26 (1971), 159.
10 Some critics, notably John Holloway, "*Hard Times:* A History of a Criticism," in *Dickens and the Twentieth Century,* ed. John Gross and Gabriel Pearson (London: Routledge and Kegan Paul, 1962), argue that the world of the circus is just as extreme as a totally factual world. This, however, is not the circus that Dickens depicts. Not total fantasy, the world of his circus is often harsh and painful; e.g., Sissy's father runs away when people no longer laugh at his act, and another performer is killed falling off an elephant. The circus troupe makes life meaningful by tempering pain with joy, balancing fact with fancy.
11 Daniel P. Deneau discusses this relationship similarly in "The Brother-Sister Relationship in *Hard Times,*" *The Dickensian* 60 (1964), 173–77.

12 Monroe Engel in *Maturity*, p. 175, calls the staircase "an extraordinary sexual image" of Louisa's "hazard at the devices of James Harthouse," and most critics repeat this. The image is not, however, Dickens' description of Louisa's downfall but of Sparsit's perception.
13 For another point of view see Geoffrey J. Sadock, "Dickens and Dr. Leavis: A Critical Commentary on *Hard Times*," *Dickens Studies Annual*, 2 (1972), 211, who argues that Sissy passively endures the evils of society and fails to embody "moral resurgency" because she does not convert the adults.

RANDOLPH SPLITTER: *Guilt and the Trappings of Melodrama in* Little Dorrit

1 George Bernard Shaw, "Foreword" to *Great Expectations*, in *Charles Dickens: A Critical Anthology*, ed. Stephen Wall (Harmondsworth, England: Penguin Books, 1970), p. 290.
2 "Dickens: The Two Scrooges," *The Wound and the Bow* (Cambridge, Mass.: Houghton Mifflin, 1941).
3 See Sigmund Freud, "Character and Anal Eroticism" and "On the Transformation of Instincts with Special Reference to Anal Eroticism," *Character and Culture* (New York: Collier Books, 1963), pp. 27–33, 202–9.
4 *Life Against Death* (New York: Vintage Books, 1959). pp. 266–69.
5 Ibid., p. 278.
6 "Little Dorrit," in *Charles Dickens: A Critical Anthology*, p. 366.
7 Ibid., p. 367.
8 See Mark Spilka, *Dickens and Kafka* (Bloomington: Indiana University Press, 1963), pp. 88, 260, and also generally for a valuable and provocative reading of Dickens.
9 See Freud, "Mourning and Melancholia," *General Psychological Theory* (New York: Collier Books, 1963), pp. 164–79.
10 See Otto Fenichel, *The Psychoanalytical Theory of Neurosis* (New York: Norton, 1945), pp. 223–24.
11 See Charles Dickens, "Autobiographical Fragment," in *Charles Dickens: A Critical Anthology*, p. 42; Leonard Manheim, "Floras and Doras: The Women in Dickens' Novels,"
Texas Studies in Literature and Language 7, no. 2 (Summer 1965), 185–86.
12 Cf. Trilling, p. 370.
13 See Freud, "Certain Neurotic Mechanisms in Jealousy, Paranoia, and Homosexuality," *Sexuality and the Psychology of Love* (New York: Collier Books, 1963), pp. 163–64.
14 See Freud, "Certain Neurotic Mechanisms in Jealousy, Paranoia, and Homosexuality," *Sexuality and the Psychology of Love* (New York: Collier Books, 1963), pp. 163–64.
15 See Northrop Frye, "Dickens and the Comedy of Humors," in *Experience in the Novel*, ed. Roy Harvey Pearce (New York: Columbia University Press, 1968).
16 Cf. Freud, "The Theme of the Three Caskets," *Character and Culture*, pp. 67–79.
17 See Freud, "Family Romances," *The Sexual Enlightenment of Children* (New York: Collier Books, 1963), pp. 41–45.
18 See Freud, "The Most Prevalent Form of Degradation in Erotic Life," *Sexuality and the Psychology of Love*, pp. 58–70.
19 G. K. Chesterton, "Charles Dickens," in *Charles Dickens: A Critical Anthology*, p. 248.
20 Dickens, "Autobiographical Fragment," pp. 38–43.
21 "Dickens and the Comedy of Humors," p. 80.

PETER CHRISTMAS: Little Dorrit

1 "Dickens: The Two Scrooges" (1939), in *The Wound and the Bow* (Boston: Houghton Mifflin, 1941), p. 56.

2 John Butt and Kathleen Tillotson trace this early idea back to Forster and to a remark in one of Dickens' notebooks. See *Dickens At Work* (London: Methuen, 1957), p. 233.

3 Many critics have misread *Little Dorrit* as Dickens' groping for the divine after an unpromising start in political reform. Surely Dickens' religion was no more than a mixture of the sentiment of his own version of the New Testament for children, the theological analysis of Unitarianism, and the philanthropy of Christian Socialism. One needs to remind those without a direct acquaintance with it that Anglicanism represents the most sterile aspect of the English mystique of compromise. Pull it to the left and it becomes Methodism; pull it to the right and it becomes Newman's papism. When, after several centuries of emasculating political compromise, it allowed itself to be associated exclusively with middle-class manners, it lost the power of recovery. The tradition of the state religion had been secularized long before Dickens inherited it; there was nothing in him to infuse a new spirituality into it.

Raymond Williams' comment (*The English Novel from Dickens to Lawrence* [New York: Oxford University Press, 1970], p. 53) on Amy and characters like her in the other works deserves to become a touchstone of Dickens criticism: "The inexplicable quality of the indestructible innocence, of the miraculously intervening goodness, on which Dickens so much depends and which has been casually written off as sentimentality is genuine *because* it is inexplicable. What is explicable, after all, is the system, which consciously or unconsciously has been made. To believe that a human spirit exists, ultimately more powerful than even this system, is an act of faith but an act of faith in ourselves." This is true. With Amy, however, Dickens was at least trying to emphasize common sense and experience rather than use the customary inexplicability.

4 Butt and Tillotson are interesting when they show with what gradual effort Dickens eventually found a balance in the novel. Amy grows in stature to counteract the impact of anger on the original conception. Butt and Tillotson dwell on the primacy of indignation in the first drafts (pp. 224–25). They conclude: "For our purpose, the most interesting feature is the prominence of the political idea; it is clear from the cover-design that chapter X, 'Containing the Whole Science of Government,' was foreseen from the start, and that its satire was a fundamental part of Dickens's conception of the novel—more so, perhaps, than the working-out of the story suggests, since the Barnacles remain rather episodic in the plot." And: "It seems likely that Little Dorrit was not at first intended to be so important a character; indeed, in manuscript, proofs, and letters we can trace the way she grew in importance, and even see her acquiring her name" (pp. 230–31; see also pp. 232–33).

At this point, no reader can afford to ignore Raymond Williams' very telling comment. Whenever one is tempted to see religion as appealing for an end to anger in the interests of higher things, Williams brings one back to earth: "Reference to a 'change of heart' is indeed now mainly known as a rationalization of resistance to change, but this is clearly not Dickens. To see a change of heart and a change of institutions as alternatives is already to ratify an alienated society, for neither can be separated, or ever is, from the other; simply one or other can be *ignored*" (p. 49).

5 In the Afterword of the Signet edition (New York, 1963), p. 530.

DEBORAH A. THOMAS: *Dickens' Mrs. Lirriper
and the Evolution of a Feminine Stereotype*

1 George Gissing, *Charles Dickens: A Critical Study* (London: Blackie & Son, 1898), p. 132.

2 Kate Millett, *Sexual Politics* (1970; reprint ed., New York: Avon Books, 1971), p. 90. Millett goes on to say that most of Dickens' "serious" female characters reflect the ideal of womanhood delineated in Ruskin's lecture "Of Queens' Gardens" (published in *Sesame and Lilies*, 1865).

3 Edwin Pugh, *The Charles Dickens Originals* (New York: Charles Scribner's Sons, 1912), p. 68.

4 V. S. Pritchett, "The Comic World of Dickens," *Listener*, 3 June 1954, reprinted in *The Dickens Critics*, ed. George H. Ford and Lauriat Lane, Jr. (Ithaca: Cornell University Press, 1961), pp. 312–13.

5 Philip Collins, "The Popularity of Dickens," *The Dickensian* 70 (1974), 18.

6 Angus Wilson, *The World of Charles Dickens* (1970; reprint ed., New York: Viking Press, 1972), p. 103; see also pp. 58–59.

7 Ian Watt, "Oral Dickens," *Dickens Studies Annual* 3 (1974), 176. See also Leonard Manheim's discussion of Dickens' recurring depiction of "the mother-figure as the butt of aggression (p. 185) and the unattainable virginal ideal, in "Floras and Doras: The Women in Dickens' Novels," *Texas Studies in Literature and Language* 7 (1965), 181–200.

8 For examples of critics, in addition to Manheim and Angus Wilson, who have extensively examined these biographical connections, see Edmund Wilson, "Dickens: The Two Scrooges," *The Wound and the Bow* (1941; reprint ed., New York: Oxford University Press, 1965); Jack Lindsay, *Charles Dickens: A Biographical and Critical Study* (New York: Philosophical Library, 1950); Edgar Johnson, *Charles Dickens: His Tragedy and Triumph*, 2 vols. (Boston: Little Brown, 1952).

9 Citations from *Mrs. Lirriper's Lodgings* and *Mrs. Lirriper's Legacy* in my text are to the extra Christmas numbers of *All the Year Round* for 1863 and 1864. The versions of Dickens' opening and closing chapters for these Christmas numbers usually reprinted in editions of his collected works under the title of *Christmas Stories* create a misleading impression of their original format, and the free-flowing first paragraph of *Mrs. Lirriper's Lodgings* just quoted in my present text is punctuated more heavily in the familiar New Oxford Illustrated edition of *Christmas Stories* than the way in which Dickens originally published it in *All the Year Round*. I have included the *All the Year Round* texts of these chapters in my edition of Charles Dickens, *Selected Short Fiction* (Penguin Books).

10 Review of *Mrs. Lirriper's Lodgings* in *Saturday Review* 16 (12 December 1863), reprinted in *Dickens: The Critical Heritage*, ed. Philip Collins (London: Routledge and Kegan Paul, 1971), p. 413.

11 John Forster, *The Life of Charles Dickens*, ed. A. J. Hoppé, new ed. (London: J. M. Dent & Sons, 1966), II, 290.

12 Stone, "Dickens and Interior Monologue," p. 58. Earle Davis has examined the relationship between Mrs. Nickleby's style of speaking and the speech mannerisms of characters impersonated by the comic actor Charles Mathews, the elder; Davis also pointed to the increasing incoherence of this conversational manner in Flora Finching and Mrs. Lirriper, in *The Flint and the Flame* (Columbia: University of Missouri Press, 1963), pp. 46–49.

13 Jane W. Stedman, "From Dame to Woman: W. S. Gilbert and Theatri-

cal Transvestism," *Suffer and Be Still: Women in the Victorian Age,* ed. Martha Vicinus (Bloomington: Indiana University Press, 1972), pp. 20–37, 211–13. Stedman notes that the role of the "dame" on the mid-Victorian stage was usually played by a man, although Gilbert broke away from this transvestite tradition.

14 With the exception in n. 9, citations in my text are to the appropriate editions of the New Oxford Illustrated Dickens.

15 *The Letters of Charles Dickens,* ed. Madeline House and Graham Storey (Oxford: Clarendon Press, 1965), I, 348, to John Forster (? December 1837).

16 Virgil Grillo notes that "The Boarding-House" is technically more advanced than the earlier tales collected in *Sketches by Boz,* although it is still in many respects an apprentice work: see *Charles Dickens' Sketches by Boz: End in the Beginning* (Boulder: Colorado Associated University Press, 1974), pp. 25–29. Grillo discusses the way in which characters in the *Sketches* anticipate figures in Dickens' later fiction, but he does not deal with the feminine stereotype in question here.

17 Henri Bergson, *Laughter: An Essay on the Meaning of the Comic,* trans. Cloudesley Brereton and Fred Rothwell (New York: Macmillan, 1911), pp. 87–88. Margaret Ganz has suggested that, while many of the characterizations in the *Sketches* remain "merely the perennial butts of farce and satire," Dickens' use of verbal incongruity in Mrs. Bloss' conversation encourages a reader to give it the kind of amused tolerance accorded to Smollett's Mrs. Jenkins, Fielding's Mrs. Slipslop, and Sheridan's Mrs. Malaprop; see "Humor's Alchemy: The Lesson of *Sketches by Boz,*" *Genre* 1 (1968), 293–95. As I argue in the remainder of this article, Dickens' treatment of this style of speech becomes increasingly tolerant in conjunction with his increase in artistic power and, especially, in Mrs.

Lirriper, goes well beyond the verbal lapses of the eighteenth-century characters. At this point, however, Dickens' skill is embryonic, and Mrs. Bloss seems only a feeble shadow of the earlier, more sophisticated creations.

18 Gissing, p. 144.

19 Sigmund Freud, "Humour," trans. Joan Riviere, *Collected Papers,* ed. James Strachey (New York: Basic Books, 1959), V, 217.

20 Margaret Ganz, "The Vulnerable Ego: Dickens' Humor in Decline," *Dickens Studies Annual* 1 (1970), 27. Mark Spilka has likewise called attention to the transcendent quality of Dickens' grotesque comedy in his *Dickens and Kafka: A Mutual Interpretation* (Bloomington: Indiana University Press, 1963). Both Ganz and Spilka relate their explanations to Freud's discussion of humor, although both perceive that Dickens' manifestation of this quality involves a greater degree of sympathy than Freud's formulation suggests; see Ganz, "Humor's Alchemy," pp. 292–93, and p. 302, n. 15; Spilka, pp. 69, 83, 84–86.

21 Stone, p. 56.

22 Ibid., p. 57. See also Davis, pp. 48, 307.

23 Northrop Frye, "Dickens and the Comedy of Humours," *Experience in the Novel: Selected Papers from the English Institute,* ed. Roy Harvey Pearce (New York: Columbia University Press, 1968), p. 63. Frye is using the term "humour" in the Jonsonian sense of "a character identified with a characteristic" (p. 56).

24 Ibid., p. 81.

25 Forster, II, 296. In a similar vein, Harvey Peter Sucksmith has analyzed the complex relationship between sympathy and irony in Dickens' novels, although he does not deal with most of his short fiction, such as the characterizations of Mrs. Lirriper and Doctor Marigold; see *The Narrative Art of Charles Dickens: The Rhetoric of Sympathy and Irony in His Novels* (Oxford: Clarendon Press, 1970).

26 Freud, 5, 218.

27   A similar view of Dickens' creative process was independently advanced at the 1973 Dickens Seminar by Hillis Miller, who credited it to an unpublished dissertation by Roger Henkle of Brown University.

WILLIAM M. BURGAN: *The Refinement of Contrast*

1   Edmund Wilson, *The Wound and the Bow* (New York: Oxford University Press, 1947; reprint ed., 1970), p. 82.

2   Research for this paper was aided by a grant from The American Philosophical Society. Quotations from the manuscript are made by courtesy of the Victoria and Albert Museum.

3   "Introduction," *The Mystery of Edwin Drood*, ed. Margaret Cardwell (Oxford: Clarendon Press, 1972), p. xxxiii.

4   I have occasionally indicated changes in punctuation, when they are important for understanding the process of revision.

5   In citing revisions made in the proofs of the monthly numbers rather than in the manuscript itself, I have relied on Cardwell's exhaustive notation of such changes. Two cases of this type are large enough to merit special mention: the deletion of the whole sentence beginning, "Among the ⟨white robes⟩ *dirty linen*," and Dickens' expansion of the account of Crisparkle's visits to Cloisterham Weir. The following is a list of other, similar changes; the reference to Cardwell is identical with that given in my text for the quotation as a whole: "⟨bleak⟩ *bleaker*"; "thunder⟨s⟩"; "⟨*framing*⟩ *frames . . . cast⟨s⟩*"; "⟨*lashing and*⟩," "⟨the⟩ *a restless*"; "⟨around⟩ *above*"; "⟨*there*⟩"; "⟨He⟩ *So, he*," "⟨reflected on⟩ *cast upon*," "⟨Outside⟩ *In the free outer air*," "teeming," "⟨*Inside,*⟩ *In the Cathedral*," "⟨dusky⟩ *murky*," "⟨for it⟩," "⟨lo⟩," "⟨and silent⟩."

6   The source of each subsequent transcription will be noted in parentheses after the quotation, as follows: in capital Roman numerals, the number of the monthly part, followed by Dickens' page number for the manuscript, and by the chapter number and page number in Cardwell. In the present case, this is as follows: (III, 2; x, 78).

7   For an account of the genesis of Dickens' pairing of clerical irresponsibility and Jasper's addiction, see Cardwell's Introduction, pp. xvii–xix.

8   See Cardwell, Introduction, p. xxii–xxiii, n. 3.

9   The novelty of prose style in *Drood* is a matter of emphasis and concentration rather than the introduction of imagery unique in Dickens' work. For example, compare with "muttered thunder" and "fiery and yet cold" the two following images from *Bleak House:* "the sun, so red but yielding so little heat" (iii), and "until we heard thunder muttering in the distance" (xviii).

10   Cardwell, Appendix B: Number Plans, p. 225.

11   "John Jasper—Strangler," *Bookman* 70 (1930), 585.

12   Cf. H. P. Sucksmith's comment, in *The Narrative Art of Charles Dickens* (Oxford: Clarendon Press, 1970), p. 160, on the manuscript of Book II, Chapter xxv, of *Little Dorrit*, in which Bar and Physician survey the sleeping city of London on the morning of Merdle's suicide: "The addition of 'who were yet asleep' further isolates the pair who are awake from the thousands of victims who remain in the most blissful of all states of ignorance."

13   See "Notes," *The Mystery of Edwin Drood*, ed. Arthur J. Cox (Harmondsworth, Middlesex: Penguin Books, 1974), p. 310; and Cardwell, Introduction, p. xxxiii.

14   On the treatment of light and detail in Bellini's paintings, see Kenneth Clark, *Landscape into Art* (London: John Murray, 1949; reprint ed.,

Boston: Beacon Press, 1961), pp. 23–24. On Ansel Adams, see Nancy Newhall, *The Eloquent Light* (San Francisco: Sierra Club, 1963), pp. 69, 164–65, et passim. Adams comment on the social import of his art is of particular relevance to Dickens: "If I feel I have any niche at all in the photographic presentation of America, I think it would be chiefly to show the land and sky as the settings for human activity. And it would be showing also how man could be related to this magnificent setting, and how foolish it is that we have the disorganization and misery that we have. I too could go back into the past for comparisons of points of view. Much of the art of the Renaissance gave man his 'setting'; recall the magnificent bits of landscape in Italian religious paintings. Again, in Dürer, both the exalted and sordid subjects are shown against the earth and sky" (p. 164). I use the term "metaphor of value" as it is defined in E. H. Gombrich, *Meditations on a Hobby Horse* (London: Phaidon Press, 1963), pp. 12–13.

15 See Sucksmith's comments, p. vii, on the difficulty of finding indications of "a certain amount of pacing up and down before revising," or a session devoted to revision.

16 G. M. Young, *Daylight and Champagne* (London: Jonathan Cape, 1937), pp. 29–30.

INDEX

Abstraction: philosophical, 17; benevolence as an embodied, 19
Adams, Ansel: landscapes of, 178; and Dickens, 199n14
Adjective: single, signifies contrast in *Drood*, 169
Admiration: expressed by feeding, 5
Adolescence: "normative crisis" of, 9; development, 9; growth in, 10
Adult reality: vision of, 133
Adult status: acquisition of, 10
Adventure: in *David Copperfield*, 87
Adventures: amorous, 24–25
Aggression: redirection of, 11; mentioned, 2, 9
Aggressiveness: of Dickens, 11
Alger républicain, 15
All the Year Round, 155
Ambiguity: of Barnaby Rudge, 45, 54
Ambivalence: in *David Copperfield*, 89
Anal: concerns of Dickens, 5; Dickens' character type, 6
Anal imagery: by Coleridge, 12–13
Analogy: between physical world and movement of human life, 59
Anal-sadistic strategy, 131
Andrews, Malcolm: remarks on chorus role, 42
Anger: righteous, 145
Anglicanism, 195n3
Anxiety: filled with terror, 77; Heidegger defines, 87; childhood images create, 89; of David Copperfield, 90
Artist-as-child: killed in Mr. Dick, 87
Artist-hero: and the demands of his art and his soul, 73
As You Like It: Touchstone's role in 41–42
Atmosphere: ominous, 170
Auctor gloriosus, 133
Autobiographical fragment, 11
Autobiographical statement, 1

Axton, William: his approach to the ocean symbol, 58

Balance: unnatural, 104; patterns of, 105; fraudulent, 108
Balance of opposites: in *Drood*, 175
Barnaby Rudge: moral mirror in, 49; Lord Gordon in, 49, 50; evil, symbols of in, 50; thematic structure of, 54
Barthes, Roland: attributes irony to the best of modern works, 73–74
"Bartleby the Scrivener." *See* Melville, Herman
Bate, Walter Jackson: biographer of Coleridge, 188n24
Beadnell, Maria: Dickens' adolescent romance with, 155; mentioned, 13
Being and Time. See Heidegger, M.
Bellini, Giovanni: landscapes of, 178
Benevolence: a viable mode of social action, 17; of the poor, 18, 21; theme of, 18, 26, 27, 30; moral value of the act of, 19; concept of universal, 19–20; appears in works of Dickens, 22; perpetual, 22; simple act of, 25; natural, 26, 31, 39; eighteenth-century philosophy of, 27; describes Falkland, 33; philosophy of, 35–36; image of Christ as paradigm of, 38
Bergson, Henri: definition of comedy, 157; and Dickens' humor, 159
Binary cast of mind, 171
Binary organization: perfection of, in *Drood*, 181
Biographia Literaria. See Coleridge, Samuel Taylor
Biography: "fiction" of, 14
Bleak House: a "dark" novel, 15; of the "dark" novel theory, 16; benevolence of the poor in, 31; views man as dark and pessimistic,